The Science of Sustainable Development
Local Livelihoods and the Global Environment

Science faces major challenges in tackling the interlinked problems of poverty and environmental sustainability. This book reviews how practical science can be applied to real-life conservation and development problems. It aims to demystify the sometimes obscure science of natural resource management, interpreting it for the benefit of those who need to deal with the day-to-day problems of managing complex natural resource systems. The book draws upon the personal experience of the authors in Africa, Asia and Latin America, but it also benefits from the best scholarship within leading natural resource management organisations, and from the realism and pragmatism of those who face these difficult environmental and developmental situations in the field. The book responds to needs expressed by the Convention on Biological Diversity, the Global Environment Facility and many other international fora where the problems of conserving the environment in poor countries are debated. It gives practical guidance to those who design and manage conservation programmes and demonstrates that new technologies are now available that enable integrated natural resource management to move from a theory to a reality. The authors argue that the threats to the natural environment posed by globalisation require an integrated response, which can yield real benefits to those living in tropical developing countries, whilst also achieving global environment objectives.

JEFF SAYER has worked extensively throughout the tropics running conservation and natural resource mangement programmes, many of them in areas where the local population is poor and is highly dependent on natural resources. He was the founding Director General of the Center for International Forestry Research (CIFOR), Indonesia and is currently a Senior Associate in the Forests for Life Programme at WWF-International, Switzerland. He holds the Prince Bernhard Chair of International Nature Conservation at the University of Utrecht, the Netherlands.

BRUCE CAMPBELL has 20 years' experience of working on conservation and development issues in the savanna systems of southern Africa, gained during his time at the University of Zimbabwe, where he established an interdisciplinary Institute of Environmental Studies. He is currently Director of the Forests and Livelihoods programme at the Center for International Forestry Research (CIFOR), Indonesia.

D1350104

The Science of Sustainable Development

Local Livelihoods and the Global Environment

JEFFREY SAYER

WWF-International, Switzerland

BRUCE CAMPBELL

Center for International Forestry Research, Indonesia

CAMBRIDGE
UNIVERSITY PRESS

PUBLISHED BY THE PRESS SYNDICATE OF THE UNIVERSITY OF CAMBRIDGE
The Pitt Building, Trumpington Street, Cambridge, United Kingdom

CAMBRIDGE UNIVERSITY PRESS
The Edinburgh Building, Cambridge, CB2 2RU, UK
40 West 20th Street, New York, NY 10011–4211, USA
477 Williamstown Road, Port Melbourne, VIC 3207, Australia
Ruiz de Alarcón 13, 28014 Madrid, Spain
Dock House, The Waterfront, Cape Town 8001, South Africa

http://www.cambridge.org

First published 2004

Printed in the United Kingdom at the University Press, Cambridge

Typefaces Bembo 11/13 pt. and Univers   *System* LATEX 2$_\varepsilon$ [TB]

A catalogue record for this book is available from the British Library

Library of Congress Cataloguing in Publication data
Sayer, Jeffrey.
   The Science of sustainable development: local livelihoods and the global environment /
   Jeffrey Sayer, Bruce Campbell.
      p.   cm.
   ISBN 0 521 82728 0 (cloth: alk. paper) – ISBN 0 521 53456 9 (pbk.: alk. paper)
   1. Conservation of natural resources.   2. Natural resources – Management.   3. Sustainable
   development.   4. Rural development.   5. Environmental management.   I. Campbell,
   B. M. (Bruce Morgan), 1953–   II. Title.
S928.S28   2003
333.7′2 – dc21   2003055143

ISBN 0 521 82728 0 hardback
ISBN 0 521 53456 9 paperback

Contents

Figures

Boxes

Tables

Foreword

When the World Wildlife Fund (WWF) was founded over 40 years ago we focussed exclusively on protecting rare species and on the establishment and management of parks and reserves. Since then we have come a long way. Today we recognise that the problems of conservation cannot be solved if we do not also address the problems of the people who live and depend upon the natural resources of forests, arid lands and wetlands. We will not be able to conserve nature if we cannot ensure the sustainability of agriculture. Reconciling rural livelihoods and environmental conservation is one of the major challenges facing humanity. The basic idea that we must manage rural landscapes in an integrated way is not new. It was clearly expressed in the World Conservation Strategy over 20 years ago. WWF, and other conservation and development organisations, have amassed a wealth of experience on how to achieve conservation and development on the ground. Yet until now we have only been partially successful. We had good theories but we lacked the practical tools for putting them into action in our programmes. We have not been good at learning from our mistakes and sometimes we have been unwilling to confront the reality that there are significant trade-offs between conservation and the livelihoods of local people.

Jeff Sayer and Bruce Campbell have spent their entire careers working at the interface of science and practical conservation. They have brought to this book a rich experience of practical realities on the ground and a comprehensive knowledge of the conservation and development literature. They have cast their net wide and have drawn upon the knowledge and insights of scientists and resource managers working in a wide range of situations from intensive agriculture to the forest frontiers. The book does not provide any ready-made solutions to natural resource management problems. But resource managers, conservation and development programme planners, natural resource scientists and especially people managing conservation and development programmes in the field will all find their ideas challenged by this book. It combines a heavy dose of hard science with a wealth of practical experience, a combination that can help all of us to achieve our objectives more effectively. The problems of conservation and development are complex in the extreme, it is essential that we strengthen the scientific basis for all our programmes and this book can help us to do so.

Claude Martin
Director General WWF Int.

Preface

In the late 1990s, Maurice Strong led an external review of the consultative Group for International Agricultural Research (CGIAR). His team included Dr Mankoto Swaminathan, Prof. Bo Bengtsson and Dr Michel Griffon. They concluded that the crop improvement work that the CGIAR had focussed on since its foundation in the 1960s had been the best investment in development assistance 'bar-none'. However, they recognised that times were changing and that the private sector, notably the large agro-industrial corporations, and a number of national research structures, for instance those of India and Brazil, were filling the niche previously occupied by the CGIAR. They advocated a new orientation for the CGIAR and a focus on the resource management problems confronting poor people in marginal areas. They urged that more attention be given to global environmental problems and to the implications of these for poor farmers, foresters and fishermen. They advocated an emphasis on integrated natural resource management research. This book is based upon the work of a task force that was established by the CGIAR to implement the recommendations of Maurice Strong's review.

The task force included scientists from a wide range of backgrounds who were all working towards the goal of managing rural tropical landscapes for the dual goals of enhancing productivity and sustaining environmental values. None of its members had a complete recipe for achieving this. But many of us had elements of answers. Within the ranks of the CGIAR and of other natural resource scientists, we found a wealth of insights and techniques that could combine to produce a new approach to science-based natural resource management. This book, therefore, draws upon the work of many of our colleagues within the CGIAR and in other natural resource management agencies and attempts to weave together the different elements that have proved successful in a diversity of situations and in dealing with a wide range of natural resource problems.

This book attempts to redefine roles for government agencies, development assistance programmes and science in achieving a more sustainable future of rural landscapes in tropical developing countries. Our overall hypothesis is that a number of external influences, particularly market forces, determine the trajectories through which rural landscapes evolve. These forces are so powerful that policy adjustments, subsidies and development projects are only able to have a limited impact on them. Conventional agricultural research produces technologies that can improve the performance of natural resource systems but they cannot reverse the underlying trajectory of the system. If we are to provide for sustainable livelihoods for the millions of people in these rural tropical landscapes, and if we are to ensure the maintenance of the global environmental benefits that they provide, then there is a need to influence these development trajectories.

The recognition of the gains to be had from managing landscapes for multiple functions has been with us for decades. *Integrated rural development, integrated watershed management, integrated natural resource management* and *ecosystem management* have all been the goals of major development efforts. These have all tended to apply total rationality to the planning of rural landscapes. Much development assistance was rooted in the belief that there was a 'best way' of managing these landscapes and that science and administrative interventions could achieve this. This deterministic, rational approach to rural development has been an enduring characteristic of the post-colonial governments of much of the developing world. It has also been the prevailing paradigm of most development assistance agencies. The basic thesis of this book is that government, aid agencies and science can all combine to influence development trajectories in the rural tropics but that neither independently nor in combination can they produce 'designer development'.

Natural resources research in the rural tropics has had a bad press. Some governments and development assistance agencies consider it a luxury that does not produce tangible benefits. We acknowledge that much natural resources research has not been very useful, but we attribute this to the way in which research has been funded and managed. Funding constraints have forced researchers to operate within the deterministic, rational vision of development. Research was expected to produce technologies ready for widespread dissemination. This vision of research was reflected in appeals from developing countries for 'technology transfer'. The entire discourse about the role of technology in development has, in our opinion, missed the point that technologies have to respond to needs: they have to fit within the context of local development trends. A technology that makes money in Japan or USA will not often be one that will solve the problems of rural people in Nepal or Burkina Faso.

We, therefore, reject the hypothesis that research is marginal in solving the problems of rural development in the tropics. We argue that research, broadly defined, may be the only basis for solving many of the intransigent problems of the developing world. But this will not be research that is carried out in artificially controlled conditions on research stations, or research designed and supervised by foreign researchers who have little sympathy for, or understanding of, the real problems of the rural poor and their environment.

The research that is needed is research that both mobilises existing knowledge and generates new knowledge. It is research that treats all management as experimental and that deals with real-life situations. It is research that enables scientists and farmers to experiment and learn together. It is action research but at a much larger scale than that usually practised.

Our review leads us to advocate a new relationship between research and management. We advocate closer partnerships between scientists and resource managers. Research must be a shared learning experience for scientists, local farmers, fishermen, forest managers and the staffs of government resource management agencies. This changed relationship is already in evidence in industrialised countries, where farmers and other resource managers have a major role in setting natural resource research agendas. Roussel et al. have argued for this new relationship between scientists and managers in the corporate sector.[1] Their vision of *Third Generation R&D* is an industrial equivalent of what is needed for the rural environment in the tropics.

A number of other recent books have probed the relationship between researchers and practitioners in the resource management field. Kai Lee's *Compass and Gyroscope* makes compelling arguments for the role of science in experimental management.[2] He argues for learning, adaptation and negotiation, where scientists and managers have complementary roles. Boru Douthwaite's recent *Enabling Innovation* provides valuable insights into the ways in which science can facilitate local innovation and now scientists can work alongside resource managers in jointly experimenting with new technologies.[3]

This book is, therefore, calling for new ways of organising science in support of sustainable development in rural tropical landscapes. It argues that scientists must not be detached observers from outside the system. They must be actors themselves. They must make long-term

---

[1] Roussel, P. P., Saad, K. N. and Erickson, T. J. *Third Generation R&D: Managing the Link to Corporate Strategy.* Boston, MA: Harvard Business School Press, 1991.

[2] Lee, K. *Compass and Gyroscope: Integrating Science and Politics for the Environment.* Washington DC: Island Press, 1993.

[3] See also Douthwaite, B. *Enabling Innovation: A Practical Guide to Understanding and Fostering Technological Change.* London: Zed Books, 2002.

commitments to working with resource managers and to studying the real-life problems of these people. They must work with resource managers to examine possible development scenarios and then use the resource managers' interventions as their laboratory bench.

The key elements of success are a willingness to make a long-term commitment to a shared development vision. Scientists must work alongside resource managers to explore the impacts of different technological interventions. Scientists and resource managers must all monitor the performance of natural resource systems so that management can be adapted to deal with unanticipated results or changing external forces. Scientists must mobilise information and knowledge from diverse sources and different scales. They must use modern information technology to combine understanding of phenomena at local levels with macro-level and extra-sectoral influences.

The sort of science that we see as essential for improved natural resource management in the tropics cannot be conducted during brief visits by scientists based in the developed world. It requires a long-term presence and an intimate involvement with local situations. This requires that there is a significant scientific capacity in the countries themselves. A major problem is that there are far too few qualified scientists in the developing countries. The past four decades of development assistance have focussed excessively on transferring ready-made technologies and have sadly neglected the need to develop the human resources needed to produce indigenous solutions. The neglect of tertiary education in our development programmes is a fundamental error that it will take decades to rectify.

We urgently need a new body of scientific competence to guide the development pathway of complex landscape mosaics and to ensure the continued flow of the wide range of goods and services that are needed by both local and global communities. We do not pretend that this book can give all of the answers. We hope it will prove interesting to the many practitioners in aid agencies and natural resource management agencies that are grappling with these problems. We hope that it will encourage renewed support for natural resource science in development assistance programmes but that this support will be used to develop resource management institutions where scientists work alongside farmers, fishermen and forest dwellers to help them to produce their own solutions to their problems.

Acknowledgements

In 1998 an independent review of the Consultative Group for International Agricultural Research (CGIAR) recommended that the centres making up the CGIAR give more emphasis to integrated natural resource management. A task force was established by the CGIAR to put this recommendation into practice. One of us, JAS, was appointed chair of this task force. The task force consisted of scientists from all 16 CGIAR centres together with leading independent natural resource scientists. Since 2001, Joachim Voss has provide inspired leadership to the task force. The governments of Holland, Japan, Norway, Denmark and Germany and the International Development Research Center of Canada supported its work. The task force has so far met on four occasions. First in Holland in 1999, then in Penang, Malaysia in 2000, in Cali, Colombia in 2001 and in Aleppo, Syria in 2002. This book is an attempt to synthesise the ideas and material presented at these meetings. It also draws heavily on our personal experience working in practical natural resource management programmes, mostly in Africa and Asia.

A number of scientists have given us special help and insights in preparing this book. Jürgen Hagmann facilitated the later workshops in Penang and Cali and also brought us the wisdom and experience of his own extensive and innovative work in Zimbabwe. Brian Walker and his colleagues at the Resilience Alliance have inspired us with their writings and Brian provided extensive comment on earlier drafts of this manuscript. Neil Byron of the Productivity Commission in Melbourne Australia (and previously Assistant Director General of CIFOR) has been an invaluable source of ideas and comments. Jacqueline Ashby of CIAT in Colombia has been the originator of much of the work on participatory and action research and a thoughtful commentator on the issues of reorganising natural resource science. Meryl Williams, Director General of ICLARM helped to organise the pivotal meeting in Penang and also helped us to access literature on the organisation of science that we might otherwise have overlooked. Michel Griffon and Jacques Valeix of CIRAD, France provided much help and encouragement and allowed JAS to work on this book whilst employed as a visiting scientist at CIRAD in Montpellier. Nigel Stork and colleagues at the Rainforest Co-operative Research Centre in Cairns, Australia hosted us while we worked on early drafts of the manuscript and gave us access to much innovative thinking on integrated natural resource management. Ravi Tadvulkar, Francisco Reifschneider and Ian Johnson of the CGIAR secretariat at the World Bank in Washington encouraged and supported this work within the CGIAR.

A number of CGIAR scientists have had a major influence on our thinking on the ideas in this book. Boru Douthwaite at IITA provided major insights through his work on technology adoption. Larry Harrington from CYMMIT contributed with his experience on small farmer innovation, Meine van Noordwijk from the World AgroForestry Centre supplied brilliant insights on all aspects of natural resources management. Dennis Garrity also of the World AgroForestry Centre and David Kaimowitz of CIFOR gave endless suggestions and support. Peter Frost of the University of Zimbabwe was a valued source of insights and sometimes painful reminders of reality. We have drawn heavily on the writings of all of the above and we hope that they will not feel that we have either plagiarised or misrepresented them.

John Poulsen of CIFOR has been a close colleague throughout this endeavour and has helped us in numerous practical and conceptual ways; we extend our special thanks to him. John has provided helpful reviews of successive versions of this manuscript. Lucya Yamin and Inna Bangun of CIFOR gave invaluable support throughout the process of preparing task force meetings and organising documents. It was a pleasure to work with them.

The meeting of the CGIAR Integrated Natural Resource Management task force in Penang in 2000 was where this book was born. Much of our work has been based on the papers presented by our colleagues in Penang (http://www.inrm.cgiar.org/documents/workshop_2000.htm). Many of these papers were subsequently published in the online journal *Conservation Ecology* and they are extensively cited in this book. We would like to thank the editors of *Conservation Ecology*, particularly Buzz Holling and Brian Walker, both for their lifetime contributions to this topic and for their enthusiasm in helping us to produce a special edition of their journal on integrated natural resource management. We thank Frits Penning de Fries and the International Water Resources Management Institute for the nomination that led to our paper on the topic of this book receiving the 2002 CGIAR Prize for outstanding scientific article. We want to mention particularly the following participants at the Penang meeting for their writings, ideas and assistance. Chapter 1: Jacqueline Ashby. Chapter 2: Jacqueline Ashby, Larry W. Harrington, Meine van Noordwijk,

Anne-Marie Izac, Jürgen Hagmann and Peter Frost. Chapter 3: Boru Douthwaite, Jürgen Hagmann, Padma Lal, Meine van Noordwijk. Chapter 4: Chris Lovell, Meine van Noordwijk. Chapter 5: Tim Lynam, Jeremy Cain, Meine van Noordwijk, Padma Lal. Chapter 6: Witness Kozanayi, Marty Luckert, Peter Frost, Chris Lovell, Nonto Nemarundwe and Bev Sithole. Chapter 7: Chris Barr, Ken MacDicken, Lini Wollenberg, Douglas Sheil, Patrice Levang. Chapter 8: David Kaimowitz, Jacqueline Ashby. Chapter 9: Larry Harrington, Chris Lovell. Chapter 10: Tony Cunningham, Peter Frost, Jürgen Hagmann. Chapter 11: Jacqueline Ashby, Chris Lovell, Boru Douthwaite. The data presented in Chapter 6 is derived from a project funded by the Department for International Development (UK).

Part I

Integrating natural resource
management

1 The challenge: alleviating poverty and conserving the environment

One of the anomalies of modern ecology is that it is the creation of two groups, each of which seems barely aware of the existence of the other. The one studies the human community almost as if it were a separate entity, and calls its findings sociology, economics and history. The other studies the plant and animal community and comfortably relegates the hodge-podge of politics to the liberal arts.

   The inevitable fusion of the two lines of thought will, perhaps, constitute the outstanding advance of the present century.

Aldo Leopold, 1935[1]

Sixty-five years ago, Aldo Leopold laid down the challenge of developing a science of integrated natural resource management. But a vast gulf still exists between the high priests of theoretical ecology, the gurus of social processes and the real world of resource managers (farmers, fishers and foresters). In this book, we will attempt to understand why the manifestly sensible goal of managing natural resources in an integrated manner has proved so elusive. Our concern is with developing countries and with the effectiveness of attempts to promote 'sustainable development' for the vast populations of the world's poor people.

   Many development assistance agencies now aspire to the dual missions of alleviating poverty and conserving the environment. Meanwhile, conservation organisations are claiming that their activities are yielding benefits for the poor. All are implying that natural resources can be managed in ways that achieve immediate benefits for local people whilst sustaining long-term local and global environmental values. However, many critics say that the lack of success of both development and conservation programmes in developing countries results from this confusion of two inherently divergent agendas.

   Huge amounts of money have been invested in various approaches to achieving integration in natural resource management. *Integrated rural*

[1] Bradley, N. L. (1998). A man for all seasons. *National Wildlife*. http://www.nwf.org/nationalwildlife/1998/tableam8.html.

development was widely attempted in the 1960s and 1970s but then abandoned. *Integrated conservation and development projects* came onto the scene in the 1970s but although they are still around their credibility as a development or conservation tool is now seriously questioned.[2] *Ecoregional approaches to development, integrated soil and water management projects, ecosystem approaches to conservation, integrated catchment management* etc. are the flavours of the first decade of the twenty-first century, but many claim that they are attempts to put old wine into new bottles. Many attempts to integrate complex sets of knowledge and the interests of diverse sets of actors into a common framework have yielded disappointing results. The desire to achieve integration persists but our seeming inability to translate the theories of integration into practical achievements on the ground is leading to widespread disillusion. In frustration, we abandon one set of integrative buzzwords and replace them with others. What is surprising is not the improvement of integrative methods over the past 40 years – rather it is their fundamental similarity. The words have changed but the paradigm remains similar (Box 1.1).

Box 1.1. Integrated natural resource management and its various manifestations

Integrated natural resource management is a conscious process of incorporating the multiple aspects of natural resource use into a system of sustainable management to meet the goals of resource users, managers and other stakeholders (e.g. production, food security, profitability, risk aversion and sustainability goals). To fulfil its aims, an integrated natural resource management approach is necessarily adaptive, interdisciplinary and involves a diverse set of stakeholders.[1]

Integrated catchment management is the process of formulating and implementing a course of action involving natural and human resources in a watershed, taking into account the social, political, economic and institutional factors operating within the watershed and the surrounding river basin and other relevant regions to achieve specific social objectives.[2]

Integrated water resource management is the coordinated planning and management of land, water and other environmental resources for their equitable, efficient and sustainable use.[3]

Community-based natural resource management is the integrated management of a multitude of open-access, common property and privately owned natural resources at the 'community' scale.

Integrated rural development was the dominant rural development paradigm of the 1960s. It shared many of the goals of integrated natural resource management as described

---

[2]McShane, T. O. and Wells, M. P. *Getting Biodiversity Projects to Work: Towards More Effective Conservation and Development.* New York: Columbia University Press, 2004, in press.

in this book but failed because the delivery mode was rooted in a top-down, western-science-knows-best mind-set.

Integrated conservation and development programmes are approaches to management and conservation of natural resources in areas of significant biodiversity value that aim to reconcile biodiversity conservation and socio-economic development interests of multiple stakeholders at local, regional, national and international levels.[4]

Ecosystem approaches are a strategy for the integrated management of land, water and living resources that promotes conservation and sustainable use in an equitable way.[5] The Convention on Biological Diversity has adopted a set of useful principles that define the ecosystem approach.

Landscape management is a term recently adopted by several international conservation groups, notably the Worldwide Fund for Nature and the International Union for Conservation of Nature and Natural Resources, to describe mosaic landscapes where one seeks to optimise environmental and production functions by managing the different landscape units in a complementary way. The French use the term '*Aménagement du territoire*' to convey roughly the same meaning.

Adaptive collaborative management is a concept promoted by the Center for International Forestry Research (CIFOR) that is based upon three linked processes: stakeholder interaction, communication and learning among stakeholders, and joint or collective action, resulting in changes or adjustments to management. These changes, in turn, affect the benefits people derive from natural resources and the quality of the resource.[6]

Multifunctional agriculture or forestry describes agriculture or forestry that deliberately avoids maximising crop yields in order to produce amenity or environmental benefits. The term has been controversial, as it is strongly associated with the European Common Agricultural Policy and its environmental payments, which are seen by competitors as hidden subsidies.

---

[1] Anon. *Report on the Workshop on Integrated Natural Resource Management Research in the CGIAR: Approaches and Lessons, 21–25 August 2000.* Penang: ICLARM. Online: http://www.inrm.cgiar.org/documents/workshop_2000.htm; Gottret, M. A. V. N. and White, D. Assessing the impact of integrated natural resource management: challenges and experiences. *Conservation Ecology,* **5** (2001), 17. Online: http://www.consecol.org/vol5/iss2/art17.

[2] UNESCO. Integrated water resource management: meeting the sustainability challenge. *IHP Humid Tropics Programme Series No. 5.* Paris: UNESCO Press, 1993.

[3] Calder, I. R. *The Blue Revolution – Land Use and Integrated Water Resources Management.* London: Earthscan, 1999.

[4] Franks, P. and Blomley, T. Fitting ICD into a project framework: the CARE experience. In *Getting Biodiversity Projects to Work: Towards More Effective Conservation and Development,* ed. T. O. McShane and M. P. Wells. New York: Columbia University Press, 2004, in press.

[5] Secretariat of the Convention on Biological Diversity. *Conference of the Parties Decisions. Decision V/6 Ecosystem Approach.* Geneva: United Nations Environment Programme, 2001. Online: http://www.biodiv.org/decisions.

[6] Buck, L. E., Geisler, C. C., Schelhas, J. and Wollenberg, E. (ed.) *Biological Diversity: Balancing Interests through Adaptive Collaborative Management.* Boca Raton, FL: CRC Press, 2001.

The lack of progress in achieving integration has led many to question its usefulness. Many have argued that the ideal of integration is conceptually appealing but is impossible to achieve in practice. For example, Sedjo (1996) has stated that 'ecosystem management lacks clear objectives and hence cannot be operationalised on the ground'.[3] Another view, and the one that we will explore in this book, is that the processes, tools and concepts that could underpin a new integrative science are not widely understood and not fully embraced, and that fundamental aspects of the way development science is organised are creating obstacles to change.

Getting researchers from different disciplines to work together with resource managers from different sectors seems sensible and easy enough. In practice, however, there seem to be language and cultural barriers that often bedevil attempts to get diverse groups of people to work together on a common problem. This is not the case in all areas of human endeavour. Large teams of diverse scientists collaborate to launch space probes, develop stunningly complex computer technology and unravel the complexity of life-threatening diseases. In a June 2000 issue of *Science* John Lawton commented that '. . . scientists and engineers from many disciplines routinely work together within institutions and organisations to improve human health. We would be startled if it were not so. The health of the planet is a different story . . . . We lack the organisations to nurture [the required integration]'.[4] The rewards of collaboration and integration for scientific endeavours with commercial applications are enormous, and the costs of reductionism are failure, bankruptcy and obscurity. However, the markets for the public goods products of integrated natural resource science are embryonic, at least in the developing world. Most natural resource organisations still reward individual achievement and fail to provide an environment where multidisciplinary teams and integration can flourish.

Nowhere is the need for integration and collaboration greater than in addressing the environmental problems confronting the developing world today. Yet most natural resource managers and researchers remain tied to their laboratories or their experimental plots. The costs of not integrating and not collaborating are colossal: the progressive deterioration of the agricultural, forestry and fishery systems upon which all life depends. These costs are not born by the scientists and government resource managers; the costs are manifest in the suffering of resource-poor farmers and deterioration of the quality of life of society at large.

[3] Sedjo, R. A. Towards an operational approach to public forest management. *Journal of Forestry,* **94** (1996), 24–27.
[4] Lawton, J. Earth science systems. *Science,* **292** (2001), 1965.

In this book, we will attempt to show why integrative approaches are essential and to demonstrate that successes from integrative science are possible and practical. We will attempt to elucidate the key processes, tools and concepts that need to be embraced if integration in natural resource management is to become operational on a scale sufficient to confront the crisis of achieving sustainable development.

The challenges facing research

The work of the research centres of the Consultative Group for International Agricultural Research (CGIAR) formed the basis of the green revolution. Scientific reviews and activist non-governmental organisations (NGOs) have all attacked the CGIAR for focussing on technological solutions to the problems of the poor and ignoring the complex realities of their lives. Critics have focussed on the harmful social and environmental externalities caused by some of the agricultural innovations that the CGIAR has produced. The harsh reality is that the benefits of more efficient production of commodity crops may accrue to better-endowed farmers and to urban consumers. The poorest of the poor may not have access to these innovations and may be further marginalised by them.

Jacqueline Ashby of the International Center for Tropical Agronomy (CIAT) at Cali in Colombia has been a leader in exploring the scientific basis for integration and participation in the work of the CGIAR. She has been responding in part to the drastic decline in the status and credibility of mainstream agricultural science since the Nobel prize-winning heights of the green revolution. In a recent article in *Conservation Ecology*, she claims that many now see conventional agriculture as a threat to the environment and to human health.[5] The perceived risks in the way food is produced and the effects of new food production technologies on the health of humans and ecosystems have become major political issues and topics for headline news. When the CGIAR was established in the 1960s, agriculture was seen as a major part of the solution to the development problems of the Third World; today, a significant body of opinion sees modern agriculture as a major part of the problem.

However, advances in agricultural science are still essential if we are to achieve the yield increases needed to meet the world's food requirements. The globalisation of trade and the food needs of a burgeoning world

---

[5] Ashby, J. A. Integrating research on food and the environment: an exit strategy from the rational fool syndrome in agricultural science. *Conservation Ecology*, **5** (2001), 20. Online: http://www.consecol.org/vol5/iss2/art20.

population will drive this process in the direction of the intensive production of uniform crop varieties by large-scale agro-industries. Poor farmers will not be able to compete in markets with modern industrial agriculture and will either have to seek their fortunes off the land or be relegated to a marginal subsistence existence. The idea that over a billion very poor farmers can be absorbed into manufacturing and services requires an exceedingly optimistic view of the potential for continuing global economic expansion. Furthermore, many fear that while food needs may be met under this scenario, it will be at the expense of climate, biodiversity and amenity values. For example, the World Conservation Strategy advocates 'reducing excessive [crop] yields to sustainable levels'.[6] Examples of well-documented public distrust in agricultural science and policy abound. Two examples are the 'mad-cow disease' scandal in the UK and the growing, international antipathy to genetically modified organisms and to uniform plantations of fast growing clonal trees.

The focus of this book is on attempts by governments and development assistance agencies to improve the livelihoods of poor people in the developing world. These poor people depend upon the 'natural capital' that supports their lives just as much as they do on the more tangible assets of money and property. Natural capital is the soil, water, climate and biodiversity upon which functioning ecosystems depend. People's concerns may be driven by a conservation ethic but this has its origins in compelling evidence of the poverty, famine and natural disasters that result from degraded ecosystems. The resilience of the poor in the face of external shocks such as war, climate variation and indebtedness depends on natural capital. The diversity of nature and the health of ecosystems are essential to people's survival in a turbulent and constantly changing world.[7]

In recent years, political support for investing development assistance money in natural resources research has weakened. Instead, funds are being channelled to better governance, public sector adjustment, disaster relief and the mitigation of environmental problems. There is a notable decline in support for agriculture, a reflection of the disenchantment with industrialised agriculture in high-income countries and the perception that development assistance to agriculture has not delivered the benefits that it promised. Agricultural research is not unique in this loss of credibility.

---

[6] IUCN 1990 cited in Adams, W. M. *Green Development*. Oxford: Oxford University Press, 1990.

[7] Conway, G. R. The properties of agroecosystems. *Agricultural Systems,* **24** (1987), 95–117; Pearce, D., Barbier, A. and Markandya, A. *Sustainable Development: Economics and Environment in the Third World*. Aldershot: Edward Elgar, 1990.

Robert Chambers of the Institute for Development Studies at the University of Sussex in the UK has analysed the way in which rural development practitioners have gone through a process of being proved consistently wrong and have lost credibility for their claims.[8] In the same vein, critics of mainstream agricultural science claim that the research establishment 'is incapable of delivering social equity, economic efficiency and ecological integrity in response to the decline of rural society and deepening crises in the depletion and degradation of water, soils, flora and fauna'.[9] The rates of return on investment in agriculture for developing low-income countries have indeed been disappointing. There is evidence that returns on investments in agricultural development projects have been even lower than in sectors such as health or education. The gains from agricultural projects are often not sustained after external donors withdraw.[10] Proponents of organisational change to support the development of sustainable agriculture do not always see a role for science in this process. Röling and Jiggins state that 'the old role of developing technologies for farmers seems to clash with the logic of [providing farmers with the adaptive skills to practice] ecologically sound farming, while a new role [for research] . . . seems not to have clearly emerged'.[11]

In the 1960s, a huge gap existed between the technologies used by resource managers in developed countries and those available to poor farmers and resource managers in the tropics and subtropics. The main objective of development assistance during the following 40 years was an attempt to transfer or adapt advanced technologies to conditions in poor tropical countries. These efforts are widely credited with having averted the large-scale famines that had been anticipated in Asia in the 1970s and 1980s. Major investments went into genetic improvement of a few commodity crops to enhance productivity and improve resistance to pests and diseases. The gains were largely confined to areas of high agricultural potential and they often benefited more prosperous farmers, missing the poorest of the poor. The initial spectacular gains in productivity of the green revolution

---

[8]Chambers, R. *Whose Reality Counts? Putting the Last First*. London: Intermediate Technology, 1997.

[9]Campbell, A. Fomenting synergy: experiences with facilitating landcare in Australia. In *Sustainable Agriculture and Participatory Learning*, ed. N. G. Röling and M. A. E. Wagemakers. Cambridge: Cambridge University Press, 1998, pp. 232–249.

[10]Pretty, J. N. *Regenerating Agriculture: Policies and Practice for Sustainability and Self-reliance*. London: Earthscan, 1995.

[11]Röling, N. G. and Jiggins, J. The ecological knowledge system. In *Facilitating Sustainable Agriculture*, ed. N. G. Röling and M. A. E. Wagemakers. Cambridge: Cambridge University Press, 1998, pp. 283–311.

are unlikely to be repeated.[12] The impacts of such research have been more modest in addressing the needs of Africa.

Green revolution science underestimated the complexity of the systems in which small-scale producers operate. Crop production, for example, is usually only a small part of a broad livelihood portfolio that may encompass a wide variety of off-farm activities such as the gathering of forest products and the raising of livestock (see Fig. 6.3, p. 131). Productivity enhancement is important but risk reduction, improved food security and the maintenance of natural and social capital are also vital. The farming systems of poor people in the tropics are subject to a multitude of exogenous influences. For instance, in semi-arid areas they are subject to highly variable rainfall. Economic conditions may change rapidly, with resulting swings in input costs and market prices. Other external shocks such as the massive rise in the acquired immunodeficiency syndrome (AIDS) in Africa or the widespread fires associated with el Niño events throughout the tropics all disrupt local resource management systems. Agricultural innovations must not only increase productivity, they must also help the poor to deal with the vagaries of their social, economic and biophysical environment.

Mainstream agricultural science has tended to try and reduce agricultural systems to their components. While reductionism has been crucial in the gains that have been achieved, it can miss the mark, as we illustrate in Chapter 6. Development assistance to agriculture has largely ignored the off-farm environment. In mainstream agricultural science, natural resource management has been synonymous with location-specific, adaptive research, mainly concerned with maintaining soil fertility. There have been few systematic attempts to help poor farmers to be resilient to the impacts of external economic, social or climatic changes.

Much development science has been portrayed as being in support of short-term growth at any cost. In many cases, agricultural research yielded short-term productivity gains at the expense of long-term degradation of the natural capital of soils, water, biodiversity and non-cultivated land. Much of this research targeted innovations that could yield quick benefits to respond to urgent needs. Researchers were committed to technologies that maximised biological uniformity and ignored the biological diversity and ecological services that might contribute to the stability and resilience of natural ecosystems. Good historical reasons explain this focus, and extensive critiques, justification and refutations of it abound. It is argued that this sort of science poses threats to the fragile societies and poor people of many

[12] Conway, G. R. *The Doubly Green Revolution: Food for All in the 21st Century*. London: Penguin Books, 1997.

developing countries. Poor countries lack formal safety nets to see their people through periods of crisis. Poor people lack the financial capital to help them to deal with crop failures caused by diseases, infrastructure break-down, social turmoil or extreme climatic events. The capital that enables these people to deal with difficult times is the social capital that allows them to cooperate and share scarce resources. But they also need the natural capital of a diverse resource base to provide them with a range of options. The immediate need may be to see them through periods of environmental, economic or social stress, but the long-term need is for a natural resource base that can provide a range of options for economic growth and social development.

In many situations, there are clear trade-offs between productivity enhancement and price minimisation on the one hand and caring for so-cial values and ecosystem health on the other. At present, the incentives in developing countries encourage producers to shift any environmental or social costs onto others. Individual farmers are faced with the stark reality that they will produce less and make less profit if they bear the full cost of resource conservation measures. The result is that many social and environ-mental costs are born by society at large rather than by individual resource managers. Development assistance has done little to help poor countries to build institutions to deal with these 'externalities'.

Dysfunctional development assistance projects

This book deals mainly with attempts to use international development assistance to address the natural resource problems of poor countries. The need for accountability and for donors to be able to target their support precisely has led to the emergence of the 'development project' as the main delivery mechanism for this aid. Donors work with their national counter-parts to define discrete, time-bound, packages of development assistance. This enables the donor to identify with, and claim credit for, individual components of the broad development agenda of the recipient country. It allows the donor to apply its own accountability mechanisms and, signifi-cantly, it allows development to be reduced to bite-sized components for which donors can assume responsibility.

The construction of a road or bridge is readily amenable to the 'project' approach. Such activities can easily be packaged as a discrete, time-bound, pre-planned project. However, the problem with natural resources is that they are components of large complex landscapes. Diverse interest groups impinge upon them. They are subject to unpredictable pressures resulting from changes in local economies, access to markets, population movements, climate change and a host of other exogenous forces. Many development projects are trying to shoehorn the complex and dynamic realities of a natural resource system into the constraints of a time-bound, tightly planned, highly predictable project. This does not usually work.

Chapter 7 describes the consequences of the application of strict project management in a research and development programme in the forests of Indonesian Borneo. Initially, flexible funding was available to support a complex programme to improve local livelihoods and conserve forests. Subsequently, special project funding from international agencies was obtained to support parts of this work. The reporting and financial management requirements of these agencies made it very difficult for all the participants in the programme to work as a team and deal with the issues in a holistic way. Meeting donor needs for quickly attaining specific milestones came to dominate over a participatory process of learning and experimentation.

Similar experiences have been reported from the Landcare programme in Australia.[13] This programme emerged spontaneously in a number of locations when farmers found that they could only deal with large-scale environmental problems by working collectively with other farmers. The programme became so successful that it began to receive significant government support. Gradually the proportion of the total funding that came from government sources increased until it exceeded that from private and philanthropic sources. In order to access this government money, it was necessary to go through significant bureaucratic hurdles – proposals had to be written and reports submitted. This became such a burden that recent commentators have suggested that the vigour and spontaneity that characterised the programme in its early years has now declined and Landcare is in danger of becoming just another government programme to subsidise better farming practices.

A main feature of the 'project' paradigm in development assistance is an attempt to reduce uncertainty. Projects seek to reduce the level of complexity and to tease-out a subset of issues that can have price tags attached to them and whose successful execution can easily be verified. This is very different to the real-life task of a natural resource manager. The job is not to attempt to reduce or eliminate complexity and uncertainty but rather to exercise judgement in dealing with the complex economic, social and biophysical environment. Good natural resource managers, for instance most poor farmers in developing countries, have always been 'adaptive managers', their success lay in their ability to make good judgements in response to the constant surprises that confronted them in their day to day activities.

[13]See Chapter 9 for further information on the Landcare project in Australia.

As donors have become more and more frustrated at their inability to integrate conservation and development successfully, they have reacted by more rigorous application of the tools of the development assistance trade. They have planned their projects in more and more detail. They have commissioned more careful diagnostic studies to reduce the possibility of surprises. They have developed more sophisticated monitoring and evaluation tools to ensure that everything is staying on track. The end result has been a generation of natural resource management projects that are so locked into a rigid donor-driven framework that they have little relevance to the real world in which natural resources and their managers have to survive.

One notable feature of the dysfunctional nature of projects is the commissioning of studies by teams of experts in order to characterise a location and diagnose its problems. These studies place great value on the knowledge that experts bring to an area. This knowledge has been gleaned from experience in many other similar situations. It typically costs between $500 and $1000 a day. However, such planning studies place little value on the knowledge of people who have lived their entire lives in the area under study. They might earn $1–2 a day as enumerators or field assistants if they are lucky. Yet it is this informal knowledge of local people that has to be the basis of most of the resource management decisions that will be taken by a project. It is the behaviour of these people that projects will strive to influence. This local knowledge is often the scarcest resource. One reason that projects often begin to become effective only after several years of operation is that it is only after quite a long period that the international project advisers become sufficiently attuned to local realities to begin to tap the informal local knowledge that is so important to success.

Pre-project studies often simply record in a form accessible to the donor a snapshot of the status quo. Their reports explain and present to funding agencies things that are self-evident and common knowledge to local people. Furthermore, the reports that are prepared in the process of project preparation inevitably tend to frame the problems from a donor or expert perspective. This has profound influences on the way in which all future interventions by the donor or its agent are oriented. Repeatedly, one finds examples of preparation missions identifying and describing problems in ways that must seem quite bizarre to local people.[14] One of us (JAS) vividly recalls the astonishment of a district officer in Tanzania when he was told that a major justification for a development project in his area was the

[14]Scott, J. C. *Seeing Like a State: How Certain Schemes to Improve the Human Condition Have Failed*. New Haven, CT: Yale University Press, 1998.

conservation of endemic birds and frogs. At the level of global biodiversity priorities, the birds and frogs were important. In terms of the livelihoods of local people, they were totally irrelevant.

We have included accounts in this book of natural resource problems as perceived by literate local people in areas targeted by projects. We asked these people to describe the conservation and development problems that they confronted in their everyday lives. The results were startlingly different to the assumptions underlying the projects.

Recent generations of natural resource management projects have generally been developed using participatory techniques, but they are still often based upon fundamental and incorrect assumptions made by donors and their advisors. Projects that seek to achieve both conservation and development are common. However, the conservation component usually addresses the conservation of species or landscapes of global value not the conservation of resources or options of immediate relevance to local people. Nonetheless, people will participate in these conservation and development projects even if given the choice, they would probably settle for the local development without the global conservation.

Everyone subscribes to the principle of ensuring 'ownership' of projects by local people, but frequently we have to invest a lot of effort in trying to secure 'their' ownership of 'our' project. There has been a notable failure for donors to accept the reality that conserving the global environment is simply not a very high priority for poor people living in rural areas in developing countries.

A common feature of project development is the preparation of maps and inventories. Participatory mapping is now a normal feature of the best natural resource management projects but still a lot is invested in maps based upon remote sensing or ground surveys by experts. James Scott has described how maps create realities and any map or chart is simply one out of an infinite number of ways of portraying those realities.[15] Even when maps are produced with local participation, the criteria or features that are mapped are often subject to the overriding influence of the outside specialists. They arrive with their own vision of what needs to be mapped. Douglas Sheil and colleagues from the Center for International Forestry Research (CIFOR) working in the forests of Indonesian Kalimantan have shown how local peoples' appreciation of forest condition and biodiversity differs markedly from the assessments of outside technical experts.[16]

[15] Scott, J. C. *Seeing Like a State*.

[16] Sheil, D., Puri, R. K., Basuki, I. *et al. Exploring Biological Diversity, Environment and Local People's Perspectives in Forest Landscapes*. Bogor: CIFOR, 2002.

The early planning stages of projects establish patterns. They launch the project upon a trajectory that is very difficult to change. If these early stages are influenced by incorrect assumptions, then major subsequent investments may be misdirected. Project planning is still frequently conducted too quickly and superficially. Some donors are now recognising that success depends upon the quality of the foundations established in the early periods of interventions. They are now allowing much more time to really get into the system − to see the situation as the principal local stakeholders see it. Some bilateral donors are now making long-term commitments to flexile support to areas or sectors. The recent USAID CARPE project in the Congo Basin and the UK forestry programme in Indonesia are excellent examples. Switzerland has for many years been exemplary in its attention to local sensitivities in its programmes in forest and mountain areas. The 'learning and adaptation' and 'adaptive programme loans' of the World Bank are also potentially useful innovations. However, the project preparation procedures of many donors are still inadequate. Many fundamental issues are settled before the process of participation has started.

Even some apparently trivial aspects of the 'project' are inimical to success. Most donors and their executing agencies want their contributions recognised. The same donors who require local ownership of projects still want their logos on the vehicles and on the cover page of publications. They still want their proposals and reports written in international languages and prepared in ways that only international experts can handle. Most donors reward creative writing ability of experts far more than they reward the resource management abilities of local people. Donors want to visit their projects, and preferably they want to bring politicians to see the good work. They want to see clear evidence of their own contributions and they also have high expectations of success. All natural resource management interventions enjoy successes and failures − often quite a lot of the latter. Yet, all the incentives favour the exaggeration of successes and the rationalisation or downplaying of any failures. Some international conservation NGOs are particularly prone to making extravagant claims of successful impact yet they also publicise the continuing decline of the habitats and species that they are claiming to conserve.[17] Yet it is these very failures that should teach us the lessons from which long-term success may emerge.

In recent years, log-frames have become popular management tools for projects. Properly used, a log-frame can indeed be a valuable basis for clarifying assumptions and facilitating a transparent process of negotiation of

[17]See for instance Lomborg, B. *The Sceptical Environmentalist*. Cambridge: Cambridge University Press, 2001.

desired outcomes. However, too many donors have allowed log-frames to be used to limit the flexibility of projects. The log-frame becomes the master rather than the tool. It ties participants into activities that were determined at the beginning of the project rather than being used to help to negotiate course changes and adaptability. Log-frames, like micro-management of project inputs, can be the enemy of the adaptability and resilience that is essential to ultimate success.

Yet another component of the project pathology is the preoccupation with delivery deadlines. For many donors, 'milestones' are the measure of success and the quicker they are reached the better. However, for natural resource management, learning and negotiation processes are far more important than technical deliverables; ultimately we are seeking behavioural change not the introduction of a particular technology. Change takes time and many projects have suffered the long-term costs of imperfect processes in their excessive haste to disburse funds and achieve deadlines. The more successful examples of natural resource management interventions have been those where small amounts of money were made available flexibly and sensitively over a long period of time. This has happened when local NGOs or even motivated individuals have championed some local conservation or development cause over a long period. There have been many failures when large amounts of money have been thrown at problems too rapidly.

One particularly worrying element of the fund disbursement paradigm is that little money reaches the ultimate beneficiaries on the ground, especially in the early phases of projects. The surveys, planning and participatory events needed to get started inevitably means that most of the money in the early stages of a project goes to the consultants. Local people often have to wait a remarkably long time before they can expect to receive any benefits. A surprisingly large number of natural resource management projects never do provide significant direct benefits to local people. They may make new technologies available and improve some social facilities, schools, roads, etc. Yet, often these benefits account for only a small proportion of the total budget and often the patience of local people is tried as they await the recompense for their investments of time and knowledge.

Projects also have a poor record at being well articulated with developments in other sectors that influence local outcomes. Failure of projects is often attributed to unpredicted changes in the macro-economic or political context. Local political support is often essential to the success of projects, but political changes may lead to this support evaporating overnight. An international market for a newly introduced crop may disappear because of changes in exchange rates etc. These are examples of the negative impacts of project bounding. The tendency for donors to circumscribe a project into a self-contained package makes it difficult for projects to be managed in ways that make them responsive to changes in their external environment.

Towards a new role for science

The simple pursuit of economic efficiency may lead, in the long term, to better lives for the average person. However, economic efficiency poses threats to the hundreds of millions of poor people whose existence still lies largely outside the modern global economy. Economic growth leads to investments in education and organisations and the emergence of strong civil societies that tend to take better care of the environment. However, during the early phases of development, severe, and possibly irreversible, environmental damage may occur. As the populations and consumption levels of developing countries grow, natural resources are coming under ever-greater pressure. The risks of environmental harm from the pursuit of economic growth are critical during this period. The advent of economic globalisation and the increasing domination of agriculture by a few large companies create special threats for the poor.[18] Equity in the distribution of benefits is emerging as a major issue. Multi-faceted threats are emerging that will require integrative responses.

There is now widespread recognition that the sustained improvement of the lives of poor farmers in developing countries will require a new kind appearing in the literature of research. There are many calls for new approaches to natural resource science.[19] A prestigious group of scientists in the USA recently 'affirmed that a bold departure from the status quo of disciplinary science was needed to address pressing national needs'.[20] What they then described is a small component of the issues that we tackle here, reaffirming our view that the departure from the status quo should be more than bold!

While we use the word 'new', we recognise that many of the elements of this new research have been around for some time. The problem is that the elements are rarely put together in an integrated package involving concepts, processes and tools, and the buzzwords are rarely subject to

[18]Korten, D. C. *When Corporations Rule the World*. London: Earthscan, 1995.

[19]See for instance Kates, R. W., Clark, N. C., Corell, R. *et al.* Sustainability science. *Science*, **292** (2001), 641–642.

[20]Kinzig, A. P., Carpenter, S., Dove, M. *et al. Nature and Society: An Imperative for Integrated Environmental Research*. Executive summary of a report prepared for the National Science Foundation, 2000. Online: http://lsweb.la.asu.edu/akinzig/report.htm.

Table 1.1. *Characteristics of approaches that use integrative principles*

Approach characteristic	Farming systems research	Adaptive collaborative management[a]	Landscape approaches	Ecosystem management[b]	Integrated natural resource management (as conceptualised in this book)
Multi-scale work generally at different scales		(√)	√	√	√
Action research part of the approach		√			√
Empowerment an issue		√			√
Takes an adaptive management approach		√	√	√	√
Multiple stakeholders recognised		√	√	√	√
Process facilitation of key importance			√		√
Systems modelling used	√	√	√		√
Breakdown of the distinction between research, management and extension					
Discusses new organisations for managing complex systems			√		√
Institutional analysis (rules, norms, devolution issues) and change are key to the approach		√	√	√	√
Knowledge management important, including informal knowledge		(√)		(√)	√
Focus on adaptive capacity, not specific technologies		√			√
Generalisable research products are based on descriptions of the learning cycle processes		√		√	√
Tools for measuring system performance are key to the approach		√	√		√
Embraces sustainable livelihoods perspectives			√		√
Focus on resources and/or people	Both	Both	Both	Resources	Both

[a] From CIFOR. See footnote 21.
[b] From Secretariat of the Convention of Biological Diversity. See footnote 22.

practical tests. In Table 1.1. we list some of the elements of the approach we put forward and compare them with the elements of some other approaches.[21,22]

Cutting-edge component research is still needed but it has to be set in local contexts and be applied in ways that recognise the special conditions of the poor. It will have to give more emphasis to management of risks, to reduction of dependence on agricultural inputs, to avoidance of long-term depletion of productive potential and to more careful control of environmental externalities.[23]

Harry Collins, the Convenor of the Centre for the Study of Knowledge, Expertise and Science at the University of Cardiff in Wales, has suggested that the role of science is analogous to that of marriage counselling. He draws the analogy with a person who goes to a marriage guidance counsellor for advice, but whose marriage nonetheless fails. Would that person feel the need to say that the marriage guidance counsellor had made 'mistakes'? Would she or he assume that in the fullness of time correct marriage guidance hypotheses would come along? Probably the person would accept that marriage guidance is not a precise science. Marriage guidance counselling is the model we need for the new complex science. In the twenty-first century, we will have to learn how to use science to increase options and make better choices and decisions rather than to provide pre-cooked remedies. Science will have to deal with evolving situations and to be a joint venture between scientists and resource managers.

Integrated approaches to research on agriculture and resource management have to accomplish seven critical changes in order to achieve a paradigm shift to increase food production and enhance ecosystem and human health.

> *Acknowledge and analyse the complexity of natural resource systems.* We must acknowledge systems complexity and bring to bear the concepts and tools of systems analysis to deal with complexity (Chapter 2).

> *Use action research – become actors in the system.* We must become part of the system in a cycle of action research (Chapter 3).

[21]CIFOR. *Local People, Devolution and Adaptive Collaborative Management of Forests. Researching Conditions, Processes and Impacts.* Bogor: Center for International Forestry Research. Online: http://www.cifor.cgiar.org/acm/download/ACMFlyer.zip.

[22]Secretariat of the Convention on Biological Diversity. Conference of the Parties Decision. Decision V/6 Ecosystem Approach. Geneva: United Nations Environmental Programme, 2001. Online: http://www.biodiv.org/decisions.

[23]Conway, G. R. *The Doubly Green Revolution.*

Consider effects at higher and lower scales. We must routinely conduct cross-scale analysis and action (Chapter 4). This means that our action research will invariably consist of cycles within cycles, and we will have to interface these with simulations of longer-term processes.

Use models to build shared understanding and as negotiating tools. We must confront complexity with conceptual and systems models, but a new type of model is needed (Chapter 5). We must have models that can facilitate discussion and stakeholder interaction: 'working' models that may be thrown away after a short period of use.

Be realistic about potential for dissemination and uptake. Is the detailed knowledge about a specific research and development site of any significance beyond the site (Chapter 9)? Anderson believes not.[24] He has portrayed natural resource management as an area for research of little strategic value, unlikely to produce internationally useful public goods and not worthy of significant levels of public sector investment. We believe otherwise: dissemination of the processes involved in successful integrated approaches will yield widespread benefits.

Use performance indicators for learning and adaptation. We need tools to monitor and evaluate system performance (Chapter 10). However, this is not 'impact assessment' as envisaged for 'transfer of technology'. Performance indicators will be essential in the learning process of adaptive management.

Breakdown the barriers between science and resource users. We will have to change the organisation of science (Chapter 11). Elite, monolithic research centres will be of little value for integrated research.

The chapters in this book treat each of the above themes in detail. In addition, in Part II, there are three case studies, covering semi-arid smallholder systems in Zimbabwe (Chapter 6), the rainforests of Borneo (Chapter 7) and the hillsides of the Andes (Chapter 8). These are not meant to illustrate best practice in approaches to complex conservation and development situations; rather, they illustrate different approaches, elements of best practice, components of success and the problems inherent in trying to use science

---

[24] Anderson, J. R. Selected policy issues in international agricultural research. On striving for public goods in an era of donor fatigue. *World Development*, **26** (1998), 1149–1162.

to improve development and conservation outcomes. Throughout the book, we use examples illustrating the lessons from integrated approaches, drawing on diverse situations (e.g. Botswana wildlife systems (see Box 1.3, below), Zimbabwean smallholder agriculture (Boxes 3.3 and 10.1), integrated conservation and development (Box 4.5), Thailand water management (Box 5.1), Indian watersheds (Box 9.1) and Australian rainforests (Box 11.1).

How integrated do we need to be?

Why, if so many people are talking about integrated approaches, are successful cases so hard to find? Part of the reason is that there has been an influential school of thought that portrayed integrated approaches as being all-embracing and integrating everything. Integrated management was often seen as requiring an ability to have a complete understanding of all the facets of a complex system. Early attempts at integrated natural resource management sought to understand the total behaviour of the system and to develop the ability to predict the outcome of any management intervention. The underlying logic of the UNESCO-led Man and Biosphere programme was an example of this approach to resource management. In reality, the skill or professionalism of integrated natural resources management lies in making judgements on what to integrate. It only makes sense to integrate those additional components, stakeholders or scales that are essential to solving the problem at hand. Natural resource scientists must have sufficient understanding of the system to make choices about where to focus attention. If this more limited view of integrated research is accepted, then there are very many examples of successful integrated research (Box 1.2).

Box 1.2. Successful examples of integrated research and management

- Integrated management of vegetation and soil in a plot or field to achieve higher nutrient use efficiency: in the research phase one would expect the researchers to have considered the volumes of organic materials available at the household and landscape levels, and perhaps national fertiliser policies.
- Interventions in the ecology of farms to achieve integrated pest management: the research would be expected to consider the group dynamics and the resources available to support pest management at the landscape level.
- Management of forested landscapes to achieve balance in yield of forest products and water, whilst retaining biodiversity.
- Adaptation of farming systems at large scales to enhance carbon sequestration.

The fundamental issue is that the marginal costs of adding each additional component, stakeholder or scale into the system under study have to be considered and have to be less than the marginal benefits of such additions. This highlights the need for a clear articulation of the problem, the establishment of appropriate research hypotheses and, above all, judgement of what has a high probability of yielding tangible benefits within reasonable time frames. Perhaps the most difficult problem facing practitioners of integrated research is the decision as to when to stop adding additional components into the system. Integrated analysis should be seen as a careful extension of the research or management domain to include those additional variables, stakeholders, scales and drivers of change that can reasonably be expected to have an influence on the sustainability and adaptability of the interventions being designed.

This is not to say that intractable problems should be abandoned because of their complexity. For instance, stakeholders may decide that the objective for a specific district in Borneo may be to eliminate poverty and conserve forest cover. Such an objective is complex in the extreme; it requires an approach that integrates across numerous components of the system − almost nothing can be left out! Research will not yield a single solution to this problem, but it may provide understanding that improves the quality of management decisions.

In Box 1.3 we demonstrate the successful 'conclusion' of an integrated approach to wildlife management in Botswana; this has centred on a hugely complex set of issues that appear to have been successfully resolved for the moment. However, further changes will occur and the adaptive management approach must continue − there is no point at which all problems are solved and further research and experimentation are no longer required. Evidence that the system is about to breakdown must be met with further institutional or management interventions. This example demonstrates the value of the integrated approach; its success was built on learning from experience in neighbouring Zimbabwe, where success was more elusive.[25] In the short term, integrated approaches to natural resource management will be more costly than sector- or discipline-based approaches. In the long term, they are more likely to yield sustainable management systems, stronger institutions and a better natural resource base. The knowledge needed for social learning and adaptive management accumulates slowly. In the Botswana case, the history of the success can be traced back to interventions in

---

[25] Campbell, B. and Shackleton, S. The organisational structures for community-based natural resources management in southern Africa. *Africa Studies Quarterly*, **5** (2001). Online: http://web.africa.ufl.edu/asq/v5/v5i3a6.htm.

Zimbabwe in the 1970s! The time and resources invested in social learning will determine how quickly development can become sustainable.

Box 1.3. Empowering local communities to benefit from wildlife in Botswana

Nico Rozemeijer and Corjan van der Jagt have documented the success of a community-based natural resource management programme in Botswana.[1] They focus on the Nqwaa Khobee Xeya Trust in Kgalagadi District, one of many such schemes. The end result is a community that has responsibility for the wildlife resources in an area of $12180\,km^2$, a vast area with three villages and 850 people. In 2000, they received US$63 000 from a safari operator in a joint venture involving hunting, photographic safaris and cultural activities. This provided about US$450 to each household. In addition, there were 75 jobs created, on average one job for every second household. In earlier times the local population had no benefits from the wildlife resource, apart from subsistence hunting. The success is based on a number of key elements.

A long history of trial and error (informal adaptive management)

In southern Africa, there has been close interaction of the key players in wildlife management in different countries so learning about successes and failures was possible. These key players, many of them ecologists, were already committed to adaptive management in the early 1980s, but it is not clear if they saw this management applying to the broader policy and institutional environment that was developing, or whether they confined it to on-the-ground wildlife issues. All key players had noted the success of giving control of wildlife to commercial farmers in Zimbabwe in the 1970s and the resulting massive expansion of wildlife as a land-use. This was followed by early, but unsuccessful, attempts of returning some benefits of hunting safaris to peasant farmers living in or next to safari areas. Then, in the 1980s, there were more empowering approaches such as CAMPFIRE in Zimbabwe.

A focus on local institutional arrangements

The architects of Botswana's wildlife programme had noted the problems in other countries, where full control was not given to local communities. They set about establishing a system whereby communities could apply for corporate status, with far-reaching management responsibilities. A community in or adjacent to a Controlled Hunting Area, allocated for community management, could apply for a wildlife quota provided it had organised itself in a participatory and representative manner that was approved by the district and wildlife authorities. The quota can be used for subsistence hunting. If the community wants more secure access to the wildlife quota and wants joint ventures with the private sector, it may decide to lease the Controlled Hunting Area from the land authority, in which case it has to comply with three conditions.

- The community had to organise itself as a representative and legally registered entity such as a trust or cooperative and demonstrate to the district authorities that a participatory process was observed.
- In this process, the community should design and adopt regulations and procedures (constitution and bylaws) that not only define its natural resource management functions but also its accountability and responsibility towards the community members.
- A land-use and management plan conforming to the wildlife management area regulations had to be prepared for the Controlled Hunting Area and approved by the land authority. A 15-year 'Community Wildlife Lease' could then be obtained.

In the study area, an attempt was made to develop a management structure that would reflect as closely as possible the ethnic and gender composition of the three settlements. Based on information obtained from the in-depth research phase, a system was agreed whereby all residents formed groups largely based on kinship. Ethnically mixed groups generally did not emerge. A man and a woman in the village committee represented each group, and two men and two women in the overall board of the Trust represent each village. Various powers have been given to the different organisational layers.

A long history of facilitated community development

The Trust, as a new organisation, needs to be given time to establish a transparent and accountable mode of operation. Some NGOs have been working for years in one community to assist in capacity building. Communities are now better prepared for negotiations with the private sector. They do not simply sell off their entire quota, creating problems of reinvestment, but are increasingly empowered to undertake economic activities under joint management, which, in turn, enhances local employment and management skills. In the study area it took three years, starting in 1996, to develop a management structure, a constitution and a land-use and management plan. The Trust was registered in 1998 and obtained user rights in 1999. The Trust then developed a tender document based on its land-use and management plan, selected a private sector partner, and signed a sublease agreement for an initial one year period.

Attention to the ecological context

To ensure ecological sustainability, the hunting quotas are set by the wildlife authorities, usually after an aerial survey. Trusts are encouraged and trained by the wildlife authorities to monitor wildlife populations in their areas but a system has yet to be put in place whereby the data can feed into the annual quota-setting process.

Attention to multi-scale multi-sector analysis and intervention

This Botswana case demonstrates very nicely that one sometimes cannot intervene in only one part of a system. The operational framework that has emerged demonstrates the need to have interventions at multiple scales. Local communities apply to district and wildlife authorities in the first instance, and then to the Land Board for a lease. The framework for the system has been set in place in terms of national legislation and policies, involving local government and land and wildlife departments. NGOs work closely with communities to build capacity in organisational development, financial control and tendering procedures and wildlife management; but they were also important in lobbying for appropriate national policies. The wildlife department sets quotas and monitors the harvest.

Summary

This is not to say that the system can now be left to run on its own. New challenges emerge and these must be met by appropriate interventions. The system must be adaptive. Two emerging challenges are the lack of clear connection to district authorities, who get little benefit from wildlife management, and the jealousy of those outside the benefit zone, especially the cattle barons belonging to other ethnic groups.[2]

[1] Rozemeijer, N. and van der Jagt, C. Botswana case study: community-based natural resources management (CBNRM) in Botswana. How community based is CBNRM in Botswana? In *Empowering Communities to Manage Natural Resources: Case Studies from Southern Africa*, ed. S. E. Shackleton and B. Campbell. Lilongwe: SADC Wildlife Sector Natural Resource Management Programme; Pretoria: CSIR; Harare: WWF (Southern Africa); Bogor: Center for International Forestry Research, 2000, pp. 1–7. Online: http://www.cifor.cgiar.org/publications/pdf_files/Books/Empowering.pdf.

[2] Postscript! This text proved rather prophetic. When returning to this text only three months later, the situation had indeed changed. The Department of Local Government had issued a directive for all funds earned by community-based natural resource management projects to be transferred to District Councils for management by them. This caused an outcry and is seen as a serious threat to community incentives and the long-term sustainability of these projects. Other surprise announcements included a ban on lion hunting and a dramatic increase in game license fees. In neither case were the wildlife management trusts consulted: see Shackleton, S., Campbell, B., Edmunds, D. and Wollenberg, L. Devolution and community-based natural resource management: creating space for local people to participate and benefit? *Natural Resource Perspectives 76*. London: Overseas Development Institute, 2002. Online: http://www.odi.org.uk/nrp/76.pdf.

Conclusion

A number of 'external' environmental, economic and social problems are now threatening the long-term performance of the agricultural, forestry, livestock and fishery systems upon which poor people depend. This creates a significant challenge for the researcher in agriculture and natural resources. It is going to be increasingly necessary to grapple with the issues of scale and complexity in natural resource systems. Integrated approaches have been used in the past, but a comprehensive framework has rarely been applied at an operational scale. There are major challenges to experimenting with such frameworks and to work out modalities to carry out effective research to manage entire natural resource systems. This in itself will be a major learning effort that requires new competencies of researchers and ways of organising research. Research organisations will need to reflect on their *modus operandi* and scientific culture and rise to the challenge of reorganising for maximum effectiveness in a more interconnected world. Our contention is that the case for more 'integrated' approaches to natural resource management is compelling. The ultimate integration of the elements of management of any natural resource may not be achievable. However, an attempt to modify existing research and development efforts to achieve higher levels of integration does, on balance, seem to be a sensible thing to do.

The challenge of integrated science laid down in the quote from Aldo Leopold at the beginning of this chapter is only beginning to be met. There are fundamental aspects in the way that science and development assistance are organised that make such innovations difficult to achieve. These obstacles are those discussed by Thomas Kuhn in his classic work on the difficulties of achieving revolutions in science.[26] Kuhn's contention is that such revolutions can only occur when a state of crisis is reached. The environmental and poverty crises that are now confronting the world may provide the trigger that is needed for change. Kuhn claims that 'Scientific revolutions are inaugurated by a growing sense, . . . often restricted to a narrow subdivision of the scientific community, that an existing paradigm has ceased to function adequately in the exploration of an aspect of nature to which that paradigm itself had previously led the way . . . the sense of malfunction that can lead to crisis is prerequisite to revolution'.

We will argue in this book that concepts and tools now exist for a science-based approach to the integrated management of natural resource systems. We will cite examples of successful natural resource management research that indicate that some of the barriers to integrated systems management are beginning to break down. We will present examples of integrative tools and concepts from different disciplines and scientific fields. We will argue that we are now at the threshold of innovative approaches to resource management that differ fundamentally from earlier discipline-based studies of natural resource problems. The methodological and conceptual problems need constant attention in order to avoid the danger of simply using the rhetoric of 'integration'.

---

[26] Kuhn, T. S. *The Structure of Scientific Revolutions*. Chicago, IL: University of Chicago Press, 1970.

If the real needs of the rural poor in developing countries are to be met, then science must deal with the natural resource system upon which they depend for their livelihoods. The farmers, fishers and foresters themselves are practising integrated management of their resources, basing their management on knowledge acquired over generations.[27] Effective research should link seamlessly with the knowledge of these clients. If scientists continue to operate in a simple technological world, they will fail to achieve the potential pay-offs that could be obtained by linking modern science to traditional knowledge and practice. However, as importantly, change is occurring in the world that defies the understanding of the local resource manager. Macro-economic changes and increased climate variability will be major determinants of the condition of human life in poor countries, and science must contribute understanding of how these phenomena will impact on ordinary people.

Similarly, the development pathways followed by people in poor developing countries will have major implications for the global environment. The world is becoming more connected and integration is emerging as an important concept in natural resource management: there is a need to integrate across disciplines, across scales (space and time), across stakeholders, across components.[28] We have to understand processes operating at scales from organisms to farms to global resource systems. Similarly, we also have to span the range from households to villages to districts up to international agreements.

The keys to integrated natural resource management

There are several features that are central to integrated natural resource management.

- In the short term, integrated approaches to natural resource management will be more costly than sector or discipline-based approaches. In the long term, they are more likely to yield sustainable management systems, stronger institutions and a better natural resource base.
- We never know enough about natural resource systems to manage them with certainty. Therefore, human interventions should

[27] Berkes, F., Colding, J. and Folke, C. Rediscovery of traditional ecological knowledge as adaptive management. *Ecological Applications,* **10** (2000), 1251–1262.

[28] Lal, P., Lim-Applegate, H. and Scoccimarro, M. The adaptive decision-making process as a tool for integrated natural resource management: focus, attitudes, and approach. *Conservation Ecology,* **5** (2001), 11. Online: http://www.consecol.org/vol5/iss2/art11.

always be experimental and should contribute to learning about the system.

- The knowledge needed for learning and adaptive management accumulates slowly. The time and resources invested in learning will determine how quickly meaningful development will occur.
- Integrated approaches to natural resources science will not yield precise recipes for managers, but they will help managers to make the right decisions and even more importantly to learn from their mistakes.
- The successful application of science to natural resources management requires changed relationships between scientists and local resource managers. Formal scientific knowledge and local knowledge must be combined in an adaptive management framework. All management must be treated as experimental and the role of science is to learn from these experiments.

2   Dealing with complexity

Research on social-ecological[1] systems, and particularly on agro-ecosystems, will inevitably be dealing with high levels of complexity.[2] Such systems are characterised by multiple scales of interaction and response, and a high frequency of non-linearity, uncertainty and time lags (Box 2.1). Multiple stakeholders seek to satisfy overlapping and often competing objectives using resources that are both spatially and temporally variable. In spite of this, development planners, many of whom come from countries with market economies, have shown a surprising faith in approaches reminiscent of 'central planning'. Development assistance often assumes levels of control and predictability that are rarely to be found in complex natural resource systems. Projects often have overly optimistic expectations of their potential to bring about predictable change in the decisions of the large numbers of households who depend upon rural landscapes to satisfy their livelihood requirements. The decisions made by these households are influenced by policies, incentive structures and access to external inputs. Decisions to adopt or not adopt new technologies or land-use practices by individuals and households depend on a multitude of factors, and the impact of external influences will vary from situation to situation.

Decisions of resource managers involve the weighing of many options. For instance, farmers weigh-up on-farm options and off-farm options that may involve temporary or permanent migration. They also contemplate whether to exploit, harvest and market resources, or whether to invest, maintain and conserve them. Where exploitation and harvesting dominate over investment and conservation, the resources are likely to degrade, but the returns for labour and short-term profitability may be high. Where soil

[1] We are grateful to Brian Walker for pointing out to us that the term social-ecological is preferable to the term socio–ecological. The latter has a connotation of an ecological system with some social aspects, the former implies an interactive system of equally important social and ecological parts.

[2] Fresco, L. O. *Cassava in Shifting Cultivation. A Systems Approach to Agricultural Technology Development in Africa.* Wageningen: Royal Tropical Institute, 1986; Scoones, I., Chibudu, C., Chikura, S. *et al.* *Hazards and Opportunities. Farming Livelihoods in Dryland Africa: Lessons from Zimbabwe.* London: Zed Books, 1996.

conservation, tree planting and other investments dominate, the resources may recover from past exploitation but may not meet current livelihood demands. Finding a balance depends very much on the interactions between land-users and other stakeholders.

Box 2.1. Complexities of research on integrated social-ecological systems

Features are:
- multiple scales of interaction and response
- high frequency of non-linear trajectories, uncertainty and time lags
- multiple stakeholders, often contrasting objectives that complicate the task of identifying research and management aims and resolving trade-offs among them
- context specificity of natural resource situations
- the need to harness the skills and tools of several scientific and management disciplines
- integration of the interactions of numerous components
- frequency of situations with common property and unclear or contested property rights.

To add further to the complexity, the resource users in these systems often function within diverse institutions, ranging from quasi-private organisations to common pool institutions established by mixtures of traditional, locally elected and central government authorities. Traditional rules governing the use of land and water resources, or forest or fishery stocks, are usually complicated and difficult for outsiders to understand.

Huge amounts of traditional local knowledge underpin the management of these complex systems. Much of this knowledge is not codified. In recent literature on knowledge management, it is referred to as *tacit* knowledge as opposed to the *explicit* knowledge of modern science. Many attempts to change the resource management practices of poor people in the tropics have paid little attention to the rich tacit knowledge that is available. This has resulted in numerous development projects doing things that run counter to the common sense of local people. This tacit local knowledge is one of the keys to dealing with complexity. Local knowledge is not only very sophisticated, it is also used in subtle ways to manage the system adaptively. This knowledge is part of the system. Modern scientific and development interventions have to be grafted onto this knowledge base and must not attempt to brush it aside. Science may simply be used to extend the array of options available and then to monitor the changes in the system and provide feedback on further interventions that may be required. The ideal situation would be a continuing iteration between formal scientific innovation and analysis and tacit local knowledge.[3]

The new technologies or practices that emerge from research can sometimes be relatively simple. They may only be options or alternatives for communities of resource users to explore. Even for simple interventions, however, the consequences of widespread adoption can be extremely complicated. Larry Harrington and colleagues from CIMMYT[4] in their recent article in *Conservation Ecology* give the following example.[5] Farmers managing irrigated cropping systems use complex practices to manage soil fertility and water quantity and quality. These include crop residue management, fertiliser and farmyard manure management, biomass transfer from outside the farm, selection of alternative fuels for household use, alternative use of canal and tubewell water, timing and frequency of irrigation and crop selection that takes account of well-drained versus poorly drained areas.[6] However, the introduction of even a relatively simple practice – zero tillage crop establishment – can improve timeliness of sowing, raise water and nutrient use efficiency, reduce water pumping, stop groundwater depletion, reduce fuel use, lower carbon emissions, change crop rotations to take advantage of the earlier grain crop sowing and (through new rotations) change soil chemistry and soil health. Some of these consequences may only become apparent at higher scales of analysis (e.g. changes in the quality and quantity of groundwater). This has led some observers to argue that it is difficult for formal science to deal with this level of complexity and that its role should only be to monitor a few key indicators of system performance and leave the details in the hands of the local resource managers.

Research that attempts to fit the full complexity of natural resource systems into rigid scientific frameworks is not easy and has provoked scepticism. Such research is widely perceived to need excessive amounts of data, to be very costly and to yield few results of immediate practical value. The farming systems research of the 1980s is an example. It is now largely discredited as it taught us little that the farmers did not already know. Fund

---

[3] The ideas on knowledge management presented here come from the work of Steve Song of Bellanet International. Further information: http://www.bellanet.org.

[4] CIMMYT is the International Maize and Wheat Improvement Center, one of the 16 centres of the Consultative Group on International Agricultural Research (CGIAR).

[5] Harrington, L., White, J., Grace, P. *et al.* Delivering the goods: scaling out results of natural resource management research. *Conservation Ecology*, **5** (2001), 19. Online: http://www.consecol.org/vol5/iss2/art19.

[6] Fujisaka, S., Harrington, L. and Hobbs, P. Rice–wheat in South Asia: systems and long-term priorities established through diagnostic research. *Agricultural Systems*, **46** (1994), 169–187.

allocation for agricultural research is often based upon analysis of the impact of research on production. It has been difficult to attribute any direct impact, in a quantitative sense, to much of the integrated research that has been conducted on complex agro-ecosystems. This is especially true where the benefits are in the form of environmental services with cash values that are difficult to determine. This has led many to conclude that integrated research on natural resource management systems is an expensive luxury.

Jacqueline Ashby of the International Center for Tropical Agronomy (CIAT) employs the concept of *holarchies* to argue forcefully for a new orientation of agricultural science.[7] The concept of holons or holarchies describes the units of analysis of complex natural resource research. The concept embodies the notion that in any natural resource system there are hierarchies of subsystems with behaviours that will influence the behaviour of other levels of the hierarchy.[8] Creating ecologically sound conditions for growing healthy animals and plants will usually mean that management must be targeted at more than one level of the hierarchy. While farm-level production may be important, it is likely that some elements of management will be at larger landscape scales.[9]

Systems, when analysed as hierarchies of interdependent subsystems, manifest the property that what is good in the short term is not necessarily good in the long term.[10] Understanding what goes on at one level does not necessarily provide sound information about what is going on at another level. For example, increasing productivity at the level of individual farm plots can lead to degradation of watersheds. Pest and disease control to improve plant health in the farming system can lead to pesticide contamination and diminished human health in the larger production-to-consumption system.

[7]Ashby, J. A. Integrating research on food and the environment: an exit strategy from the rational fool syndrome in agricultural science. *Conservation Ecology*, **5** (2001), 20. Online: http://www.consecol.org/vol5/iss2/art20.

[8]Allan, T. F. H. and Starr, T. B. *Hierarchy Perspectives for Ecological Complexity*. Chicago, IL: University of Chicago Press, 1982; Giampetro, M. and Pastore, G. Multi-dimensional reading of the dynamics of rural intensification in China: the amoeba approach. *Critical Reviews in Plant Sciences*, **18** (1999), 299–329.

[9]Holling, C. S., Schindler, D. W., Walker, B. H. and Roughgarden, J. Biodiversity in the functioning of ecosystems: an ecological synthesis. In *Biodiversity Loss: Economic and Ecological Issues*, ed. C. A. Perrings, K. G. Maler, C. Folke, C. S. Holling and B. O. Jansson. Cambridge: Cambridge University Press, 1995.

[10]Giampetro and Pastore, Multi-dimensional reading.

The new vision of integrated research

What then is needed if agricultural and natural resource research is to comprehend and manage complexity? Buzz Holling has described the generic features of research on complex environmental systems, and his ideas are summarized in Box 2.2. However Holling's framework was conceived for developed countries with well-developed institutions. In situations of extreme poverty and lack of local empowerment, additional elements are needed. Action research, not analyses from outside the system, is a powerful tool in these situations and organisational change, knowledge management and learning assume major importance.

Box 2.2. Generic features of research on complex systems

Holling's analysis of research on complex systems has the following framework.[1]

- Environmental problems are essentially systems problems where aspects of the behaviour of the systems are complex and unpredictable, and where causes, while at times simple, when finally understood are always multiple. *Therefore interdisciplinary and integrated modes of inquiry are needed for understanding. Further, understanding (not complete explanation) is needed to form policies.*

- The causes of problems are fundamentally non-linear in their dynamics. They demonstrate multi-stable states and discontinuous behaviour in both time and space. *Therefore, the concepts that are useful come from non-linear dynamics and theories of complex systems. Policies that rely exclusively on social or economic adaptation to smoothly changing and reversible conditions lead to reduced options, limited potential, and perpetual surprise.*

- Environmental problems are increasingly caused by slow changes, reflecting decade-length accumulations of human influences on air and oceans and decade-to-century transformations of landscapes. These slow changes cause sudden changes in fast environmental variables that directly affect the health of people, productivity of renewable resources and vitality of societies. *Therefore, analysis should focus on the interactions between slow phenomena and fast ones and monitoring should focus on long-term slow changes in structural variables. The political window that drives quick fixes for quick solutions simply leads to more unforgiving conditions for decisions, more fragile natural systems and more dependent and distrustful citizens.*

- The spatial span of connections is intensifying so that the problems are now fundamentally cross-scale in space as well as time. National environmental problems can now more and more frequently have their source both at home and half a world away: witness greenhouse gas accumulations, the ozone hole, AIDS and loss of biodiversity. Natural planetary processes mediating these issues are coupled to human, economic and trade linkages that have evolved since the mid twentieth century. *Therefore, the science that is needed is not only interdisciplinary, it is also cross-scale.*

- Both the ecological and social components of environmental problems have an evolutionary character. The problems are, therefore, not amenable to solutions based on knowledge of small parts of the whole, nor on assumptions of constancy or stability of fundamental relationships, be they ecological, economic or social. Assumptions that such constancy is the rule might give a comfortable sense of certainty but is spurious. Such assumptions produce policies and science that contribute to a pathology of rigid and unseeing institutions, increasingly stressed natural systems and public dependencies. *Therefore, the focus best suited for the natural science components is evolutionary; for economics and organisational theory it is learning and innovation, and for policies it is actively adaptive designs that yield understanding as much as they do products.*

[1]Holling, C. Investing in research for sustainability. *Ecological Applications,* **3** (1993), 552–555; Box derived from Sithole, B., Frost, P. and Veeman, T. Searching for synthesis: integrating economic perspectives with those from other disciplines. In *Uncovering the Hidden Harvest: Valuation Methods for Woodland and Forest Resources* (People and Plants' Conservation Series), ed. B. M. Campbell and M. Luckert. London: Earthscan, 2002, pp. 198–227.

In recent years, a proliferation of innovations have reflected the paradigm shift towards an integrated approach. However, no coherent unity of thought or organisation has yet appeared. Scientists have called for a broader focus and created new names for these approaches, all of which emphasise integration and attention to complexity, but there is no widespread recognition and best practice for this new integrated thinking. One objective of this book is to begin to define such best practice.

Research on complex systems is dealing with patterns that are repeated in an irregular way. The research cannot be based on the assumption that a generic pattern will emerge. Hence, integrated research will not produce technological silver bullets like those from research on single components of an agricultural system. It must, instead, focus on the strategic and on *how* rather than *what* to change in agriculture. Natural resource management research has to evolve from a focus on plans, maps and regulations to an acknowledgement of the complex, sometimes chaotic, reality in the field, with a large number of actors making their own decisions, often outside the framework provided by plans, maps or regulations.

A framework of system components to be covered in integrated research is presented in Fig. 2.1[11] A good understanding of ecological, biophysical, economic and social processes is needed to anticipate, model

[11]Swift, M. J., Bohren, L., Carter, S. E., Izac, A. M. and Woomer, P. L. Biological management of tropical soils: integrating process research and farm practice. In *The Biological Management of Tropical Soil Fertility,* ed. P. L. Woomer and M. J. Swift. Chichester: John Wiley, 1994, pp. 209–227.

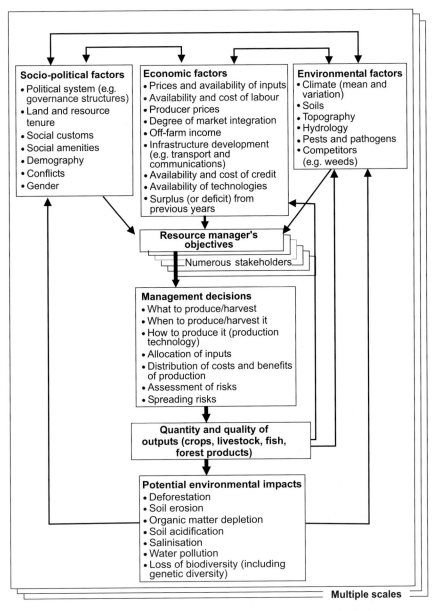

Fig. 2.1. Some of the major components of social-ecological systems. (Modified from Swift *et al.*, 1994. See footnote 11.)

and manage change. Yet, however good this understanding, many decisions will still have to be made by farmers and scientists reacting to the unfolding of events. Almost all natural resource management systems involve multiple stakeholders, with multiple perceptions and objectives. There are likely to be a series of mechanisms by which their interests are integrated and traded off. To be effective and relevant, integrated research has to be carried out at an appropriate scale and in a realistic context. At the level of smallholder farming systems, for example, research should be carried out mainly in the farmers' fields, where problems exist, rather than on research stations. This would invariably involve a participatory approach. We envisage most integrated research occurring within a specific geographical area, with appropriate linkages made to other scales in order to capture off-site effects and external drivers of change. There are, however, other models of integrated natural resource management that apply to domains that are not geographically continuous, for instance to a particular farming system discontinuously distributed across a large area. There may also be single problems that require an integrated approach to be applied across a very large area, for instance the restoration of degraded lands in Northeast Asia, and the management of desertification in Africa and Australia.

The elements of an integrated approach to research and management are presented in Fig. 2.2. The key elements of the interlinked package are listed below, and discussed in more depth in the sections that follow.

1. *The reorientation of the objectives of research.* In mainstream agricultural research, the prime objective is to improve yields of the dominant crops using plot-specific technologies. In other natural resource fields, the technological options are often also related to productivity improvement (e.g. improving yields of timber or fish). This conventional research seeks to produce technological solutions to specific problems. Research-based management of natural resource systems has a different objective. It does not seek total explanation but rather it seeks to improve the efficiency of learning and innovation. Given the complexity and dynamism of systems, one of the prime objectives of such research should be to improve the adaptive capacity of the resource managers and to enhance system resilience.[12]

2. *Giving attention to a specific set of concepts and issues.* Such research has to give attention to a number of concepts and issues. First, there are

[12] While in most circumstances it would be appropriate to enhance system resilience so that stress and disturbance can be withstood, in some cases systems are in an undesirable and resilient state, in which case the task would be to shift the system to another state.

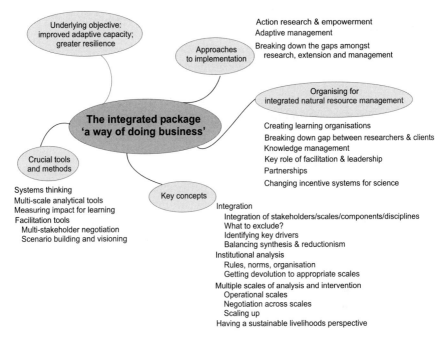

Fig. 2.2. The major features of integrated research and management.

numerous forces that influence a natural resources system. So the most important question becomes 'what to exclude'. The combined experience and judgement of scientists and local resource users will be the best basis for making such decisions. Science will then have to be used to understand the performance of the system and not just that of its components. Considerable emphasis will be given to understanding decision-making processes and investigating institutional arrangements (this chapter). And the appropriate balance between reductionism and synthesis will have to be sought. Most important is the multiple scales of analysis and intervention that need to be considered (Chapters 4 and 9).

3. *Added weight to action approaches to implementing research.* Faced with such daunting complexity and multiple actors, we advocate an adaptive approach, based on social learning and action research (Chapter 3).[13] An important element of this is the empowerment of disadvantaged stakeholders in order to ensure that all negotiations

[13] Holling, C. S. (ed.) *Adaptive Environmental Assessment and Management.* (*International Series on Applied Systems Analysis.*) New York: John Wiley, 1978; Walters, C. *Adaptive Management of Renewable Resources.* New York: Macmillan, 1986.

are fair. This requires that the distinction and the power differentials between researchers, extension workers and local managers are broken down.

4. *Giving extra weight to some specific analytical tools.* The problems posed by complex systems require that tools are drawn from systems analysis. A variety of tools to tackle multi-scale issues will be necessary (modelling, databases, geographical information systems, communities of practice, decision and negotiation support tools, etc.; see Chapter 5). Impact assessment will also be needed to measure system performance, but less as a tool for ex-post evaluation and more as a tool for adaptation, learning and performance enhancement. Impact assessment will also provide insights for further negotiation amongst stakeholders (Chapter 10). Given the diversity of stakeholders, facilitation will be important. Scenario building and visioning can be valuable in helping diverse stakeholders to share their knowledge and expectations.

5. *Restructuring the organisation of science.* Integrated research is not going to be successful if conducted within the present organisational models for research. Radically new forms of organisation are needed, where not only are disciplinary barriers removed but also those between research, extension and management (Chapter 11). Knowledge management will be required to deal with the diversity of information held by different actors and for applying it at various scales. More weight will have to be given to the sharing of informal or tacit knowledge. Partnerships will become essential to deal with the multi-scale and multi-sector issues. For scientists to perform in their new role, a radical revision of the incentive system will be required. Scientists' rewards will need to be linked to the performance of the system and not to the production of journal articles.

Adaptation, not sustainability, as the focus?

'Sustainability' as a concept received enormous attention in the 1980s and 1990s. However, if we accept that natural resource systems are inevitably going to change, how can we hold 'sustainability' sacred? For instance, who would have predicted in 1970 that peasant farmers in southern Zimbabwe would contribute 60% of the national grain supply by the mid 1980s (up from less than 5%)? Who would have predicted that gold panning, unknown in the 1970s, would be a key income source in the late 1980s? Who would have predicted a 10-fold increase in woodcraft marketing from 1990 to the mid 1990s, and who would have predicted widespread human mortality with massive implications for household expenditure, labour and remittances as a result of the human immunodeficiency virus and acquired immunodeficiency syndrome (HIV/AIDS) by the late 1990s? If we focus on, for example, sustainability of particular farming systems, we are locking farmers into those systems, whereas the evidence suggests a need for constant adaptation to new conditions. Sustainability as traditionally used by natural resource scientists implies maintaining the status quo. Sustainable development implies improving human livelihoods while maintaining options to allow for adaptation to change. So our objective is not sustainability, it is sustainable development and that means evolution and adaptation, at all levels, from the individual cropping system to the entire planetary environment (Fig. 2.3).[14]

Many existing sustainability indicators derive from the 'maintaining the status quo' paradigm; they do not recognise that there can be multiple 'sustainable states' and that many of them involve people switching to entirely new ways of life. Sustainable livelihood options outside of agriculture are not normally considered in resource management discussions, but these options will inevitably form the escape route for the majority of today's rural poor. This has already happened in the 'developed' world as a result of agricultural transformation[15] and the expansion of employment in manufacturing and services. Research to support sustainable development and enhance adaptability is going to be different from that on the sustainability of yields. The latter has specific land-use practices as its target and can do experiments and make models of their longer-term behaviour. Sustainable development and adaptive capacity research have to consider the range of options available and the way these options themselves change in time and differ between stakeholders.[16]

Changing the emphasis from technologies to decision making and institutional change

Integrated natural resource management research is more concerned with better decision making, maintaining options and resilience, establishing

[14]van Noordwijk, M., Tomich, T. P. and Verbist, B. Negotiation support models for integrated natural resource management in tropical forest margins. *Conservation Ecology*, **5** (2001), 21. Online: http://www.consecol.org/vol5/iss2/art21.

[15]Tomich, T. P., Kilby, P. and Johnston, B. F. *Transforming Agrarian Economies: Opportunities Seized, Opportunities Missed*. Ithaca, NY: Cornell University Press, 1995.

[16]Walker, B., Carpenter, S., Anderies, A. *et al.* Resilience management in social–ecological systems: a working hypothesis for a participatory approach. *Conservation Ecology*, **6** (2002), 14. Online: http://www.consecol.org/vol6/iss1/art14.

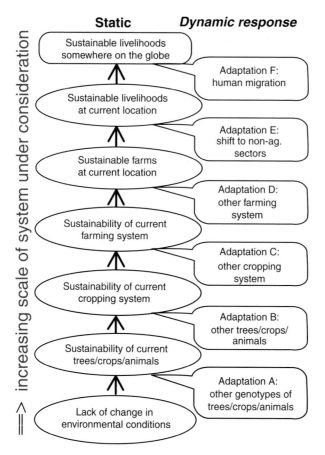

Fig. 2.3. Adaptive capacity as the missing link between sustainability (persistence) and sustainable development at different levels of organisation (ag., agricultural). (From van Noordwijk *et al.*, 2001. See footnote 14.)

appropriate institutional arrangements for resource management and reconciling conflicting management objectives *than* with producing technological packages. While we advocate a reorientation of the balance between technological research and other kinds of research, we are not abandoning technology. Research on natural resource systems should lead to tangible benefits on the ground – it must solve problems.[17] The motivation to engage

[17] Hagmann, J. R., Chuma, E., Murwira, K., Connolly, M. and Ficarelli, P. Success factors in integrated natural resource management R&D: lessons from practice. *Conservation Ecology*, **5** (2002), 29. Online: http://www.consecol.org/vol5/iss2/art29; Garrity, D. P., Amoroso, V. B., Koffa, S. *et al.* Landcare on the poverty–protection interface in an Asian watershed. *Conservation Ecology*, **6** (2002), 12. Online: http://www.consecol.org/vol6/iss1/art12; Harrington *et al.*, Delivering the goods.

jointly with stakeholders in experimentation and learning is that there is some 'plausible promise' or 'best bet' for a beneficial change.[18] Successes will invariably be built around specific intervention possibilities that achieve adoption and uptake.

Many conceptual models of integrated natural resource management focus on decision making processes.[19] Padma Lal of the National Centre for Development Studies at the Australian National University has noted the complexity of the processes leading to decision making by natural resource managers. Decisions to adopt or not to adopt new technologies by individuals or households depend on cycles of learning and adaptation. They are based upon a multitude of factors and external influences that will vary from situation to situation and be dependent on incentive structures, information flows and so on. Central to the decision-making process is the analysis of trade-offs and competing interests, and the resolution of conflicts. In the process of designing improvements in decision making, the research will throw up technological problems. Some of these will be addressed through systems-level process research, which is interdisciplinary (e.g. a water × soil × vegetation problem on hillsides). Others will require discipline-based, component research (e.g. a plant pest problem).

The most that outside actors can hope to do is to facilitate and support a process of negotiation among the stakeholders and to empower weaker stakeholders to engage with more powerful ones. Partners in action research should be equals; researchers who hold themselves aloof from the resource managers are unlikely to be effective. Michael Mortimore writes:

> My own research teaches me that there are solid grounds for regarding resource managers, even poor ones, as autonomous, responsible, experimental, and, though risk-averse, also opportunistic. Constraints not ignorance deter poor households. It follows from such an optimistic interpretation that they don't need to be lectured, cajoled, pressured or motivated but offered choices of technology, . . . information, experience, and an enabling economic environment that make the effort worthwhile. Given

[18]Douthwaite, B., de Haan, N. C., Manyong, V. and Keatinge, D. Blending 'hard' and 'soft' science: the 'follow-the-technology' approach to catalyzing and evaluating technology change. *Conservation Ecology*, **5** (2001), 13. Online: http://www.consecol.org/vol5/iss2/art13.

[19]Lal, P., Lim-Applegate, H. and Scoccimarro, M. The adaptive decision-making process as a tool for integrated natural resource management: focus, attitudes, and approach. *Conservation Ecology*, **5** (2001), 11. Online: http://www.consecol.org/vol5/iss2/art11; van Noordwijk *et al.*, Negotiating support models.

an 'autonomous' rather than a 'dependency' view of small-scale resource managers, the objective of systems research is empowerment (through targeted information, access, participatory experimentation, institutional change etc).

A major focus of natural resource management is the development of new institutional arrangements and policies that foster integration in different contexts and across scales – from village level institutions to central policies and laws. Institutional development will be particularly important in the situation where common property and open access resources prevail, especially where these resources are valued differently at different scales. The existence of a globally endangered but locally valueless species in an area of extreme human poverty provides a classic example. Why would poor farmers forego development opportunities in order to conserve an animal or plant whose sole value is its global rarity? Chapter 3 explores the institutional arrangements necessary for social learning. Chapter 4 deals with the importance of understanding organisational scale. Chapter 9 addresses the problems of planning for dissemination and uptake and Chapter 11 suggests ways of reorganising for effective research-based management.

Becoming part of an action cycle

Researchers need to become actors in the systems they are working with; they cannot remain outside the system as totally objective observers. The gulf between researchers and their clients has to be bridged. External analysis is of only limited value in predicting the behaviour of social systems. Greater insights can be gained by manipulation of the system. Kurt Lewin captured this in his observation that: 'If you want to know how things really work, just try to change them'.[20] This explains why an external 'clinical' systems analysis and static intervention design, as practised in classic farming systems research or in classic adaptive management, has failed to address the 'real issues which make things work' or fail.[21] Jürgen Hagmann suggests: 'We were still being surprised by revelations of social dynamics after five years of intervention'.[22]

Consequently, we have to confront the reality that we can never understand and control all the factors in complex, non-linear systems from

[20] Lewin, K. Action research and minority problems. *Journal of Social Issues*, **2** (1946), 34–46.

[21] Bawden, R. On the systems dimension in FSR. *Journal of Farming Systems Research–Extension*, **5** (1995), 1–18.

[22] Hagmann *et al.*, Success factors in integrated natural resource management R&D.

'outside'. However, action research enables us to analyse and interpret a system's reaction to change and helps us to understand the behaviour of the whole system better. Instead of analysing as many separate components of a system as possible and then looking at how they interact, the action research intervention would induce change on certain selected components of the system. This should reveal which other parts of the system need to be understood. In practice, this implies a focus on parts of the system in order to study the dynamics of the whole system. The part is not the whole, but it can provide a short cut to understanding it.

Participation and shared learning are central to this exploration of the system. This can be achieved through action research at various levels, from the household up to international conventions. These approaches mobilise the common sense and tacit knowledge of multiple stakeholders who routinely deal with complexity. We deal with these and related topics in depth in Chapter 3.

Adaptive management is a key component of much integrated research because it implies monitoring the behaviour of the system and seeking to determine patterns and causality of change in order to trigger management interventions. Much of the stimulus for advocating an adaptive approach is the recognition that it may not be possible to collect and analyse sufficient data to understand the entire system adequately.[23] The organisations for carrying out this research need to engage all interest groups as full partners, thus creating learning communities that are together developing new approaches. Engagement must be at all stages of the process: from problem identification through to the implementation of solutions.[24] Adaptive management as currently understood in a significant part of the literature is focussed mainly on biophysical management.[25] We envisage a major shift of focus to applying it to the entire social–ecological system, and this is not a simple undertaking.

Many of the difficulties faced by development research can be traced to poor problem identification. However, in natural resource systems, it is not a simple procedure to identify problems – there will usually be a complex

[23]Johannes, R. E. The case for data-less marine resource management: examples from tropical near shore fisheries. *Trends in Ecology and Evolution*, **13** (1998), 243–246; Walters, *Adaptive Management of Renewable Resources*.

[24]Chambers, R. *Rural Development: Putting the Last First*. Harlow, UK: Longman Scientific and Technical, 1983.

[25]Walters, C., Korman, J., Stevens, L. E. and Gold, B. Ecosystem modeling for evaluation of adaptive management policies in the Grand Canyon. *Conservation Ecology*, **4** (2000), 1. Online: http://www.consecol.org/vol4/iss2/art1.

of problems, with different stakeholders holding different views on which are most important.

Given the combined elements of action research, multiple stakeholders and decision making and negotiation, a key feature of most interventions in natural resource management will be good process facilitation. Facilitated discussions to ensure shared understanding between stakeholders and researchers should be a core component of action research.

Moving across scales

A key feature of integrated research is its attempt to integrate across spatial and temporal scales (Box 2.3): it can never involve just a single snapshot in space or time. Action research may be 'integrated' at various levels, from households to villages up to the highest institutional levels (Chapter 4).

Box 2.3. Agroforestry initiatives: comprehending complexity

Agroforestry as a science had its roots in the naïve expectations that close associations between trees and crops can not only serve multiple functions but also serve these functions better than a spatial segregation of agriculture and forestry. With the increased understanding that competition typifies many of these intimate mixtures,[1] the focus in agro-forestry research has evolved from plot-level interactions between trees, soils, crops and animals to the way landscape elements, including trees and forest patches, interact to produce local as well as external environmental service functions. These service functions include sustained production, risk reduction, clean water, maintenance of terrestrial carbon stocks and conservation of biodiversity. Some of these functions can indeed be combined at plot level; others may be better combined in landscapes. Understanding lateral flows of, for example, water, nutrients, soil, fire and organisms between components of the landscape, and the channels (e.g. roads, streams) and filters (e.g. strips of vegetation) modifying those flows, is the key to recognising options for a landscape integration of functions. For example, where high nutrient supply to agricultural crops is not compatible with quality standards for surface or groundwater, a nutrient filter by tree or other vegetation around streams and ditches may lead to an acceptable solution.

The Alternatives to Slash and Burn programme, a broad consortium of international and national research organisations led by the World Agroforestry Centre (International Centre for Research in Agroforestry (ICRAF)) has made progress in the analysis of these issues at the forest margins in the humid tropics and in the rehabilitation of degraded lands. Meine van Noordwijk, a systems ecologist based at ICRAF, notes that the complex agroforests developed by farmers as alternatives to food-crop-based agriculture integrate local as well as global environmental functions. However, when management is intensified to maximise production, the systems may lose some of these non-local values.

The constraints to agroforestry development involve issues of property rights and market functions, as well as technological and ecological barriers. According to the scale at which stakeholders are involved, we can distinguish between natural resource management problems at village level, those involving upland/lowland linkages in catchments (within country or trans-boundary) and those that relate local stakeholder decisions to global issues such as biodiversity conservation or greenhouse gas emissions.

In Sumatra, unsustainable systems used by recent migrants are mostly the result of government planned transmigration programmes rather than of spontaneous poverty-driven land-use practices.[2] Farmers do develop agroforests, based on rubber, damar and other local or introduced trees, as sustainable and profitable alternatives to food-crop production based on slash and burn; however, this opportunity has stimulated rather than slowed down forest conversion. In the absence of active boundary enforcement mechanisms for nature reserves, this has negative impacts on biodiversity.

In mountain zones, opportunities for migrant farmers to plant profitable tree crops such as coffee and cinnamon have increased forest conversion, with variable impacts on forest functions. A combination of logging, large plantation-style projects, government-sponsored migration and activities of both local and recent migrant smallholders drives current forest conversion; much of the conversion is planned and sanctioned by government and encouraged by public policy. Small remnants of 'shifting cultivation' remain in Sumatra, but largely in the form of settled fallow rotation, and these do not lead to significant land degradation. The new land-use systems differ significantly from the systems based on natural forest, in terms of their sustainability, profitability, carbon stocks, greenhouse gas emissions and biodiversity.

[1] Sanchez, P. Science in agroforestry. *Agroforestry Systems*, **30** (1995), 5–55; Sinclair, F. L. and Walker, D. H. Acquiring qualitative knowledge about complex agroecosystems. Representation as natural language. *Agricultural Systems*, **56** (1998), 341–363.

[2] van Noordwijk, M., Tomich, T. P. and Verbist, B. Negotiation support models for integrated natural resource management in tropical forest margins. *Conservation Ecology*, **5** (2001), 21. Online: http://www.consecol.org/vol5/iss2/art21.

Natural resource management always involves negotiating trade-offs between different interests at different scales. The scales at which it is possible to get a reasonable consensus on desired outcomes may limit the scales at which natural resource management can be integrated. Integration of natural resource management seems to work best in situations where indicators of success are negotiated amongst a small number of stakeholders: for example, upstream and downstream farmers in the Murray Darling basin in Australia, erosion prone farmers and watershed managers in the Tennessee valley or small numbers of villagers in southern Zimbabwe. It will become progressively more difficult to achieve true science-based integrated management in a situation where a large number of stakeholder groups are engaged at various scales.

Becoming systems thinkers

The complexities of resource management systems are seldom sufficiently acknowledged. Alternatively, they may be acknowledged but the solutions or tools used simplify them to the point where they have no relation to reality. Models can be developed for a better understanding of complex system dynamics or to assist the decision-making process, but integrated natural resource management should not be seen as synonymous with predictive models of whole systems (Chapter 5). Large predictive models are unlikely to be of much use within the swiftly moving action research process. Nonetheless, particular predictive models can be valuable tools in articulating our current understanding of any natural resource system. Action research will often benefit by being interfaced with systems models to explore longer-term scenarios. It is within the framework of systems' thinking that diverse technological options for addressing given resource management problems can be most effectively developed.

Knowledge management

Agreement on desired outcomes presupposes an ability to monitor and manage for those outcomes. This will require managing knowledge (Chapter 5). This encompasses data management, monitoring and information sharing. A starting requirement for any integrated natural resource management will be a comprehensive data set for the management area, preferably spatially referenced. A shared understanding of changes in a system's properties will be important. However, the significance of informal knowledge must not be downplayed. Steven Song at Bellanet International likens knowledge to an iceberg, with our formal knowledge sticking out above the surface of the water and a vast amount of informal, tacit knowledge below the surface. Different stakeholders will have knowledge of the system that may not be amenable to simple formalisation. Different researchers will have insights into the system, many of which will not have been formalised through analysis and publication. Ensuring the sharing of informal knowledge will in many cases be as important as sharing scientific data. 'Knowledge management' as a concept embraces much more than data – it is about how organisations learn and share information in order to retain their comparative advantage in a rapidly changing environment. It fits squarely within integrated research on complex systems.

Scaling-up: going beyond the specific

Because integrated research considers numerous variables, many of which are locality specific, it has been criticised for only yielding local solutions. Scientists practising integrated research must respond to this criticism (Chapter 9). However, if natural resource systems are characterised adequately and their attributes are measured across their full range of variation, resource management models will yield results that have application across broad ecological and social domains.

Scaling-up will not always be an appropriate concept, however. The dissemination of the research products of conventional agricultural research, for example high-yielding crop varieties, follows a simple linear route from researcher to extension worker to farmer (the 'transfer of technology' model). Resource management research does not yield technological packages amenable to this sort of dissemination. In resource management research, the farmers, extension officers and researchers are all stakeholders, participating from the initiation of the research. Scaling-up to benefit many people is largely a function of planning and investment at the outset to create the enabling environment that allows for dissemination and uptake. Widespread adoption is most likely to happen if top-down and bottom-up approaches to development are properly reconciled; both are likely to be needed for the effective delivery of benefits from research.[26] The cycles of adaptation and learning that resource users experience in experimenting with new technologies are the key to widespread adoption; repeated learning cycles ensure an improvement in the 'credibility' of the innovation and facilitate its incorporation into existing management systems by ever larger numbers of producers.[27]

Measuring impact in complex systems

Any natural resource management research innovation will have impacts at a number of spatial and temporal scales.[28] The work of Jürgen Hagmann and colleagues in southern Zimbabwe provides an example of impacts at multiple scales. These authors undertook research that spanned the scale from plots to

---

[26]Lovell, C., Mandondo, A. and Moriarty, P. The question of scale in integrated natural resource management. *Conservation Ecology*, **5** (2002), 25. Online: http://www.consecol.org/vol5/iss2/art25; Hagmann *et al.*, Success factors in integrated natural resource management R&D.

[27]Douthwaite *et al.*, Blending 'hard' and 'soft' science.

[28]Harrington *et al.*, Delivering the goods; Lovell et al., The question of scale in integrated natural resource management; Jones, P. G. and Thornton, P. K. Spatial modeling of risk in natural resource management. *Conservation Ecology*, **5** (2002), 27. Online: http://www.consecol.org/vol5/iss2/art27.

farms to policies; their work resulted in successful interventions at the plot level and important reorientation of thinking within the extension service at the national level.

Measurement of the impact of natural resource management and of the research that supports it is at least as complex as measuring the impact of education, improved public health, etc. (Chapter 10). Impacts of integrated research are more difficult to isolate than those of more focussed component research. The impact of integrated natural resource management will tend to be manifest through improved performance of the system and the improved ability of farmers and other decision-makers to adapt to external changes. This can be tracked through indicators of system performance and will reflect the combined impacts of research, management and other, external, drivers of change. Causal relations between actor behaviour and systems performance can be determined. However, impact assessment is less important for ex-post project evaluation than for on-going learning from successes and failures.

Moving to new forms of organising and conducting science

What has been said above leads inevitably to the conclusion that we need new ways of organising science and a new incentive structure for conducting science (Chapter 11). Integrated natural resource management implies a closer relation of research to management – in its ultimate expression a breakdown of the distinction between research and management. The research will not normally be planned or designed independently of management. An integrated approach requires that organisations have the capacity to deal with multi-sector, multi-stakeholder and multi-scale issues.

In terms of project planning, this approach requires a high degree of flexibility, as the initially planned activities have to be adapted after each cycle of learning and exploration, when new, more important problems reveal themselves. Project time frames of two to four years are much too short for this sort of research. Developing sustainable institutions for natural resource management takes many years.

Conventional scientific culture has many elements that are not favourable to achieving integration. For example, much research focusses on controlled 'plots' or 'demonstration areas' and the need to show changes that can be directly and immediately attributed to research interventions. Development practitioners often view this sort of research as an unnecessary burden.

The integrated approach is favoured by the existence of strongly integrated organisations or a single management organisation for a geographically circumscribed area. Examples of the latter, such as the Tennessee Valley Authority in the USA and the Wet Tropics Management Authority in northeast Australia (Box 11.1, p. 231), seem to exist only in the developed world. The US Forest Service ecosystem management approach in the Pacific northwest is an example of an integrative process but operating in a relatively simple system. It has the advantage of only dealing with a moderate number of stakeholders in a context of secure property rights and strong legal frameworks.

Not getting lost in the system

A common criticism of integrated natural resource management is that it attempts to describe a multi-component system in which everything is connected to everything else and that such complexity defeats useful analysis. Given the complexity of resource and livelihood systems, the main challenge is to focus on the impacts being sought and not get lost in hundreds of peripheral research questions. Just because a natural resource system is highly complex does not mean that research and management have to address every element of that complexity. Pragmatism is essential. Fuzzy holistic approaches to natural resource management must be avoided at all costs. A clear articulation of a problem, plausible solutions and tangible potential benefits must still underlie all research investments. There are some guidelines that can be followed in attempting to make the system of study tractable.

- Based on the principle of systemic intervention, Jürgen Hagmann and colleagues tried to react to events and problems as they occurred within farmers' reality, rather than to anticipate and prescribe. The 'guiding star' was provided by their vision and goal as interventionists (their strong desire to improve rural life and their belief that rural people are able to develop and use their own potential to manage resources adaptively) and by farmers' own goals. The review of successes and failures then determined the continual adaptation of management interventions. When issues arose that were outside the competence of the team, outside specialists were brought in through strategic partnerships and networking.
- Brian Walker and colleagues in the Resilience Alliance argue that complexity is not boundless but has its own natural subdivisions and boundaries, and that three to five key variables often drive any particular system.[29] The trick will be to identify these variables,

[29]Holling, C. S., Folke, C., Gunderson, L. and Maler, K-G. *Resilience of Ecosystems, Economic Systems and Institutions.* Final report submitted to John D. and Catherine T. MacArthur Foundation. Gainesville:

taking care that slow variables are not forgotten. Slow variables change imperceptibly, but when they reach a threshold the system may switch rapidly into a new state.

- Participatory and action research approaches deal with complexity by drawing on the common sense and tacit knowledge of participants.

Defining and focussing upon a subset of processes and components is the key to defining the practical limits to the elements of complexity that have to be addressed in any piece of research. The ability to identify these key drivers of change successfully may be one of the most important steps in research-based attempts to achieve sustainable resource management. As we will reiterate throughout this book, the value of adding new components to research or management models must exceed the cost of doing so.

Integrating across disciplines

Peter Frost, of the Institute of Environmental Studies at the University of Zimbabwe, has analysed the role of interdisciplinary research in natural resource management programmes. He argues that the advances in scientific knowledge and understanding made over the past few centuries have come about through the widespread adoption of reductionism in science.[30] Reductionism involves the study, at increasingly finer levels of detail, of the mechanisms and processes underlying the patterns that we observe around us. To make the problems tractable for observations and experiments, apparently extraneous components and processes are omitted and, ultimately, often forgotten; site, setting and history are usually ignored.

A natural consequence of reductionism is that scientists have become increasingly focussed on, and specialised in, addressing the ever more detailed questions about causal relations. This has produced separate disciplines within science; as they mature, these spawn subdisciplines that grow and become distinct. The consolidation of scientific endeavour into disciplines has been paralleled by the establishment of a supporting infrastructure of university departments, research teams, research councils, funding agencies, review bodies and scientific journals, all organised at some level of aggregation along disciplinary lines. This structure undoubtedly serves

Resilience Alliance, 2000; Gunderson, L. and Holling, C. S. (eds.) *Panarchy: Understanding Transformations in Human and Natural Systems*. Washington, DC: Island Press, 2002.

[30] The first portion of this text is based on the writings of Peter Frost in Campbell, B. M., Chuma, E., Frost, P., Mandondo, A. and Sithole, B. Interdisciplinary challenge for environmental researchers in rural farming systems. *Transactions of the Zimbabwe Scientific Association*, 73 (1999), 39–57.

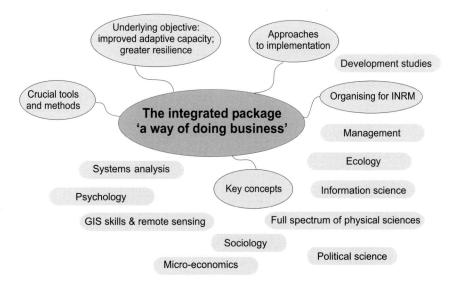

Fig. 2.4. The array of disciplines that is likely to be involved in research on social–ecological systems, overlaid on the major features of such research. (GIS, geographic information system; INRM, integrated natural resource management.)

science well in its analytical phase, but how relevant is it when we want to use scientific knowledge and understanding to resolve complex environmental, social, economic and other problems?

Scientists from many disciplines can contribute to improved natural resource management (Fig. 2.4). But the communities of scientists who make up the different disciplines tend to approach natural resource management problems in very different ways, and interdisciplinary agreement has proved remarkably elusive. Kuhn[31] has argued that

> to an extent unparalleled in most other fields [practitioners of disciplinary science] have undergone similar educations and professional initiations; in the process they have absorbed the same technical literature and drawn many of the same lessons from it. Usually the boundaries of that standard literature mark the limits of a scientific subject matter, and each [discipline] ordinarily has a subject matter of its own . . . Members of a scientific [discipline] see themselves . . . as the men (sic) uniquely responsible for the pursuit of a set of shared goals, including the training of their successors. Within such groups communication is relatively full

[31] Kuhn, T. S. *The Structure of Scientific Revolutions*. Chicago, IL: University of Chicago Press, 1970. A great deal of the argumentation in this landmark book applies to the difficulties of changing natural resource science in the direction of greater integration.

and professional judgement relatively unanimous. Because the attention of different scientific [disciplines] is, on the other hand, focused on different matters, professional communication across [disciplines] is sometimes arduous, often results in misunderstanding, and may, if pursued, evoke significant and previously unsuspected disagreement.

Simply bringing together all the relevant understanding from a wide array of disciplines (i.e. multi-disciplinary research), does not in itself guarantee success. An approach is needed that bridges the disciplines, takes account of history and context and, in many instances, makes people and their institutions the focus of the research. Successful interdisciplinary studies require people to think about and operate at the interfaces between disciplines rather than within them. Ideally, they would work together to conceptualise the problem, frame the questions, collect and analyse the data and write up the results. How to stimulate and maintain this kind of interaction and co-operation is a key issue in undertaking this kind of research. It is important that unidisciplinary frameworks are not allowed to dominate the diagnostic, problem-definition or visioning stage.

This does not mean that there will not be a need to apply the tools of specific disciplines to individual technical problems that fall under this overall conceptual framework. Problems of crop improvement or disease, harvesting or post-harvest technology and many others will be best addressed with the methodologies of conventional disciplines. However, constant iterations among disciplinary specialists, resource managers and integrative scientists are required in order to ensure that context is not lost and externalities are not being inadvertently created (Fig. 2.5). A major challenge for leadership will be to maintain the balance between in-depth disciplinary studies and approaches aimed at integrative understanding.

Economists have coined the term transaction costs for the costs (mostly time) related to negotiation, discussion and conflict resolution between partners. The transaction costs of interdisciplinary work are high. Close and frequent interaction is necessary: meetings, written communications, workshops and informal interaction are important. A considerable amount of time will have to be invested in planning, discussing and presenting research results, and in team building and facilitation.

In many academic fields, interdisciplinary endeavour is not rewarded. A colleague in Europe who worked in Zimbabwe relates how his job description in his first year of work was to publish three papers in any of the top 10 economics journals. He was able to meet this target by increasing the theoretical content of his draft manuscripts and stripping them of any non-economic data (e.g. data collected in participatory rural

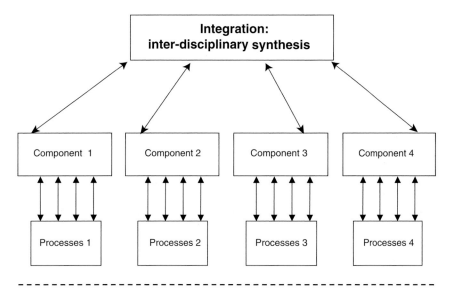

Fig. 2.5. Interdisciplinary science focusses on integration (synthesis) of components and processes functioning at lower levels of organisation. The study of these lower-level components and processes is the subject of single- or multi-disciplinary studies.

appraisals). As a result, his work was less relevant to real problems. Inter-actions between disciplines are often seen as compromising good science! Those who practice interdisciplinary research risk losing their credibility amongst more conservative colleagues. If we want to contribute to solving the world's conservation and development problems, then we must accept this risk. Interdisciplinary research is essential in dealing with complex systems but it will only succeed if there are sufficient incentives, rewards and time.

The keys to complexity

Integrated natural resource management as described here is more a changed approach to research and management than a specific set of technologies; it is a way of doing business rather than a new research paradigm. If agricultural and other production systems are understood as complex social–ecological systems, this will drive research to deal with long-term effects and environ-mental externalities. It will produce research products that are increasingly strategic in nature. It should 'democratise' the research process by involving a broad set of stakeholders in processes of adaptive management. Dealing with this complexity of biophysical factors, stakeholder interests and social and economic influences has a number of requirements.

- A fundamentally changed relationship is required between scientists and resource managers. The science of integrated natural resource management will not be conducted in the laboratory or on the research station. It will involve the study of patterns and causality in real-life farms, forests and fisheries.

- None of the components of the new vision are of themselves particularly new. If there is a paradigm shift then it lies in considering the new research as an interlinked package of numerous elements and a change in the relationships between the actors.

- Through action research, researchers become actors rather than undertaking 'neutral' analysis from outside the system. Action research mobilises the common sense and tacit knowledge of participants in dealing with complexity.

- Integrated research must transcend many of the boundaries between disciplines, and among research and development organisations, line agencies and ministries. It must have modest expectations of direct impact on components of the system. It may not yield scientific breakthroughs but it will help to generate options and resolve problems. Integrated research can improve the processes of negotiation and compromise that are needed to reconcile conservation and development trade-offs. It will yield improvements in the performance of the natural resources system.

- At any one time, there will only be a small number of significant drivers of change in a system and these must be the focus of research. Just because a natural resource system is highly complex does not mean that research and management have to address every element of that complexity.

- Interdisciplinary research will only succeed if there are changes in the incentives and reward systems of scientists. Scientists must be judged on their contribution to the improved management of natural resources systems and not on the delivery of papers or technological widgets. This requires time for the development of relationships between scientists and local resource managers and this process can often benefit from professional facilitation.

3 Getting into the system: multiple realities, social learning and adaptive management

One thing sets humans apart from other organisms: they are very good at learning and adapting. The farmers, foresters and fishers who are the supposed beneficiaries of natural resources research are constantly experimenting and innovating. The persistent failure of formal research and development assistance projects to recognise this reality is, therefore, something of a surprise. Far too many researchers and development practitioners act as though resource users are passive recipients of new ideas and technologies developed in the laboratory or on the research station. In the previous chapter, we argued that farmers are more sensitive to many elements of the complexity of their environment than many researchers. In this chapter, we extend this argument to the issues of innovation and adaptation. We contend that farmers' judgements of which innovations are viable and which are not will often differ from, and may be better than, those of the scientists. Furthermore, farmers are past masters at adaptation. They are constantly reading the faint signals that they receive from their environment – the date when a migrant bird arrives, the weather at a certain phase of the moon – and adapting their agricultural calendar or choice of crop accordingly.

Development projects and research institutes have been stubborn in their unwillingness to accept the realities of learning and adaptation by farmers and other resource managers. Typically, teams of consultants characterise and diagnose resource management problems. They develop a detailed plan for how the problem might be addressed over a project lasting for three to five years; every detail of the project is programmed and then it is handed over to a consulting company for execution. These sorts of R&D projects are based upon perceptions of situations at a single point in time. They ignore the inevitability of change and surprise. They assume a level of predictability of system performance that almost never exists in real life.

Many will argue that we are portraying a situation that has ceased to exist. That modern research and development projects are using the tools of participatory and action research and that this provides for adaptability and flexibility. We agree that much progress has been made in recent years. However, many of the projects that practise participatory and action research and aspire to foster adaptability do so within boundaries that are rigidly defined by the disciplinary background and personal experience of aid agency advisers and those implementing the project. Projects regularly curtail farmers' options or marginalise their local knowledge when they should be building upon that knowledge and expanding the range of options. There are rather few projects where farmers and scientists genuinely learn and experiment together as equal partners in a research endeavour. In industrialised countries, the farmers are usually the 'owners' of the problems and the researchers provide a service in response to the farmers' demands. In the developing world, it is usually the researcher who decides what the problem is and then sets about telling the farmer the solution.

Public sector planners, researchers and development practitioners are strangely locked into the paradigm of totally predictable, 'steady-state' resource systems. This is reflected in our constant calls to achieve sustainability. Sustainability is portrayed as maintaining the status quo. Producing the same yield of the same crops forever into a stable and predictable future. It is obvious that this is not a useful concept in the real world. Resource systems change over time. The relative profitability of different crops changes; forests respond to modifications in their environment or the mix of species in a fishery constantly alters. Global climate change and the integration of markets are amplifying these changes. Research and development activities that do not recognise the inevitability of change, or that attempt to control it, are doomed to failure. Research and development must build upon and enhance the learning and adaptation abilities of resource users. One starting point is to end the widespread arrogance of research and development: the assumption that modern science is superior to local knowledge. One characteristic that is shared by many of the successful resource management initiatives discussed in this book is that the R&D specialists have shown humility in their dealings with local resource managers. They have had the patience and respect to share knowledge and experimentation with the clients of their research. This has to become the norm not the exception. Scientists and extension workers have to move from imparting acquired knowledge to being learners and facilitators.

In mainstream productivity enhancement research, the prime goal is to deliver technologies and planting material to improve yields of the dominant crops. However, in a multi-stakeholder situation with small-scale producers, there will be multiple objectives, and it is unlikely that any single production objective will suit everyone. Standardised 'cookie-cutter' technologies that can be used in many contexts will only be part of the solution. The complexity and dynamism of systems requires that one of the prime goals will be to help resource users to deal with change, and thus enhance the adaptive capacity of the system. Science must improve the ability of the farmers, fishermen and foresters to sustain a flow of the diverse products and services that they depend upon. Research will need to strengthen the farmer's ability to manage a broad range of production factors and to increase their flexibility and ability to respond to multiple exogenous influences. A major objective will be to help the managers to achieve the skills and acquire the technologies that will enhance their control over their own destinies.[1] High-technology research on the components of agricultural systems is still vital but it has to be constantly reviewed to ensure that it is correctly placed in the context of changing local biophysical and socio-economic conditions.

Jürgen Hagmann and colleagues write that their experience with complex and dynamic livelihood systems led them to conclude that the only thing that is constant is change itself. What they considered sustainable in 1990 subsequently proved unsustainable. Therefore, sustainability in resource management is subject to a continual value-dependent, political and social negotiation process that cannot be usurped by outsiders. Sustainable development depends upon a social learning process in which the goal is increasing human capacity to solve problems and adapt to changing conditions.[2] Sustainability is determined less by technical expertise and consensus than by negotiation and trade-offs among stakeholders. Collective adaptive capacity is the key determinant for sustainable development.

Adaptive natural resource management requires a learning paradigm with a flexible combination of concepts and methodologies.[3] Recent writings on new scientific concepts have much to teach us,[4] for example experiential learning or learning by doing, systems thinking or looking at the big picture, and self-organisation (Box 3.1). We need to develop human and

---

[1]Lynam, T., Bousquet, F., Le Page, C. *et al.* Adapting science to adaptive managers: spidergrams, belief models, and multi-agent systems modelling. *Conservation Ecology*, **5** (2002), 24. Online: http://www.consecol.org/vol5/iss2/art24; Lal, P., Lim-Applegate, H. and Scoccimarro, M. The adaptive decision-making process as a tool for integrated natural resource management: focus, attitudes, and approach. *Conservation Ecology*, **5** (2001), 11. Online: http://www.consecol.org/vol5/iss2/art11.

[2]Holling, C. S., Berkes, F. and Folke, C. Science, sustainability and resource management. In *Linking Social and Ecological Systems. Management Practices and Social Mechanisms for Building Resilience*, ed. F. Berkes and C. Folke. Cambridge: Cambridge University Press, 1998; de Boef, W. S. Tales of the Unpredictable. Learning about Institutional Frameworks that Support Farmer Management of Agrobiodiversity. Thesis, Wageningen University, 2002.

[3]Röling, N. and de Jong, F. Learning: shifting paradigms in education and extension studies. *Journal of Agricultural Education and Extension*, **5** (1998), 143–161.

[4]Wheatley, M. *Leadership and the New Science. Discovering Order in a Chaotic World*, 2nd edn. San Francisco, CA: Berrett-Koehler, 1999.

social capital and combine it with hard science and a good dose of common sense.

Box 3.1. An adaptive management lexicon

Adaptive management is surrounded by a complex array of terms and concepts, many of which appear to us to mystify rather than clarify the issues. Here is a selection together with our interpretations of them.

Constructivism. Building on one's own mental model or common sense through learning and experimentation.

Positive-realism. Basing everything on objective scientific analysis.

Experiential learning.[1] Learning by doing emerges from the educational approach which says that it is better for people to find out things for themselves than to be taught them in more formal ways. In natural resource management, it captures the idea that people should not be taught new ideas or technologies but should be helped to experiment and find these things for themselves.

Social learning.[2] A change in a widely shared set of beliefs is achieved by communities learning together through shared experiences. The significance of this for natural resource management is that it provides a counter to the 'tall poppy syndrome': the idea that in many cultures anyone who stands out from the crowd has to be cut down to size. Promoting new ideas or technologies by promoting a small number of exemplary farmers often failed when these individuals were ostracised by their peers. Projects that foster group learning tend to have a higher success rate.

Collaborative learning. This appears to be a synonym for social learning. It is the term preferred by Daniels and Walker in their insightful book *Working through Environmental Conflict*.[3]

Adaptive-learning cycles. Continual reinforcement of learning by experimentation and feedback.

Actor-oriented approaches. Approaches that recognise that people are not passive recipients of information but respond to outside information on the basis of the mental models that they have built over years of experience.

Lifeworlds. The idea that everyone has a different view of the world based upon their experience and learning. Therefore, everyone will react differently to any new idea or technology.

Soft-systems methodology. The use of systems analysis techniques to address situations where there is no clear agreement on the objectives of the system or even on the definition of the system. Systems analysis techniques are used to structure the debate.[4]

[1] Kolb, D. A. *Experiential Learning. Experience as a Source of Learning and Development.* Englewood Cliffs, NJ: Prentice Hall, 1984.

[2] Reich, R. B. (ed.). *The Power of Public Ideas.* Cambridge, MA: Harvard University Press, 1988.

[3] Daniels, S. E. and Walker, G. B. *Working Through Environmental Conflict: The Collaborative Learning Approach.* Westport, CT: Praeger, 2001.

[4] Checkland, P. B. From optimising to learning: a development of systems thinking for the 1990s. *Journal of Operational Research and Society*, **36** (1985), 757–767; Checkland, P. and Scholes, J. *Soft Systems Methodology in Action.* New York: John Wiley, 1990.

In this chapter we draw on the work of Boru Douthwaite and colleagues at the International Institute for Tropical Agriculture (IITA). Douthwaite's recent book should be essential reading for natural resource management practitioners.[5] The concept of an adaptive learning cycle – how we can learn together for change – is central to achieving science-based innovation. The idea that scientists must become actors – stakeholders – in the natural resource systems where they work is also fundamental.

A clash of two paradigms

Boru Douthwaite and colleagues at IITA see one of the greatest challenges for natural resource management as being the shift that is needed towards a new understanding of the role of science.[6] Jürgen Hagmann and his co-authors pursue a similar theme in arguing that there is a need to get away from the idea that the resource managers themselves are the 'insiders' and the researchers are the 'outsiders'.[7] All agree that there has to be a softening of the barrier between scientists and local farmers, foresters and fishermen. Natural resource management by these local resource users is always 'integrated' as people have to deal with the complexity of natural resources in their daily lives. The knowledge, culture, values and norms of rural people are all aimed at a capacity to act and organise themselves to deal with changing natural resource and other challenges. However, the 'outsiders', the scientists and advisors, are also stakeholders; they are aiming to influence decisions of the

[5] Douthwaite, B. Enabling innovation: a practical guide to understanding and fostering technological change. London: Zed Books, 2002.

[6] Douthwaite, B., de Haan, N. C., Manyong, V. and Keatinge, D. Blending 'hard' and 'soft' science: the 'follow-the-technology' approach to catalyzing and evaluating technology change. *Conservation Ecology*, **5** (2001), 13. Online: http://www.consecol.org/vol5/iss2/art13.

[7] Hagmann, J. R., Chuma, E., Murwira, K., Connolly, M. and Ficarelli, P. Success factors in integrated natural resource management R&D: lessons from practice. *Conservation Ecology*, **5** (2002), 29. Online: http://www.consecol.org/vol5/iss2/art29.

other actors. And real decisions are largely based on the people's existing perceptions of reality and not a mechanical response to external advice.

This simple observation suggests that external efforts to influence local resource management must be based upon what Berger and Luckmann have described as constructivism.[8] External interventions will only make a difference if they contribute to the reality constructed in the minds of resource managers. In simple language, this means that decisions must be made, owned and internalised by those managers. Outsiders can be most effective if they have a facilitative role in this learning process. They can help by creating an environment in which the multiple, complex objectives of stakeholders are articulated and where diverse views are respected. Collective accountability for natural resources requires the construction of a common vision rooted in local people's values. This can lead to the adoption of new social norms. Existing local organisations will usually provide a better basis for this process than new institutions established by projects.

If everyone saw the world in the same way, then resource management would simply be a case of agreeing on a few tried and trusted methodologies with the stakeholders involved and then following a formula to implement them. Unfortunately, life is not that simple. Some natural resource scientists still feel that 'if we cannot come up with something better than what the farmers are doing we should give up and go home'. These practitioners generally embrace the technology transfer approach (Box 3.2) in which scientific knowledge is assumed to be superior to farmer knowledge. Proponents of this approach are scornful of participatory approaches that eulogise farmers' knowledge. The attitudes of these scientists harden when they have to work with farmers who ignore realities that seem blindingly obvious to researchers. Understanding and accepting that people see reality differently, and the ability to negotiate shared visions of reality, are fundamental to successful natural resource management. Constructivism is based upon the idea of multiple realities. Achieving a balance between the constructivist paradigm and the positivist–realist paradigm that underpins the 'science-is-best' approach is the fundamental change that is needed if integrated approaches to natural resource management are to succeed.

Box 3.2. Transferring technology

Conventional agricultural researchers have been able to assume a simple, rather linear, view of the technology development and transfer process (Fig. 3.1), described by Chambers

---

[8]Berger, P. L. and Luckmann, T. *The Social Construction of Reality. A Treatise in Sociology of Knowledge.* Garden City: Anchor Books, 1967.

and Jiggins as 'transfer-of-technology'.[1] The success enjoyed by the technology transfer approach in starting the green revolution has helped to ingrain the approach to such an extent that it has been commonly applied to the development and transfer of many types of technology other than improved germplasm.[2]

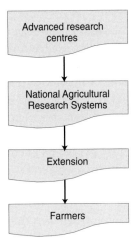

Fig. 3.1. The transfer of technology view of the way innovations originate and are passed down to farmers. (Adapted from Chambers and Jiggens. See footnote 1 in this box.)

Since the 1982 publication of Rhoades and Booth's landmark paper describing the 'farmer-back-to-farmer' approach,[3] there has been a growing realization that the technology transfer approach is flawed. For example, in a recent comprehensive review of research on soil fertility in West Africa, Bationo *et al.* concluded that: 'Over the past years a considerable number of technologies to improve the productive capacity of African soils have been generated. These technologies have not been transferred or implemented by the intended beneficiaries'.[4] The unhappy situation is that in many parts of Africa farmers have little choice but to continue to degrade their soils and their environment. It is just this scenario that integrated natural resource management must address. The questions remain. How will resource managers achieve their goals in practice? What tools and methodologies are resource management practitioners going to employ?

[1]Chambers, R. and Jiggins, J. *Discussion Paper 220: Agricultural Research for Resource Poor Farmers: A Parsimonious Paradigm.* Brighton: Institute of Development Studies, University of Sussex, 1986.

[2]Kaimowitz, D., Snyder, M. and Engel, P. *Linkage Theme Paper 1: A Conceptual Framework for Studying the Links between Agricultural Research and Technology Transfer in Developing Countries.* The Hague: International Service for National Agricultural Research (ISNAR), 1989.

[3]Rhoades, R. E. and Booth, R. H. Farmer-back-to-farmer: a model for generating acceptable agricultural technology. *Agricultural Administration,* **11** (1989), 127–137.

[4]Bationo, A., Lompo, F. and Koala, S. Research on nutrient flows and balances in West Africa: state of the art. *Agriculture, Ecosystems and the Environment,* **71** (1998), 19–35.

Positive-realism is associated with 'hard' science, that is, science that sets up hypotheses and tests them with repeatable and quantifiable experiments. 'Hard science' is rooted in the belief that the world has an independent reality that scientists discover in their experiments. The knowledge gained from hard science is independent, absolute and separate from the knower. Because this knowledge has passed the rigor of the scientific process, it is seen as superior to farmers' indigenous knowledge. Hence, the technology transfer approach, applied in its purest form, stipulates that the job of agricultural scientists is to employ the scientific method to understand, structure and model reality in order to develop technologies of benefit to farmers. It is then the job of extension to project the scientists' knowledge to the minds of farmers as accurately as possible, and the responsibility of the farmers to receive it. Farmers are expected to be passive recipients in that they are not expected to adapt the message if it is based on good science and properly delivered. If farmers do not adopt, it is their fault for being backward. In the research into farming systems of the 1980s, scientists attempted to subject farming systems to dispassionate analytical science: they viewed the farming systems as part of a controlled experiment. The participatory action research of the 1990s has gone a long way in recognising the complexity and unpredictability of farming systems: the researchers have been getting inside the system.

Constructivism is associated with soft science, that is, science that looks at social phenomena that cannot be reduced to component parts and is not repeatable outside of its complex context. Case studies that paint a rich, thick picture of phenomena are a mainstay of the soft sciences. Soft scientists contend that, contrary to the realist–positivist position:

- knowledge is not passively received and 'mapped on' to a learner's brain but is actively 'constructed' by the learner; this construction process is often social because the mental maps may be culturally defined, and because 'sense-making' may be undertaken by a group through negotiation
- an individual's faculty to learn and understand is adaptive; cognition serves a person's need to process information to organise and understand conceptually the world they experience in order to help them to thrive in that world.

The actor-oriented approach

Resource management must consider both social and technical elements of a system in context, giving equal emphasis to both. For example, when researching irrigation we need to observe the irrigation organisation and not just the irrigation technology. A focus on irrigation technology is a focus on technical and biophysical attributes. However, proper understanding also requires an analysis of how various actors interact to confront problems of water management and distribution. These relationships help us to understand how and why change might be adopted. This is what the *actor-oriented* approach developed at the Wageningen Agricultural University attempts to do.[9] Boru Douthwaite and colleagues argue strongly that this approach should become a central thrust of natural resource management.

The main goal of the actor-oriented approach has been to understand the reactions of different stakeholders to technical and social change. Long describes *intervention* as an attempt from outside a system 'to organize and control production' within it.[10] The focal point of interest in the actor-oriented approach is the manner in which people negotiate and transform the technology that they have admitted into their system. People will react to the intervention by manipulating and transforming it to fit their own mental maps of reality. They may simply ignore the technology and try to maintain their *lifeworld* unchanged. It is these types of reaction that the actor-oriented approach seeks to identify and study. Methodologically, this is significant because the intervention provides an entry point into a complex situation.

If the introduction of a new technology is going to cause problems or create opportunities, the social interface is where these difficulties have to be negotiated in a face-to-face situation. The interface will be between individuals or social units representing different interests and backed by different resources. It is by identifying these interfaces and studying their dynamics that we can understand how interventions will need to be modified by everyday life.[11]

Lifeworlds are the realities that people unconsciously construct for themselves. They are the sum total of the mental maps and models that people have built to allow them to cope in their environments. Schütz and Luckmann describe lifeworlds as a 'lived-in and largely taken-for-granted world'.[12] This 'taken-for-granted' nature of lifeworlds makes them difficult

[9] Long, N. Agency and constraint, perceptions and practice. In *Images and Realities of Rural Life*, ed. H. de Haan. and N. Long. Assen, the Netherlands: van Gorcum, 1997, pp. 1–20.

[10] Long, N. *Encounters at the Interface: A Perspective on Social Discontinuities in Rural Development.* Wageningen, the Netherlands: Wageningen Agricultural University, 1989; Douthwaite, *Enabling Innovation.*

[11] Arce, A. and Long, N. Bridging two worlds: an ethnography of bureaucrat peasant relations in Western Mexico. In *An Anthropological Critique of Development: The Growth of Ignorance*, ed. M. Horbart. London: Routledge, 1993, pp. 123–134.

[12] Schütz, A. and Luckmann, T. *The Structures of the Life-world*, Vol. 1. London: Heinemann, 1974.

- Monitor options
- Share results & interactive communication of ideas, processes, experience
- Monitor processes (including stakeholder interactions)
- Extract and build on positive experiences and analyse reasons for failure

- Implementation
- Create enabling conditions for scaling-up

Negotiation on interests and collective action
- Land-use negotiation
- Negotiating the institutional framework
- Exposure to options: identify best bets
- Identification of research needs
- Identification of disciplinary foci
- Linking responsibilities and tasks to local organisations
- Identification of preconditions for scaling-up
- Development of performance indicators

System formalisation
- Identifying key components
- Identifying scales & boundaries
- Develop throw-away model
- Scenario analysis & identification of leverage points

Implementation of an integrated approach

Implementation phase

Evaluation phase

Reflective phase

Updating

Exploratory phase

- Review of shared problems
- Renegotiate and re-plan collective action

Facilitate platform building
- Development of visions
- Identification of shared problems, needs and goals
  (Including capacity building for disadvantaged groups where necessary)

- Stakeholder/institutional analysis: decision-making rationales, interests, mental models
- Historical trend analysis
- Resource assessment, including participatory mapping
- Analysis of external influences
- Exploratory vision, needs and problem analysis
- Identification of scale of analysis and possible interventions

Fig. 3.2. The learning cycle in integrated natural resource management research.

to study because, unless challenged to do so, people often do not understand the concept or realise the limits of their own lifeworld.[13] The methodological importance of the lifeworld concept is that it explicitly acknowledges that people have different realities. It puts the understanding of these realities as a primary research activity. This is very different from more traditional approaches that put a premium on the scientist's understanding of the problems and solutions.

The approach – learning together for change

The concept of 'learning together for change' is drawn from Jürgen Hagmann.[14] Recent advances in natural resources research have drawn heavily upon advances in our understanding of social learning.[15] This tells us that resource management must be based upon continuous dialogue and deliberation amongst stakeholders. Ultimately, in the ideal scenario, all management is experimental and all research involves managers – there is little distinction between management and research. Roussel and colleagues, writing about the industrial sector, have described this new relationship between researchers and managers as 'Third generation R&D'.[16] They portray this type of research as being a bit like jazz; it requires constant improvisation. This implies that researchers can no longer remain exclusively external actors but need to engage themselves in action research to develop appropriate solutions together with resource users. Good process facilitation is an essential component of its implementation.

Figure 3.2 provides an example of the concrete processes that are needed to put these concepts into practical use. This operational framework does not claim to be complete or universal.[17] The learning cycle is depicted as a neat formalised cycle of reflection–implementation–evaluation

---

[13]Long, N. From paradigm lost to paradigm regained. The case of actor-oriented sociology of development. In *Battlefields of Knowledge: The Interlocking of Theory and Practice in Social Research and Development*, ed. N. Long and A. Long. London: Routledge, 1992, pp. 16–43.

[14]Hagmann, J. *Learning Together for Change. Facilitating Innovation in Natural Resource Management Through Learning Process Approaches in Rural Livelihoods in Zimbabwe*. Weikersheim: Margraf Verlag, 1999.

[15]Maarleveld, M. and Dangbegnon, C. Managing natural resources: a social learning perspective. *Agriculture and Human Values*, **16** (1999), 267–280; Daniels, S. and Walker, G. Rethinking public participation in natural resources management: concepts from pluralism and five emerging approaches. In *Proceedings of an International Workshop on Pluralism and Sustainable Forestry and Rural Development*. Rome: Food and Agriculture Organization, 1999, pp. 29–48; Hagmann, *Learning Together for Change*.

[16]Roussel, P. P., Saad, K. N. and Erickson, T. J. *Third Generation R&D: Managing the Link to Corporate Strategy*. Boston, MA: Harvard Business School Press, 1991.

[17]The framework is drawn from the work of Hagmann *et al.*, Success factors in integrated natural resource management R&D; Lal *et al.*, The adaptive decision-making process as a tool.

and updating. Such simplicity would be rare; different phases will overlap and there will be a whole series of concurrent cycles moving at different speeds. For example, capacity building of disadvantaged groups to enable them to participate on an equal footing with more powerful groups may be complete before the main implementation phase is attempted (see Fig. 4.1, p. 81). The complexity of the process points again to the need for excellent process facilitation. Rigorous formalisation of the learning cycle will tend to hamper creativity and adaptation.

In Fig. 3.2, many of the elements of an integrated approach are listed. Meine van Noordwijk and colleagues from World Agroforestry Centre have considerable experience with integrated approaches in Indonesian landscapes. They consider the following as key elements of the research cycle.

- Identifying clear, realistic *objectives*, together with stakeholders. This will help to avoid getting lost in the complexity of the system.
- Defining performance *indicators* that reflect the way these objectives will be met. Once again, this helps to maintain focus on a few key variables that will need to be monitored.
- Attempt to see things from the local manager's perspective and respect the fact that local people will have different *mental models* to those of outside scientists. Taking the 'manager' seriously implies trying to understand the mental model that underpins farmers' decisions. This opens the way for introducing new technologies that enlarge the array of options from which farmers can choose.
- Making use of the mental models for *planning* the way desirable impacts can be obtained for minimum inputs: developing a common vision.
- *Implementation* of these management plans and visions.
- *Learning* from how the real world (its ecology, economy, society and polity) actually responds to the changes induced by the plans, including the feedbacks created by ecological, economic, social and political interactions within and across scales.

A key component of the action learning cycle is the component involving joint action. Experiential learning and discovery play a key role in enhancing the creativity and capacity of innovative local resource managers.[18] Jürgen

---

[18] Kolb, D. A. *Experiential Learning. Experience as a Source of Learning and Development*, Englewood Cliffs, NJ: Prentice Hall, 1984; Hamilton, N. A. *Learning to Learn with Farmers*. Thesis, Wageningen University, the Netherlands, 1995. This is a case study of an adult learning project conducted in Queensland, Australia 1990–1995.

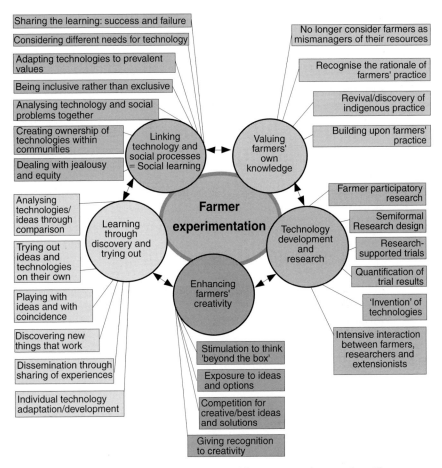

Fig. 3.3. Important components of farmer experimentation. (From Hagmann *et al.*, 2002. See footnote 7.)

Hagmann and colleagues, working with smallholder farming systems, have achieved some remarkable successes – based largely on their approaches to farmer–researcher interaction. They have shown how farmer experimentation is central to the learning process (Fig. 3.3),[19] and that it relates to several other important features that are key to building the adaptive capacity of farmers (Fig. 3.3).

> *A methodology for discovery and experiential learning.* It creates curiosity and a spirit of trying and discovering.

[19]Hagmann *et al.*, Success factors in integrated natural resource management R&D.

A way to value farmers' own knowledge. Farmer experimentation improves the understanding of biophysical processes by farmers and reveals the interrelationships between farmers' knowledge and scientific knowledge. This contributes to a better mutual understanding and raises the status of farmers' knowledge, which in turn raises confidence in their own solutions.

A way to enhance farmers' creativity. The curiosity and the confidence that is created generally encourage and trigger creativity in finding solutions. People develop their own solutions rather than waiting for answers from outside.

A methodology that links technical and social processes and generates social learning. A collective experimentation process automatically raises technical and social issues. Technologies will be adapted to social conditions if farmers try them out and share their experiences with others.

A methodology for research and technology development. This helps researchers and farmers to work effectively together and develop technologies.

Although they started with on-farm 'trials', they soon learned that experimentation is much more than testing a certain technology (Box 3.3). Participatory research has an important role to play as is demonstrated by the team working on forages for smallholders (Box 3.4). However, this has to move towards being part of a social learning process.

Box 3.3. Learning and adapting for innovative resource management in southern Zimbabwe: getting into the system

Work by Jürgen Hagmann, Edward Chuma, Kuda Murwira and others in southern Zimbabwe provides many useful insights into the research approaches that can enhance the adaptive capacity of resource users.[1] This work began in 1988 with conventional 'on station' experiments with new tillage systems to conserve soil and water. This evolved into on-farm research on conservation tillage in the early 1990s. The interactions with the farmers produced important new insights and led the team to move towards a more interactive relationship with the communities. The linearity from researcher to extension agent to farmer as the pathway for innovation did not work in this case, even if it was improved through feedback loops from farmers to researchers through on-farm trials. A participatory approach was developed inspired by elements of Paolo Freire's writings on a 'pedagogy of liberation'. The approaches suggested in Hope and Timmel's *Training for Transformation* were applied.[2] These ideas led the team to shift its focus towards developing awareness amongst farmers for self-reliant development and addressing more diverse stakeholders. They began to accept that innovation is more of a social process than an issue of technology transfer (Fig. 3.4).[3]

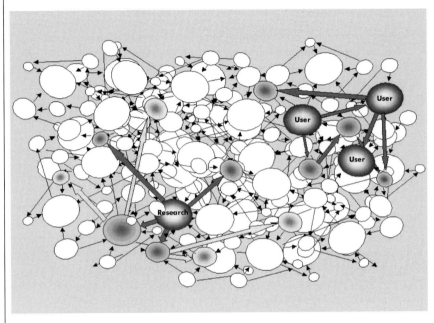

Fig. 3.4. Innovation as a social process where the influences of research on the users are highly complex and unpredictable. (From Kuby 1999. See footnote 3 in Box 3.3.)

Hagmann and his team learnt that unless farmers themselves learn about and develop technologies together with researchers, adoption rates remained low. The team developed numerous tools and methods for enhancing participation and for learning (see also Box 10.1, p. 213).

Farmers' own experimentation, communication and sharing of knowledge from farmer to farmer through participatory technology development became the focus. This led to a variety of technologies being tested and developed successfully, but the research team failed to achieve any significant adoption of innovations as long as they worked with individual farmers only. This applied not only to collectively managed resources, but also to individually managed farmers' fields. The social pressure and norms in the society did not leave much freedom for individuals to innovate. 'Natural' innovators were the object of jealousy and were often avoided and victimised rather than copied (the tall poppy syndrome). The core lesson was that the social environment needs to be conducive to the spread of social and technical innovations. Operationally, this meant that the team had to create opportunities for negotiation and learning at community level.

From 1994, the workentered a new phase based upon a more integrated concept of community-based innovation. The aim was to facilitate social, economic, ecological and organisational innovations through experiential learning, thus enabling people to manage their environment adaptively. Testing the new approach to innovation in resource management became the main research focus.

Hagmann and his colleagues found that innovation is driven by much more than research. It involves a whole system of actors and sources of inspiration, creativity and motivation to do things differently. Researchers, extension agents and farmers are just three actors in this non-linear, dynamic system in which the direct cause and effect of a certain activity is almost impossible to assess. Research can no longer stay 'outside' and investigate objective, transparent and predictable elements of a system. Researchers need to understand themselves as part of the system, contributing to innovation processes that are not controllable.

Integrating 'hard' and 'soft' issues in research and extension was very important in supporting farmers effectively. In Zimbabwe, two different types of research were carried out and integrated through the process.

- Research on the process of resource management (mainly 'soft' institutional and participatory action research, e.g. on local organisational development, communication interfaces, innovation and knowledge development, institutional change and competence development). This action research integrated the local knowledge and scientific knowledge as it was grounded in farmers' reality.
- 'Process-supporting research' on technological and social issues and problems (mainly more conventional 'hard' research, e.g. on soils, land use, soil and water management technologies, degradation, livelihood analyses).

Both types of research were required to achieve impact at the different levels. Often 'hard' studies (e.g. on land degradation) were used to demonstrate the need for soft approaches (building capacity for adaptive management) or for deepening the basis and outcomes of farmer experimentation and assessment. The frame of 'soft' action research permitted the valuation of 'hard' research. The research questions for 'hard' research emerged out of the action research and the results were fed back into the process to help the stakeholders make informed decisions.

[1] Hagmann, J. R., Chuma, E., Murwira, K., Connolly, M. and Ficarelli, P. Success factors in integrated natural resource management R&D: lessons from practice. *Conservation Ecology*, **5** (2002), 29. Online: http://www.consecol.org/vol5/iss2/art2).

[2] Freire, P. *Pedagogy of Hope. Reliving Pedagogy of the Oppressed*. New York: Continuum, 1997; Hope, A. and Timmel, S. *Training for Transformation, a Handbook for Community Workers*. Gweru: Mambo Press, 1984.

[3] Kuby, T. *Innovation is a Social Process. What does this Mean for Impact Assessment in Agricultural Research?* Eschborn: German Development Cooperation (GTZ), 1999.

[4] de Boef, W. S. Tales of the Unpredictable Learning about Institutional Frameworks that Support Farmer Management of Agro-biodiversity. Thesis, Wageningen University, 2002.

[5] Hagmann, J., Chuma, E. and Murwira, K. Kuturaya: participatory research, innovation and extension. In *Farmers' Research in Practice: Lessons From the Field*. L. van Veldhuizen,

A. Waters-Bayer, R. Ramirez, D. Johnson and J. Thompson. ed. London: Intermediate Technology, 1997, pp. 153–173.

Box 3.4. Adoption of new forage crops in Southeast Asia

The experience of 'Forages for Smallholders' project of the International Center for Tropical Agronomy (CIAT) illustrates how a mix of participatory learning and research supported an integrated approach to food production and natural resource management.[1] Its aim was to introduce legumes and grasses into small farm production systems in Southeast Asia. The approach fostered adaptive management that was responsive to, and supportive of, variability in ecosystems.

The introduction of a large variety of new multi-purpose legume and grass species used participatory methods that enabled farmers to learn about diversity, and to devise a variety of niches for different species in their systems. Use of a menu of diverse options for participatory learning was fundamental to the approach. Farmers learnt, invented and validated new ways of using diverse species. There has been an increase in complexity as farmers gained experience. With time, farmers' preferences for varieties and characteristics changed. At first, animal feed, contour hedgerows and intensive cut-and-carry plots emerged as the main ways in which farmers integrated several species into their agricultural system. Then other ways of integrating legumes and grasses as living fences, ground cover and small grazed plots started to evolve for many different end-uses. Farmers began to choose new species and varieties and to try new ways of combining plants and animals, such as growing shrub legumes for forage as part of contour rows for soil erosion control.

The mix of participatory learning and research fostered adaptive management that enabled the project to encompass the diversity and complexity of agricultural systems. Researchers' initial ideas about appropriate options for each farming system differed from those of farmers and were revised in recognition that the farmers' grasp of the complexity was different from that of researchers.

Researchers' innovations have also been introduced, although not always in ways that researchers expected. For example, on steeply sloping lands, farmers introduced contour planting of *Paspalum atratum*, which establishes much more rapidly and cheaply than the widely promoted *Vertiver zizanoides* grass and can also be used for fodder. It competes with associated crops, but not to the same extent as other barriers. Farmers took an integrated approach to managing small areas planted with legumes for forage, with the use of alternative feed sources from adjacent forest and 'waste' areas. Farmers thus highlighted for the project the potential of managing both types of land-use for the preservation and increased use of indigenous species.

[1] Stür, W. W., Horne, P. M., Hacker, J. B. and Kerridge, P. C. (eds.) Working with farmers: the key to adoption of forage technologies. *ACIAR Proceedings* No. 95. Canberra: ACIAR, 2000.

Getting into the system

The entry point for initiation of an integrated project is crucial to success. The manner of entry will influence the way in which problems are perceived. It may also have a profound influence on future relations amongst stakeholders and set the trend for buy-in to a long-term process. It is important that the initial phases of any integrated natural resource initiative are not dominated by any subset of potential stakeholders. In the integrated approach that we are proposing, integration across disciplines and integration across a range of stakeholders with variable levels of power, confidence, resources and so on need to be built in right from the start.

Much supposedly interdisciplinary work originates when scientists from a single discipline involve other disciplines in addressing a problem. Many collaborative international programmes in the natural resource arena have this characteristic, with biophysical scientists often in the driving seat. The conceptual framework for the research comes from the paradigms of the initiating discipline, and buy-in by other disciplines is then weak at the best.

In the learning cycle that we have outlined (Fig. 3.2), the first phase is the exploratory phase. Ideally there should be early entry into full-scale multi-stakeholder engagement (the reflective phase). However, the political agendas of the various stakeholders can derail such a process. There is need to ensure that the facilitators understand the political landscape, its historical development and its relationship to resources, current management initiatives, etc. Ideally, tools used in the exploratory phase should bring disciplines together from the start and ensure interaction between stakeholders and researchers. Potential tools, drawn from the participatory rural appraisal toolbox, include stakeholder analysis, participatory mapping and historical trend analysis.

It is unlikely that, in the exploratory phase, all stakeholders will be drawn together in a single forum. As David Edmunds and Eva Wollenberg of the Center for International Forestry Research have written, many approaches to multi-stakeholder negotiations mask abuses of power and ignore enduring structural inequity.[20] Such approaches are likely to expose disadvantaged groups to greater manipulation and control by more powerful stakeholders. As negotiation and decision making are so central to integrated approaches, understanding the political landscape becomes a central endeavour in the exploratory stage. Such an understanding will give a firm foundation to the facilitators for the subsequent phases. Throughout the

---

[20]Edmunds, D. and Wollenberg, E. A strategic approach to multistakeholder negotiations. *Development and Change*, **32** (2001), 231–253.

action cycle, stakeholders will be jostling for power and power balances will change. Consequently, there is a constant need to understand the politics of resource management.

In the reflective stage, the focus moves to visioning and negotiation. David Edmunds and Eva Wollenberg argue for a strategic approach to multi-stakeholder negotiations, involving several steps.

- Seeking out possibilities for alliances amongst select stakeholders, rather than trying to achieve an apolitical agreement among all possible stakeholders. They give the example of a process facilitated by the World Wildlife Fund (WWF) for claims to traditional forest areas in the Kayan Mentarang National Park. WWF chose not to invite timber companies for fear that they would dominate decisions. They invited villagers to negotiate with an equal number of government officials. Initial proposals were worked out in separate sessions and then negotiated with a facilitator.
- 'Situating' the legitimacy of all decisions and agreements. This means analysing the reasons for non-participation or participation, how groups are represented and the role of facilitators and convenors.
- Approaching negotiations as one strategy among several: lobbying, capacity building, networking, etc.
- Improving the preconditions of successful negotiations, particularly the capacity of disadvantaged groups to participate effectively.

Visioning is an ideal tool to facilitate cross-disciplinary analysis and to hear the voices of different stakeholders, if good process facilitation is available. It can be used to understand better the landscape and the larger scale forces for change.[21] Visioning is a first step towards redefining current development pathways. It has been suggested that the adaptability of community management can be improved not only by responding to changes but also by anticipating changes. Visioning is widely used in the corporate sector but has also been developed as part of participatory research and development in rural contexts.

The above outlines some of the tools for getting into a system, but one does not want to get into a fuzzy, all-embracing system in which one soon gets lost. A number of researchers argue that one should focus on best bets or, as Boru Douthwaite has described them, 'plausible promises'.

---

[21] Wollenberg, E., Edmunds, D. and Buck, L. Using scenarios to make decisions about the future: anticipatory learning for the adaptive co-management of community forests. *Landscape and Urban Planning,* **47** (2000), 65–77.

These are often seen as being particular technological solutions to problems. Jürgen Hagmann writes that rural people can be approached much more easily through technical issues than philosophy; hence the technical issues are often the best entry point. In the learning cycle proposed by Boru Douthwaite, the focus is on technological interventions (Box 3.5). While this may be partially true, we would extend the best bet concept, to include changing bylaws, modifying policy instruments etc.

Box 3.5. Learning cycles in technology innovation

Boru Douthwaite and partners have developed a practical guide on how to launch and manage the innovation process by starting with a best bet and then building a development community of motivated users.[1]

1. *Start with a best bet or plausible promise.* The first step to induce change is to produce a 'best bet': something that convinces potential stakeholders that it can evolve into something that they really want. Mokyr believes that the process of inventing plausible promises is by its nature something that 'occurs at the level of the individual'.[2] It is not something that lends itself to a broad consensus approach. The best bet does not need to be refined or polished: it can be imperfect and incomplete. In fact, on the one hand, the less finished it is, the more scope there is for the stakeholders to adapt it and thus gain ownership of the technology. Yet, the more problems there are, then the greater the chances that the key stakeholders will give up in frustration.

2. *Find a product champion.* The next step is to identify the innovator or product champion. He or she needs to be highly motivated, have the knowledge and resources to sort problems out and be a good communicator. The product champion will need to build a development community, attract people and keep them happy working for the common cause.

3. *Keep it simple.* Do not attempt to dazzle people with the cleverness and ingenuity of the prototype's design. A best bet should be simple, flexible enough to allow revision, and robust enough to work well even when not perfect.

4. *Work with innovative and motivated partners.* Allow the participants in the process to select themselves through the amount of resources they are prepared to commit. Do not give participants anything for free that has a resale value. Otherwise, people may be motivated to adopt in order to get something for nothing. In addition, people generally value something more highly if they have paid for it, and they will be more committed to sort out the problems that emerge. However, it must be made clear to the first adopters that they are adopting an unperfected product and that they are working with you as codevelopers. You should be prepared to offset some, but not all, of the risk they are taking in working with you.

5. *Work in a pilot site or sites where the need for the innovation is great.* The environment will influence your codevelopers. Their motivation levels will be sustained for

longer if they live or operate in an environment where your innovation promises to provide great benefits.

6. *Set up open and unbiased selection mechanisms.* Once you have the key stakeholders working with you to generate novelties in design, you need ways of selecting and promulgating the beneficial changes. Initially, the product champion usually plays this role. An effective selector must be able and prepared to recognise good design ideas from others. Even if the product champion can be open-minded and unbiased, he or she may have problems convincing others. One option is to set up a review mechanism that is well respected by your key stakeholder community.

7. *Do not release the innovation too widely too soon.* For the innovation to evolve satisfactorily, the changes the stakeholders make to it need to be beneficial and, as those generating the novelties will have gaps in their knowledge, product champions should restrict the number of codevelopers so that they can work with them effectively. When people show enthusiasm for a prototype, it is very tempting to release it as widely as possible, but this should be resisted. The technology will always be less perfect than one initially thinks.

8. *Do not patent anything unless it is to stop someone else trying to privatise the technology.* People cooperate with each other because they believe that all will share the benefits. The process is, therefore, seriously damaged if one person or group tries to gain intellectual property rights over what is being produced.

9. *Know when to let go.* Product champions need to become personally involved and emotionally attached to their projects to do their jobs properly. This makes it easy for them to go on flogging dead horses long after it has become clear to everyone else that the technology is not going to succeed. Equally, project champions can continue trying to nurture their babies long after they have grown up and market selection has begun. It is, therefore, a good idea to put a time limit on the product champion's activities.

[1] Douthwaite, B. *Enabling Innovation: A Practical Guide to Understanding and Fostering Technological Change.* London: Zed Books, 2002.

[2] Mokyr, J. *The Lever of Riches: Technological Creativity and Economic Progress.* Oxford: Oxford University Press, 1990.

Staying in the system: facilitation of participatory learning and action

No one makes the case stronger for the importance of process facilitation than Jürgen Hagmann.[22] Good facilitation, leadership and interpersonal relationships of project members are all key to the success of integrated approaches. Knowing the 'correct' technical way to manage the resource

[22] This section is largely drawn from Hagmann *et al.*, Success factors in integrated natural resource management R&D.

is likely to be a very small part of the final solution. In the experience of Hagmann and his team, process facilitation proved to be the foundation of learning across a number of sites with different facilitators. The quality of facilitation was more important than any particular tool or learning aid, and this skill proved to be very difficult to learn by development agents and local people.[23] The core of reflective facilitation is about asking the 'right' questions at the 'right' time. It is important to enhance people's self-reflection and self-discovery without pre-empting the responses or pushing in a pre-conceived direction. Questions should aim to make people reflect upon the consequences of their present perceptions and behaviour. This should lead to careful consideration and subsequent ownership of the solutions that they find.

Hagmann and colleagues found that the values of ownership, participation, emancipation and social learning were crucial in the construction of new realities. Local ownership was created through channelling interventions through local organisations. The intervention of the research team was geared towards strengthening organisations, by enhancing accountability, improving leadership and facilitating critical self-awareness. A key role for research is to understand group dynamics and facilitate the formation and effectiveness of groups.

Community values had probably the greatest influence on farmers' decisions. Through good facilitation, these core values (e.g. social harmony, collectiveness, inclusiveness, environmental values) were brought into the open and so could be debated in relation to present behaviour. These facilitated debates often triggered deep self-reflection and, over a number of iterations, often led to the emergence of new social norms. The main difficulty is 'steering' the facilitation process. Jürgen Hagmann lists several conditions that must be met to ensure successful facilitation.

Clarity of vision and values. The vision needs to be built upon values such as participation, ownership, inclusiveness, people's self-development, openness, transparency and accountability. With this vision as a guiding star, the facilitator is able to handle situations flexibly and to pose the 'right' questions to enhance learning. Thus the facilitator needs to be a step ahead and lead the process but must not determine its outcome. Often, this vision can be enhanced through

[23] Groot, A., Marleveld, M. *Gatekeeper Series No. 89: Demystifying Facilitation in Participatory Development.* London: International Institute for Environment and Development, 2000; Röling, N. G. Towards an interactive agricultural science. *European Journal of Agricultural Education and Extension,* 2 (1996), 35–48.

exposure to successful cases that provide a real and concrete example of such a vision.

Empathy and the 'culture of enquiry'. The facilitator needs to be able to empathise with the group members so that he/she can react appropriately. Empathy goes beyond knowledge about group dynamics; it is a skill that depends on personality and on emotional intelligence.[24] Another skill is the 'culture of enquiry', which is the ability to question apparently simple things and to get down to details. Often the real problems lie in the details, which need to be disclosed before a solution can be developed. Often the mental models of people need to be made apparent and deconstructed through their own reflection so that new ways of thinking and acting can be generated.

Clarity on process design and intermediate steps. Jürgen Hagmann argues that facilitators will have major problems guiding the negotiations unless the process design is clear. Beginners in process facilitation need a clear 'operational framework' as a 'rail' to guide them. Such a framework defines the objectives, key questions and issues, core methodologies and partners for each process step. Only after thorough training and experience in these steps are facilitators able to understand and implement them confidently. They can then modify them according to their own experience, empathy and common sense. Understanding the process with its usual ups and downs also helps to reduce the frustrations often experienced when things do not go in the desired direction. Once having gone through a whole process cycle, facilitators know that these are part of any non-linear learning process and they can handle these situations by placing them in context.

Readers will believe that the writers of this book unconditionally accept the new norm of participation. We do, but with reservation. There is too much rhetoric and too little attention to some of the original intentions of those promoting participation; in many cases, participatory approaches have been manipulated for bureaucratic purposes; 'toolboxes' are being applied mechanically, and efficiency in project delivery is overriding more important goals of empowerment. The reservations regarding participation are clearly articulated by the contributors in the book *Participation: The New Tyranny*.[25] David Mosse illustrates how local knowledge, instead of determining

---

[24]Goleman, D. What makes a leader? *Harvard Business Review*, Nov/Dec (1998), 92–102.

[25]Cook, B. and Kothari, U. *Participation: The New Tyranny*. London: ZED books, 2001.

participatory planning processes, is structured by the agenda of the external agent conducting the participatory exercises. Bill Cooke and Uma Kuthari suggest that participatory approaches have to pay greater attention to understanding power and its manifestations and dynamics. John Hailey notes that participation should not be reduced to some formulaic processes but should be rooted in a dynamic relationship of mutual trust and respect. Frances Cleaver calls for better understanding of local norms of decision making and representation, of how these change and are negotiated. The time is ripe for a critical reappraisal of participatory approaches.

Keys to getting into and staying in the system

Researchers are not dispassionate outside observers; they are interested parties and need to recognise that they are part of the system they are researching. Successful engagement has resulted in positive outcomes, as has been illustrated, for example, in the Zimbabwean smallholder farming system (Box 3.3).

- Researchers must actively engage with their clients and begin to understand their lifeworlds rather than putting a premium on the scientists' perspective and solutions.
- Learning cycles, in which stakeholders reflect, implement and evaluate their actions, will be crucial, but there are cycles within learning cycles, and improvisation will be more important than formalisation.
- The entry point into the learning cycle is likely to have a profound impact on future relations amongst stakeholders.
- Understanding group dynamics, and facilitating the formation of effective groups, will greatly improve social learning.
- Good process facilitation will be key to the implementation of such research-based development.

4   Issues of scale

Some of the most contentious contemporary issues confronting natural resource managers relate to scale. Global-scale changes in economies, climates,
biological diversity, forests and deserts are having profound impacts on local
livelihoods. Conversely the aggregate impact of actions by individual farmers, foresters and fishers are mitigating or reinforcing many of the global-scale
changes. International responses are grappling with the reality that the costs
and benefits of these changes, and of measures to mitigate them, do not
accrue equally to all people. The quickest and most effective way to slow
climate change would be to reduce fossil fuel use in industrialised countries. However, the inhabitants of those countries are unwilling to suffer the
decline in their standard of living that would result. One way to conserve
biological diversity would be to lock-up the world's remaining rainforests in
parks and protected areas, but the inhabitants of the countries where these
forests occur are unwilling to forego the economic benefits of exploiting the
forests and the land that lies under them. Within industrialised countries, it is
now common for those who incur the costs of environmental protection to
be compensated by those who enjoy the benefits. Billions of euros are spent
every year in the European Union to pay farmers to use their land in ways
that maintain environmental values. In Europe, these payments are no longer
called subsidies: they are payments for the amenity values, wildlife and landscapes that are now amongst the products of multi-functional agriculture.
However, progress in developing international markets for environmental
services has been excruciatingly slow. Practical ways of getting money into
the hands of poor people in developing countries as an incentive for not
clearing tropical forests have yet to be developed. Similarly, effective mechanisms to enable poor people in developing countries to make money by
growing trees to sequester carbon are proving elusive. Reconciling global
environmental needs with local development needs will be one of the greatest challenges facing natural resource managers in the coming decades.

All natural resource management systems have multiple scales of
interaction and response; interventions at global, national and household
scales invariably have impacts at other scales. A key feature of integrated

research is its attempt to reconcile these spatial and temporal scale issues. It is rarely effective to manage natural resources on the basis of observations made at a single point in space or time. In this chapter, we focus on the scale of investigation, action and impact. We consider temporal scale, spatial scale from plots to global scales and institutional scales from household norms of behaviour to global policy instruments. We also consider scaling relationships – how different levels in a hierarchy relate to each other. Scaling-up the application of lessons gained in particular research sites to the broader landscape (extension, dissemination and adaptation across space and time of technologies or practices) is the subject of Chapter 9.

Temporal scale

In the real world, different processes take place at different speeds; some processes may be studied over short time frames while others may have to be studied over decades. The latter can be accomplished using historical data or through simulation modelling (Chapter 5). The examples given in Chapter 6 of hydrological modelling in Zimbabwe highlight the importance of analysing variations over long time frames before reaching conclusions on the causes of resource depletion. Point-in-time studies in Zimbabwe had attributed groundwater depletion to bad land management. Historical data analysis and simulation modelling showed that rainfall variation was the key determinant of groundwater levels.

Slow variables present particular challenges. These variables affect the dynamics of more rapid processes and when they reach thresholds or trigger breakpoints they may cause sudden and surprising shifts in systems. Accumulations of toxic chemicals in soils, water and organisms, gradual erosion of soil fertility and depletion of groundwater are all slow variables that need to be tracked in studies of complex resource systems.[1] Slow change can take the form of accumulations of human influence on the environment, over decades, centuries or millennia. Some abrupt changes can radically alter resource systems almost instantly; forest fires, cyclones or changes in exchange rates are all examples of fast variables. Short-duration development projects often founder because they tend to ignore slow variables and focus exclusively on more rapidly changing phenomena. Caution has to be exercised to ensure that adaptive learning frameworks do not exclude consideration of slower variables. Learning processes must be based upon a series of overlapping, interlinked and superimposed patterns of variability

[1] Gunderson, L. and Holling, C. S. (eds.) *Panarchy: Understanding Transformations in Human and Natural Systems.* Washington, DC: Island Press, 2002.

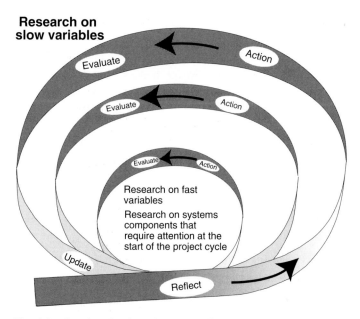

Fig. 4.1. Overlapping learning cycles for processes with different temporal characteristics.

going at different speeds (Fig. 4.1). Within the time frame of a single project, some phenomena will have been through many cycles, while others may not even complete a single cycle.

Biophysical–spatial scale

National programmes for integrated catchment management and integrated water resource management are commonly established at the scale of river basins, typically 5000 to 500 000 km². The boundary ascribed is almost always the watershed. In contrast, integrated management is also a feature of many community-based natural resource management programmes where the scale is the micro-catchment, typically 5 to 50 km². Many 'watershed development' programs are being undertaken at this scale in developing countries, primarily through non-governmental organisations.

However, there are dangers in making generalised conclusions on the basis of research conducted at a single spatial scale: what is good for the river basin may not be good for the people in the micro-catchment and vice versa. Much natural resource management is conducted without due attention to its impacts at smaller or larger scales.[2] Thus work at the household level may require component studies at the plot level or intrahousehold level to understand the important processes that lead to the emerging characteristics at the household level. Work at the farm level will also generally require work at higher levels (e.g. at the landscape level) to follow the externalities of farm activities.

Research by K. G. Saxena and colleagues from the G. B. Pant Institute of Himalayan Environment and Development illustrates the dangers of ignoring the local impacts of large-scale watershed management programmes (Box 4.1).[3]

Box 4.1. Rehabilitation of degraded lands in the Himalayas: issues of spatial and institutional scale

Studies by K. G. Saxena and colleagues show how the approaches to management differ dependent upon the geographic scale of the problems being addressed and the scale of responsibility of management institutions.[1] Their study was carried out in the village of Khaljhuni on the margin of the Nanda Devi Biosphere Reserve in the central Himalayas in India. There were two main institutional actors in the area. The local villager institutions were concerned with the portfolio of activities that supported local livelihoods. They focussed on livestock, agriculture and harvesting of non-timber forest products, particularly bamboo and medicinal plants. The state and central government forest institutions, by comparison, were concerned with large-scale catchment protection, global and national biodiversity values and timber crops.

The study aimed to find approaches to land cover restoration that reconciled the immediate livelihood needs of the 115 million Himalayan mountain people and those of the much larger numbers who live in the downstream Indo-Gangetic plains. Mountain people experience higher levels of poverty than the inhabitants of the plains: 40% of the Indian Himalayan region is degraded. Major investments have been made in both poverty alleviation and watershed protection but almost always by institutions operating within sectors. The study is one of few that attempted to integrate across spatial and institutional scales.

The area had a history of failed attempts by the forest department to establish conifer plantations. Seedlings were raised in central nurseries but suffered damage in transport to plantation sites. Local people were paid to plant the trees but these same people would subsequently set fires and otherwise damage the plantations to open up

---

[2]Holland, J. H. *Hidden Order. How Adaptations Build Complexity*. New York: Addison-Wesley, 1995; Allan, T. F. H. and Starr, T. B. *Hierarchy Perspectives for Ecological Complexity*. Chicago, IL: University of Chicago Press, 1982.

[3]Saxena, K. G., Rao, K. S., Sen, K. K., Maikhuri, R. K. and Semwal, R. L. Integrated natural resource management: approaches and lessons from the Himalayas. *Conservation Ecology*, **5** (2001), 14. Online: http://www.consecol.org/vol5/iss2/art14.

the areas for their cattle. This also created the need for further paid labour to re-establish plantations on the damaged sites.

Saxena and his colleagues used participatory methods to work with local people to determine approaches to reforestation that would meet both large-scale biodiversity and watershed needs and the local people's subsistence and cash income needs. They determined that, rather than conifers, local people favoured a mixture of multi-purpose broad-leaved trees, bamboos and medicinal plants. They also negotiated the terms upon which people would contribute to the restoration of this vegetation. The people still insisted upon being paid for the actual tree planting but they were prepared to collect seedlings from nearby forests as planting material and to provide manure to fertilise the plantations. An informal consensus was reached with the entire village community on what was to be planted and how the costs would be shared.

The total cost of reforestation, as negotiated by Saxena and his team, was US$305/ha, compared with US$160–190/ha for the forest department's conifer plantations. However, the forest department costs do not reflect the fact that many areas have had to be planted more than once.

Saxena and his team monitored the growth and survival of their village plantations for seven years. The village plantations outperformed the forest department conifer plantations on several counts. The trees survived and grew well; watershed and soil properties were improved, and significant carbon was sequestered. There was also some evidence that pressures on the adjoining biodiversity reserve were diminished. At the local level, more fuel and fodder was available and a number of people were obtaining incomes from harvesting and selling medicinal plants and bamboo.

The overall conclusion was that the up-front costs of establishing plantations that were sustainable at both local and larger scales were high. Significantly greater time investments were needed for negotiation and decision making. A consensus had to be forged. Labour costs for planting had to be met. However, the economic analysis conducted by Saxena suggests that there was a significant net benefit to society as a whole from these higher investments

[1] Saxena, K. G., Rao, K. S., Sen, K. K., Maikhuri, R. K. and Semwal, R. L. Integrated natural resource management: approaches and lessons from the Himalayas. *Conservation Ecology*, **5** (2001), 14. Online: http://www.consecol.org/vol5/iss2/art14.

Organisational scale

Boundaries are central to natural resource management since they specify the area over which jurisdictions apply as well as the roles that particular actors are assigned.[4] Specifying areas over which jurisdictions apply is,

[4] Lovell, C., Mandondo, A. and Moriarty, P. The question of scale in integrated natural resource management. *Conservation Ecology*, **5** (2002), 25. Online: http://www.consecol.org/vol5/iss2/art25.

nevertheless, easier said than done, not least because administrative boundaries, infrastructure links, ethnic groups, user groups, community limits
and informal networks seldom correspond with biophysical boundaries. To
complicate matters further, natural resource management usually involves
the integrated management of a multitude of common property, open-
access and privately owned resources such as croplands, pastures, forests and
water. Each resource has an associated complex of often-conflicting interests held by 'stakeholders' both inside and outside the particular resource
boundary.

The choice of organisational scale for integrated research and management can conceptually be made from a continuum ranging from the
'big government' to a 'small is beautiful' option.[5] Small units mitigate the
transaction costs of organising for collective action and are generally associated with mutuality of interest and greater social cohesion arising from
easy day-to-day contact. However, the small is beautiful approach can result
in a multiplicity of fragmented jurisdictions that lack coordination when it
comes to tackling bigger problems of both a local and trans-local nature.
These bigger problems that cannot be tackled in isolation at localised scales
are better addressed by bigger, unitary jurisdictions, but such jurisdictions
are often directed from a remote centre out of touch with local priorities
and aspirations.

There are two contrasting views of how management units for natural resource management should be defined. Those at the centre may define
small units on the basis of the subdivision of big units. The danger here is
that communities may end up with responsibilities for resource management
without corresponding authority. It may be difficult for local institutions to
assert their jurisdiction and defend local interests against outsiders. Alternatively the areas of concern to local interest groups may be aggregated into
bigger coordinated units (Box 4.2). The danger here is that lack of capacity
and poor linkages between lower and middle-level institutions may inhibit
integration and coordination across the landscape.

Box 4.2. The CAMPFIRE programme in Zimbabwe

Zimbabwe's natural resource governance structures and processes have for quite some time
been dominated by 'big government'. They have been sector based and over-centralised.
However, recent reforms have led to changes that appear to address the scale problem. The
country's flagship in participatory natural resource management is the Communal Areas

---

[5]Murphree, M. W. Boundaries and borders: the question of scale in the theory and practice of common property resource management. In *Proceedings of the Eighth Biennial Conference of the International
Association for the Study of Common Property*, Bloomington, Indiana, 31 May to 4 June, 2000, pp. 1–35.

Management Programme for Indigenous Resources (CAMPFIRE) in which communities are empowered to manage wildlife and to benefit from doing so.[1] The programme is based on the concept of the 'producer community' – held as the basic unit of social organisation through which communities can be empowered to manage local resources. The original idea was to focus on 'producer communities' at the subdistrict level,[2] but, in terms of institutional scale, the programme has been variously implemented at the levels of village development committees, ward development committees, traditional villages and even entire districts. The village and ward development committees are structures created under a Prime Minister's directive of 1984, purportedly to democratise the process of planning for local development. However, they are demographically defined administrative units superimposed on traditional villages, with which they do not correspond in terms of boundaries, membership or roles. These have been assumed to represent the 'communities' in which the local people have had a major stake in defining themselves and their roles and responsibilities. They have generally met with greater success when they have been relatively small in size.

[1] Lovell, C., Mandondo, A. and Moriarty, P. The question of scale in integrated natural resource management. *Conservation Ecology*, **5** (2002), 25. Online: http://www.consecol.org/vol5/iss2/art25.
[2] Martin, R. B. *Communal Areas Management Program for Indigenous Resources (CAMPFIRE)*. Harare: Department of National Parks and Wildlife Management, Branch of Terrestrial Ecology, Government of Zimbabwe, 1986.

Identifying interest groups and understanding their relationships is a key part of natural resource management. The process generally benefits from external facilitation to foster organisational development and to help find compromises between potentially conflicting interests.[6] It is inevitable that the solutions, in the form of appropriate institutional arrangements and 'deals done', will mostly be location specific, often with high transaction costs (see Box 4.3, below). However, a conducive policy and regulatory environment at the 'next scale up' is essential to achieve higher scales of integration and coordination.

Combining multi-scale models and databases

In spite of the importance of scale issues in the integrated management of natural resources systems, there are surprisingly few examples of rigorous analytical approaches to understanding the management implications of scale

[6] Ravnborg, H. M. and Ashby, J. A. *AGREN Network Paper 65: Organizing for Local-level Watershed Management: Lessons from Rio Cabuyal Watershed, Colombia*. London: Overseas Development Institute, 1996.

relationships. Peter Jones, a scientist at the International Center for Tropical Agronomy (CIAT), and Philip Thornton, of the International Livestock Research Institute (ILRI), do provide one excellent example of how the linking of models developed at different scales can have useful practical applications. They have developed links between models of maize and pasture production systems in the drylands of southern Africa. Their work provides one of the few practical examples of the use of models to make predictions across spatial scales.[7] They used crop and pasture simulation models, which are excellent tools for assessing the weather-related production variability associated with particular management strategies. However, such models usually require long data sets of daily weather from meteorological stations combined with input parameters from single plots.

CERES–Maize is one such model; it simulates the growth, development and yield of the maize crop. The model shows daily growth and this requires daily weather data (maximum and minimum temperature, solar radiation and rainfall). A similar model, but one requiring fewer data, is **Watbal**, a water balance model that provides robust estimates of the potential growing days for a pasture. Jones and Thornton use these models together with **MarkSim**, a model that generates daily weather predictions. MarkSim can be used to interpolate rainfall data for places where such data do not exist. A characteristic of this approach is that each point is evaluated in isolation. While this may be satisfactory for plot-level analysis, it is unsuitable for analyses at broader scales, where a shortage of domestic food or cattle feed usually also affects your neighbours. When harvests are good, the market price often plummets. The spatial coherence and variability of weather is manifest at a wide range of scales. In their study, Jones and Thornton used a clustering algorithm within MarkSim to group climates in the study area and to produce regional patterns of climates. This illustrates how models at one scale may have to be modified for use at another scale to capture emergent properties at the new scales.

Jones and Thornton also include climate change in their prediction, using the results of a global circulation model to extrapolate to the year 2055. The model, **HadCM2**, has a spatial resolution of about $417 \, \text{km} \times 278 \, \text{km}$ at the equator, and, therefore, an interpolation method was used to estimate variables to the same grid as MarkSim.

CERES-Maize also requires soil data. This was drawn from the Food and Agriculture Organization (FAO) digital soil map of the world. Qualitative assessments of agricultural suitability for maize production were

---

[7]Jones, P. G. and Thornton, P. K. Spatial modeling of risk in natural resource management. *Conservation Ecology*, **5** (2002), 27. Online: http://www.consecol.org/vol5/iss2/art27.

made for all the soil types in the study area. These were then assembled as representative profiles from the database for each of the soil types compiled by the International Soils Reference and Information Center (ISRIC). Using further models and databases, it was then possible to estimate water-holding capacities.

Jones and Thornton used a range of models and databases. They linked plot-level models such as CERES-Maize with global models (such as HadCM2) and have used databases from several organisations in this sophisticated analysis. They have run six scenarios, involving 3975 treatments (unique combinations of soil and weather inputs for the 1042 sample points) of CERES-Maize, each replicated 29 times. The 115 250 runs for each scenario took about six hours of computer time.

They found that the probability of high maize yields in the face of climate change is reduced at the Mozambique, Tanzanian and Zimbabwe case study sites. Maize yields at the Congo site are badly affected at the lower end of the yield spectrum, although the probabilities of obtaining yields above about 1.7 tons/ha are almost the same as in 1975. Conversely the lower yield probabilities are strongly conserved at the Zimbabwe site, but higher yields become far less probable. Yields at the Mozambique site are uniformly low, rarely exceeding 2 tons/ha, but hardly ever fall below 1 ton/ha. Yields are predicted to increase in highland areas where the crop responds to rising temperatures. In general, there is an increase in the standard deviation of maize yields. Similar trends are found with pasture growth. Resource management must take these differences into account. At the Mozambique site, a low but constant source of domestic food supply may free resources for other enterprises, whereas in the other two sites, domestic and regional food stocks must be saved against the day when maize yields may fail.

Despite the uncertainties in the analysis, by 2055 or so climate will clearly change and this will have impacts on crop and livestock production. The highlands may become more suitable for maize (higher night temperatures, and more rain in places), while the marginal areas in the lowlands may become even more marginal. Agricultural production will shift because of climate change. These changes can be overlaid with the intensification arising as a result of population increases where the general trend is likely to be one of more specialisation in farming systems. Such information will allow interventions to be better targeted, help to inform policy-makers of possible shifts in the patterns of production, and help to give indications of where policy and infrastructure adjustments might be needed in the future. In the current example, the possible spatial shifts in maize cultivation may have large impacts on targeting maize-related technology. This illustrates that designing natural resource management strategies is a moving target. In this case, maize production will probably become increasingly risky in some areas whereas in others it may actually stabilise. It may be wise to concentrate on intensification, with a concomitant increase in input levels, both in areas that are relatively risk free at present and in those that will still be so in the next 50 years. The risky areas may be better left to grazing, although the increasing risk of low levels of pasture growth may indicate that additional work on fodder conservation could be a good investment.

Natural resource modelling is a highly scale-specific process with strong cross-scale effects. Models will need to change with scale as wider spatial linkages are incorporated. Jones and Thornton have demonstrated a method where plot level models can be run over large land areas and the results aggregated to provide useful information at the regional level. They have clearly shown how output from much lower resolution global models can be broken down using a higher resolution weather grid and interpolation technique. The study has achieved, perhaps for the first time, integration from process-level plant-growth models to global climate models: the full gamut of the scaling problem. Much remains to be done to integrate these approaches into reliable landscape resource management models, but this research is paving the way for using models to deal with some of the very challenging problems of relating local land-use to global environmental change (Box 4.3). The next step will be to use such models to help people explore scenarios and develop strategies for adaptation and resilience.

Box 4.3. Reconciling local sustainability with global climate change mitigation

Recent concern about the impact of climate change on local natural resource systems and the potential for farms and forests to be managed in ways that sequester carbon add major new scale dimensions to natural resource management. Resource users need to be given both the means to adapt to changed climates and the incentives to do so. Only then will they modify their management systems in order to sequester carbon, reduce methane emissions or otherwise contribute to the mitigation of climate change. It is hard to see how this could be achieved without much better spatial data on carbon stocks and their rate of change than that which is available today.

The Clean Development Mechanism (CDM) proposed under the Kyoto Protocol of the Framework Convention on Climate Change commits governments to carbon sequestration projects that also support broader sustainability objectives. Joyotee Smith and colleagues from the Center for International Forestry Research in Indonesia have been exploring the problems of using carbon forestry investments to support rural livelihoods.[1]

They examined the 11 pilot phase CDM projects in developing countries to determine the extent to which they had succeeded in their dual objectives of sequestering carbon and contributing to local sustainability.

The work highlighted the problems of measurement and leakage that have bedevilled most attempts to pay for environmental services in developing countries. Leakage is the problem of knowing the impact of subsidising the planting of trees in one location on the profitability of planting trees in other locations. Measurement is the problem of knowing how much carbon was sequestered as a result of the investment over and above what might have been sequestered without CDM funds. These problems are manageable if the starting point is bare land with no people. When CDM projects operate in locations where forests already exist and are under common property or common pool management regimes, then leakage and measurement present serious challenges.

The CDM projects studied by Smith and her team ranged from payments to local people to plant trees in Mexico to buying-out of logging concessions in Bolivia. In the latter case the carbon benefit came not from sequestration as such but from the deforestation averted. The overall conclusions are somewhat ambivalent. Investing CDM funds in forestry activities that also support local livelihoods and environmental values is certainly possible. However, since each local situation is different and they are all complex, the transaction costs of this approach to CDM are very high. If carbon markets are based upon simple economic efficiency then the cheapest way of sequestering carbon will be in large monoculture industrial style plantations. The position of the Bush administration in the USA has put the future of the CDM in doubt. If it, or something similar, eventually goes ahead then some form of incentive or premium will be needed to offset the high transaction costs of approaches that target the co-benefits of local livelihoods and broader environmental values.

The conclusions of this work echo those of the study of Himalayan watersheds (Box 4.1). Integration across scales is possible, and for many environmental objectives it is necessary, but it comes at a price. Many of the economic benefits of scale integration are public goods or do not accrue to the investors – in these circumstances integration is only likely to occur if it is supported by effective laws and fiscal measures.

[1] MacDicken, K. and Smith, J. *Capturing the Value of Forest Carbon for Local Livelihoods: Opportunities Under the Clean Development Mechanisms of the Kyoto Protocol.* Bogor: CIFOR and University of Maryland, 2000.

Scale relationships

Solutions to resource management problems at one scale may or may not solve problems at the next scale, and they may actually cause problems 'downstream'. Rules or relationships that hold at one scale often do not transcend scales. Indeed, the temporal and spatial scale issues, with their associated social and physical contexts and dynamics, confirm that resource management practices identified at one scale of investigation will often be location specific and often time specific. The contexts and dynamics associated with single scales of investigation, and the additional feedbacks and interactions that become important with increasing scale, pose serious challenges for natural resource research (Box 4.4).

Box 4.4. A conceptual model of nested scales of investigation in integrated research

Lovell and colleagues have discussed the problems of overlapping boundary areas and the requirement for considering interactions on nested scales.[1] For example, groundwater decline is a key degradation issue in the twenty-first century. Aquifer levels have fallen in recent decades in several major grain-producing regions of the world. This decline is popularly attributed to groundwater mining. However, significant gaps in knowledge and understanding of the processes of groundwater decline remain (Table 4.1) and limit our identification and implementation of appropriate management actions.

Table 4.1. *Examples of studies at different scales*

| Examples of studies at different scales | Scales of investigation | |
	Spatial	Temporal (projection in some cases)
Pilot devolution of control for natural resource management, e.g. through environmental education, capacity building, village government	User-group, village, ward, council, ministerial	Years
Promotion of collective responsibility for groundwater through programmes that support group-based activities and discourage private exploitation	Water supply sector	Years
Work with user groups, non-governmental organisations and government, apply knowledge gained in the related local studies to develop and field test appropriate technical, legal, financial and institutional incentives for effective management	User-group, village, ward, council, ministerial	Years

Table 4.1. (*cont.*)

Examples of studies at different scales	Scales of investigation	
	Spatial	**Temporal (projection in some cases)**
Model the importance of spatial and temporal variability of rainfall and land management to the reported groundwater decline	Field, aquifer, micro-catchment, river catchment	Wet year, average year, dry year, '20-year' cycle of variability
Partition the decline to natural recession and human use, and partition the natural recession to deep flow, lateral flow and vegetation water use	Field, aquifer, micro-catchment, river catchment	Year
Simulate the impacts of increasing population and changes in land-use and climate	User-group, village, ward, council, field, aquifer, micro-catchment, river catchment	Wet year, average year, dry year, '20-year' cycle of variability
Cost–benefit analysis of potential macro-economic interventions, e.g. import grain from water-rich areas to reduce need for local production	Regional, 'global'	Years, decades

[1]Lovell, C., Mandondo, A. and Moriarty, P. The question of scale in integrated natural resource management. *Conservation Ecology*, **5** (2002), 25. Online: http://www.consecol.org/vol5/iss2/art25.

The widespread adoption of practices that are appropriate at one scale may result in undesirable impacts at other scales. For example:

- improved plot-level water-use efficiency may not, in fact, lead to improved water use at the level of the whole irrigation system
- changes in land-use or crop management on hillsides may improve or may downgrade the quantity and quality of water available to downstream users
- more efficient fishing practices used by one person may destroy fish stocks if used by everyone.

The problems posed by the failure to understand relationships across scales has been the subject of the work by Meine van Noordwijk and other colleagues at the World Agroforestry Centre. He has shown that much earlier (and some contemporary) work makes naïve extrapolations about aggregating data from measurements at small scales.[8] For example, plot-level measurements of sediment loss have been used to justify statements that 'erosion is one of the main causes of nutrient loss from Africa', while, in fact, very little sediment reaches the seas or oceans from African rivers. Plot-level erosion leads to a considerable lateral flow, impoverishing soil in one place and enriching it in another, albeit sometimes at the bottom of a lake.

At the heart of integrated research, and thus at the heart of this entire book, is the problem of anticipating, modelling, monitoring and assessing scale relationships – and then managing the externalities, unexpected complexities or impacts that emerge at higher scales of analysis. This requires an understanding of the interactions among institutional and ecological processes. An understanding of the consequences of these scale relationships can be used as feedback to redefine approaches to dissemination and replication. The objective must be to ensure that the widespread uptake of new technologies does not result in undesirable externalities (Chapter 11).

Integrated conservation and development projects

Integrated conservation and development projects (ICDPs) are an approach to reconciling global-scale environmental objectives with local-scale development needs. Hundreds of millions of dollars have been spent on ICDPs throughout the developing world since the term was first introduced for the Luangwa Valley Conservation and Development Project in eastern Zambia in the late 1960s. The basic premise of all these projects was that people could be persuaded to adopt ways of life that would maintain biological diversity and other global environmental values. The incentive has normally been the provision of technical assistance to help people to develop new livelihoods that do not degrade the local environment. In some cases, the projects helped people to develop livelihoods that depended upon the maintenance of the target of conservation. Ecotourism in national parks

[8] van Noordwijk, M., Tomich, T. P. and Verbist, B. Negotiation support models for integrated natural resource management in tropical forest margins. *Conservation Ecology*, **5** (2001), 21. Online: http://www.consecol.org/vol5/iss2/art21.

is a good example. Providing that the number of tourists is sufficiently great in relation to the opportunity costs of not developing the land for other uses, then these ICDPs can work. There are good examples in Costa Rica.

However, many ICDPs have assumed that agricultural innovations could allow people to practice environmentally friendly development around protected areas. This often flew in the face of clear evidence that people were better off when they pursued normal economic efficiency. Worse still, when the technologies introduced by ICDPs proved genuinely profitable, people often exploited them in the only land that was available to them – the protected area. For example, when cloves, introduced as a buffer zone crop around the forests of the East Usambara Mountains in eastern Tanzania, proved profitable, the local people cleared the native forest to expand their clove plantations.

The basic problem with ICDPs was that they assumed that poor people would be persuaded by education or a sense of environmental responsibility to forego the development opportunities being followed by other members of society. ICDPs rarely provided the subsidies or other financial or regulatory incentives that might have caused people to adopt alternative development pathways.[9] ICDPs have too often been naïve ideas of project proponents based upon what Beinert has described as their 'technical imagination of what might be possible'.[10]

Most ICDPs have failed to convince local stakeholders that they offered plausible pathways to development. In industrialised countries, ICDP-type situations have usually been addressed through a combination of subsidies, tax incentives or regulation to favour environmentally desirable land-uses over those that are considered less desirable. Thomas McShane of World Wildlife Fund International and Michael Wells have recently completed an in-depth review of ICDPs and have concluded that there are keys to success, as outlined in Box 4.5.[11] Using such keys can lead to successful outcomes for conservation and development.

[9]McShane and Wells and many others have commented on the disappointing performance of ICDPs: McShane, T. O. and Wells, M. P. *Getting Biodiversity Projects to Work: Towards More Effective Conservation and Development*. New York: Columbia University Press, 2004, in press.

[10]Beinert, W. Agricultural planning and the late colonial technical imagination: the lower shire valley in Malawi, 1940–1960. In *Proceedings of a Seminar on Malawi: An Alternative Pattern of Development*. Edinburgh, 12 and 25 May 1984. Edinburgh: Centre of African Studies, University of Edinburgh, 1985, pp. 95–148.

[11]McShane and Wells *Getting Biodiversity Projects to Work*.

Box 4.5. Lessons from integrated conservation and development projects

McShane and Wells considered the following features key to success in integrated conservation and development projects.[1]

1. Clarity about goals and objectives is essential. Biodiversity goals are often in partial opposition to development goals and this is rarely acknowledged and addressed explicitly.

2. The constraints imposed by the project structures of many conservation and development agencies are still inhibiting real engagement with local stakeholders and preventing the integrated management of natural resource systems.

3. Interventions must occur at different scales. Too many of the interventions of conservation and development agencies are scale-specific – they address local symptoms but ignore underlying policy constraints or they deal with macro-level issues but ignore local realities.

4. Policy change is as important as field-level intervention. The two should ideally go hand in hand and local action should help people to influence the policies that impact upon their lives.

5. Community-based development requires strong local institutions. Defensible land tenure, property and access rights are vital and securing these rarely receives enough attention in conservation and development programmes.

6. Sound institutions, at the local, district and national level, are essential. Many otherwise excellent concepts for reconciling conservation and development founder because they are not supported by the institutional structures concerned.

7. It is important to acknowledge and address trade-offs between conservation and development objectives. Too many programmes have raised funds on the basis of false claims about potential win–win outcomes.

8. Poverty alleviation is indeed linked to environmental deterioration, but many conservation and development programmes proceed on the basis of very simple and incorrect assumptions about the nature of the dependence of poor local people on natural resource systems.

9. Adaptive management and learning are often preached but rarely practised. This requires constant monitoring of design and management and the systematic testing of assumptions and adaptation of activities.

[1]McShane, T. O. and Wells, M. P. *Getting Biodiversity Projects to Work: Towards More Effective Conservation and Development.* New York: Columbia University Press, 2004, in press.

Lateral flows and filters

Meine van Noordwijk uses the terms 'lateral flows' and 'filters' to provide a theoretical basis for understanding scale relationships in mosaics of forest and agricultural land. Scale relationships depend on lateral flows of entities such as organisms, fire, smoke, water, sediment, nutrients, people, money and ideas. Filters are anything that can intercept a lateral flow; examples are shelterbelts or legal boundaries. Many external effects of land-use change are caused by lateral flows. For example, people cross boundaries at village, district, national or continental scale. The number of migrants (or its proportion in the total population) decreases with increasing scale because governments impose more restrictions – filters – on the movement of people at higher spatial scales. Biodiversity is also a concept with a complex scaling relationship. The richness of taxonomic or genetic entities at any scale is dependent both on the richness of units at a smaller scale – alpha diversity – and on the degree of similarity of those units – gamma diversity. Habitat discontinuities provide filters and eventually lead to reduced diversity at all scales.

Filter elements can be easily overlooked as they typically occupy a small fraction of the total area. However, they can have a large impact per unit area occupied. They can, therefore, be regarded as 'keystone' elements of a landscape and should be the focus of research if we want to understand how the landscape functions as a whole. Conserving or establishing filters to intervene in lateral flows may provide attractive options to mitigate the impacts of local decisions, compared with elimination of the 'root cause'.

Examples of this type of 'mitigation' can be found in the filtering and temporary storage of carbon dioxide in terrestrial ecosystems, which slows down the rate of increase of the atmospheric concentration caused by fossil fuel use. Another example is a riparian filter strip that mops up the flows of excess nutrients from intensively used agricultural land and reduces 'downstream' impacts of such nutrients. There are several key questions on the way filters function.

- How effective are different types of filter?
- How quickly will they saturate at high rates of flow?
- How fast can the filters regenerate between events?
- Do filters have a direct value and can they be treated as a separate 'land-use practice'?

Institutionally, landscape filters may require special attention. Private-resource access is hard to secure for linear elements in the landscape. This is especially so if they are far way from home and potentially external to the enterprise. Unless local institutions secure access to the fruits, nobody will plant trees in vegetative filter strips along streams even if they contain fertile soil and have a favourable water supply.

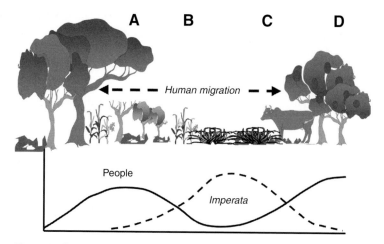

Fig. 4.2. Schematic land-use transformations from forests ('more people, less forest') via *Imperata* grasslands to rehabilitated lands with various agroforestry options ('more people, more trees'). A, Forest margin: slash and burn. B, Shorter fallows: soil degradation. C, *Imperata* fire climax: people move out. D, *Imperata* rehabilitation via agroforestry. (From van Noordwijk 1994. See footnote 12.)

Each type of natural resource may have a typical scale at which it can be meaningfully managed, depending on the patterns of lateral flow relative to the local stocks of the resource. This scale, however, depends on the situation. Groundwater may be a resource that is used, replenished and thus managed at the village scale (as in the Zimbabwe example; Chapter 6), or be part of aquifers that span hundreds of kilometres and require management at the scale of large streams and rivers.

The lateral flow, or migration, of people is one of the main conditioning factors in natural resource management at scales relevant for policy. For example, people moving to, and pushing back, the forest margin are a major source of land-use change, with potentially desirable short-term economic outcomes, but longer-term losses of environmental services at a national, regional or global scale. A number of phases can be recognised when people move into the margins of tropical forests. An initial degradation stage leads into a rehabilitated stage and people begin to plant trees (Fig. 4.2).[12] Rules such as taxes and administrative restrictions on the sale of logs and wood aimed at reducing the forest degradation stage may be a

[12]van Noordwijk, M. Agroforestry as reclamation pathway for *Imperata* grassland use by smallholders. In *Proceedings of a Panel Discussion on Management of Imperata Control and Transfer of Technology for Smallholder Rubber Farming System*. Indonesia: Balai Penelitian Sembawa, Pusat Penelitian Karet Indonesia, 1994, pp. 2–10.

major constraint in the rehabilitation stage. They reduce the incentives to plant indigenous trees but may encourage people to plant exotic species.

The keys to scale

Multiple scales of analysis and intervention can have positive outcomes for conservation and development, as has been illustrated in numerous examples (e.g. Boxes 1.3, (p. 23) and 3.3).

- Failure to recognise and address different impacts at different temporal, geographic or institutional scales is a major weakness of many natural resource management programmes.
- The equitable sharing of the local and global costs and benefits of environmental protection measures is a major issue for natural resource management. At present, there are too many instances of poor people in developing countries incurring the costs of global environmental protection measures.
- Insufficient attention is at present being given to slow variables. The gradual build-up of toxic chemicals, fire hazard, disease risk and the long-term decline of groundwater and biological diversity in managed systems or fragmented protected areas are all examples of slow variables.
- The significance of flows and filters as mediators of scale impacts requires more attention. Filters can range from strips of vegetation in between farmers' fields, dams to store water at temporal scales and regulations to inhibit movement of people at geographic scales.

5   Models, knowledge and negotiation

Nothing provokes as much controversy in integrated natural resource management as the use and misuse of simulation models. Advocates proclaim the awe-inspiring capacities of computer models. The detractors point to the enormous investments in data gathering to feed models that can rarely, if ever, predict outcomes better than a skilled practitioner. However, in reality we all work with models. Everyone takes decisions on the basis of mental models built up from our knowledge of a resource system and the lessons we have learnt from past attempts to manage it. Computers can be used to formalise these models and to explore the potential impacts of different management interventions. The range of possible modelling approaches runs from simple box and arrow diagrams to help people to share their understanding of linkages in a system through to hugely complex simulation models that aim to predict every permutation of possible responses to policy and management interventions. In this chapter, we review some of the applications of modelling to natural resource management but emphasise that models should be seen as just another management tool whose use is determined by the nature of the problem at hand.

The problems of dealing with multiple objectives and actors, non-linearity, unpredictability and time lags in natural resource systems suggests that modelling will have an important role to play. In this chapter, we focus on the use of various types of model to help with decision making and negotiation. We propose the use of models as an *aid to conceptualising and investigating the interactions across scales between the linked biophysical and human components of a system*.[1] This definition emphasises that a model need not be computer based although the reality is that computers have the potential to make these models much more useful.

We aim to understand and manage the full complexity of natural resource systems and we criticise 'reductionist' or 'component' research that, we claim, fails to deal with problems in their true context. There remains,

[1] Cain, J., Moriarty, P. and Lynam, T. *Designing Integrated Models for The Participatory Formulation of Water Management Strategies*. Unpublished document.

however, a strong body of opinion amongst scientists and practitioners that modelling is a distraction and invariably ends up being driven by the curiosity of the modeller. This reticence is reinforced by the heavy data requirements of large and complex simulation models and on the fact that models have a 'black box' character to all but the builders of the models. There is also a surprising lack of theoretical content of many models, even in the case of some large and complex simulation models, as noted by Marty Luckert, a resource economist at the University of Alberta.

> When disciplinary specialists want to integrate their theory into the modelling simulation framework, they find the model platform lacking. For example, many integrated models require decision-making components where individuals, households, communities or some such actor makes resource allocation decisions over time while considering risks and the decisions of the other actors. As an economist one would want to set up household production models that incorporate game theory and allocate resources optimally, cross-sectionally, and over time in the presence of risk. Given that more specialised disciplinary models have had very difficult times trying to do this, I doubt that any simulation models that incorporate numerous actors, numerous production activities etc. can do this. My experience has been that simulation-modelling frameworks are frequently not able to integrate state of the art disciplinary theory.

Disciplinary research can offer the necessary 'building blocks' to make quantitative simulations with a certain probability and precision but the linking of models across disciplines and scales is in its infancy. This is an emerging field and progress is being made.

Model uses and stakeholder participation

If modelling of systems is to be used, it makes sense to use it early in the research and management process. At this stage, models can be useful in helping to conceptualise the system. They enable us to build a common understanding of problems and issues; they assist in setting priorities and they guide the implementation phase of the work by identifying leverage points for interventions. At the earliest stage, the model may be at the level of a simple box-and-arrow diagram (Fig. 5.1).[2] When moving to a computer-implemented model, data inputs may at first be best guesses. One role of

---

[2]Lynam, T., Bousquet, F., Le Page, C. *et al.* Adapting science to adaptive managers: spidergrams, belief models, and multi-agent systems modeling. *Conservation Ecology*, **5** (2002), 24. Online: http://www.consecol.org/vol5/iss2/art24.

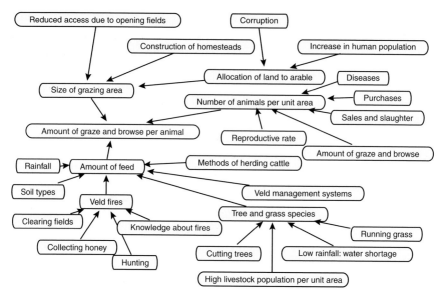

Fig. 5.1. Spidergram of factors affecting the amount of graze and browse available to livestock in Mahuwe. This was prepared with stakeholders from the study area. (From Lynam *et al.*, 2002. See footnote 2.)

this type of modelling is to clarify to the various participants in the research programme the types of information that they must provide.

Models can be used for communication and mediation in a collective decision-making process.[3] Although models may not play a direct role in the actions themselves, they do form the stimulus–response framework that guides the nature of the actions and their implementation. Public administrators, non-governmental organisations (NGOs), researchers, farmers, migrants, wealthy households, poor households, male-headed households and female-headed households have different representations, or mental models, of the system. The management of natural resources is a collective learning problem; consequently, during the implementation phase of the learning cycle, integrated models can be used as a tool in stakeholder negotiations. The different scenarios envisaged by the various stakeholders can be made explicit, and their impacts explored using a model.

Models can play an important role in devising monitoring protocols as well as providing a useful set of evaluative tools to investigate when

[3]Bousquet, F., Barreteau, O., Le Page, C., Mullon, C. and Weber, J. An environmental modelling approach: the use of multi-agent simulations. In *Advances in Environmental Modelling*, ed. F. Blasco and A. Weill. New York: Elsevier, 1999, pp. 113–122.

critical thresholds or conditions are likely to be reached. Simulation models become valuable tools when the evaluation phase of the learning cycle is reached. The models can be used as tools to assist with impact assessment (Chapter 10).

All modelling steps should normally involve stakeholder participation.[4] Not only does this ensure that all objectives are identified and understood but it also helps to ensure that management plans formulated to meet those objectives have stakeholder support and are likely to be implemented. Furthermore, stakeholder participation will make available otherwise inaccessible knowledge. It will often reveal unforeseen ways in which objectives can be reached.

It is important to decide the appropriate level of stakeholder participation in integrated modelling. Stakeholder participation can be limited to simply providing data for model construction. However, there are many successful cases of local resource managers being trained in modelling techniques and then going on to construct and use models independently. The appropriate level of participation will depend on why the model is being used, but also on the abilities and interest of the relevant stakeholders. Clearly, different levels of participation will be appropriate to different stakeholders. When designing a participatory approach to integrated modelling, it is useful to identify those who will either make the resource management decisions or who have a direct and significant influence on them. These stakeholders should be encouraged to participate as closely as possible in model construction and, if possible, carry out analyses themselves. It may be sufficient for other stakeholders (i.e. those with no direct decision-making power) to contribute to model development by identifying their objectives and discussing (together with other stakeholders) how these might be achieved. Care should be taken that consultation does not become just a cosmetic exercise but genuinely leads to the model reflecting stakeholder perspectives. The integrated model is not an end in itself, but a means to the successful formulation and implementation of management programmes. Therefore, the potential long-term benefits of stakeholder participation should be recognised.

The building of conceptual frameworks does not necessarily involve computer-based approaches. These simple models can be readily accessible to everyone. However, even the building of box-and-arrow diagrams can be facilitated by systems modelling software. Proprietary software such as STELLA allows easy construction of such figures and allows one to move rapidly into a systems dynamic model. While systems dynamic modelling

---

[4] Cain *et al. Designing Integrated Models.*

was until recently relatively inaccessible to the non-expert, the off-the-shelf software now available makes it accessible to everyone. Using such software, we were able to build a useful land-use and forestry model for Mzola State Forest and adjacent communal areas in a two-week period during a modelling training course (see Fig. 10.3, p. 222).

Most modellers are aware of the importance of keeping the model transparent to stakeholders. Given the complexity of natural resource systems, models can rapidly become inaccessible to all but the model builders. Even in a model with numerous submodules, builders of specific submodules will not know the workings of other submodules. Everyone espouses transparency in model building but reality usually falls far short of this ideal. All models are also based upon some assumptions and there is a tendency to fail to make these explicit. An assumption that may seem self-evident to a Western aid worker or scientist may not be at all plausible to the inhabitants of a remote forest frontier area. Stating, and if possible testing, assumptions is an important step in any use of models.

Modelling to help villagers to improve their adaptive capacity

Local managers are, almost by definition, adaptive; all resource managers will learn from their experiences – and in a community of several hundred households there are always a few people who are trying different things and those who are watching to see what works. In the adaptive management literature, the latter are referred to as passive adaptive managers. Active adaptive management requires that managers probe the systems to explore the fullest possible range of outcomes. It is important to recognise that learning by doing is a long and time-consuming process. It is clearly a risky strategy – and particularly so when the experiments are being implemented on the only set of resources of a kind: the ones upon which you and your family are totally dependent. It is understandable that people who are dependent upon poor resources are cautious in their experimental management: they tend to be conservative as they cannot afford to take risks. Modelling can go some way towards reducing the risks and costs of experimentation, but not all the way. The most important role that modelling and simulation can play is in probing the system and expanding the range of options in the adaptive management process.

Systems dynamic modelling has yielded valuable results when conducted with stakeholder participation. It is possible to do this with local people who have no prior experience with computers, though the numbers of cases where this has been attempted can be counted on one hand. Tim Lynam and colleagues, from the Tropical Resource Ecology Programme in Zimbabwe, provide one of the few examples of the use of computer-based modelling with such smallholder farmers.[5] The farmers assist in the development of models and model results are fed back to them using participatory techniques such as role-plays. The initial experience with these types of participatory modelling exercise is that they can provide a very cost-effective way for scientists and resource managers to share their knowledge and understanding; they can also be fun for all involved.

The objective of the work of Lynam and colleagues was the design of vegetation management strategies in a semi-arid area, of about 400 km^2, in the eastern Zambezi valley in Zimbabwe. The focus was on improving the productivity of common pool resources yielding livestock feeds as well as other goods and services that households use (e.g. timber, wild fruits, thatching grass). Recognition of the failure of so many similar development initiatives prompted the Zimbabwean research team to ask themselves what it was that would most meaningfully contribute to the sustainability and replicability of their initiatives. The answer appeared to be the enhancement of the capacity of other farmers in similar, but not identical, situations to adapt the system to their specific conditions.

Several participatory rural appraisals were held with the communities and village committees to identify broad community objectives for woodland resource management. The issues were explored using graphical representations (called spidergrams[6]) that enabled people to identify components of an answer to a given question and to weight each component of the answer (as an example see Fig. 5.2). Once these factor spidergrams were developed, the workshop participants defined the states that each node in the spidergram might adopt. Thereafter the relationships between factor states in each of the input variables (nodes) and the core objective state were defined. These relationships provided the basis for development of a Bayesian network.[7] These provide a probabilistic and relatively, although not entirely, static representation of the relationships between input variable states and the states of the variables of interest. Research staff developed the computer implementations of the Bayesian networks (Fig. 5.3) during the evening and workshop participants manipulated these the following day.

---

[5]Lynam *et al.*, Adapting science to adaptive managers.

[6]Lynam, T. J. P. Adaptive analysis of locally complex systems in a globally complex world. *Conservation Ecology*, **3** (1999). 1 Online: http://www.consecol.org/Journal/vol3/iss2/art13.

[7]Jensen, F. V. *An Introduction to Bayesian Networks*. London: UCL Press, 1996.

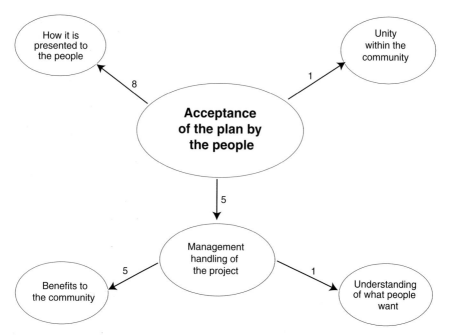

Fig. 5.2. Factors affecting the local acceptance of management plans developed through the research process. Numbers on the spidergram arms indicate the relative importance of each factor at each level as scored by the village participants – the least important factor is always scored with 1. (From Lynam *et al.*, 2002. See footnote 2.)

The resulting model indicated that three sets of interacting factors were influencing the availability of graze and browse. The first factor was the size of the grazing areas. This was a major concern as corrupt local leaders were allocating grazing lands to new settlers for fields and home sites. The second component was the amount of graze or browse available on each unit of land, while the third component was the number of animals. The model provided a first iteration of a locally developed exercise of the issues that were of primary concern to the project. The project could thus focus attention on those aspects of the problem that were of most importance to local people: the amount of land available for grazing. Perhaps more importantly, the model provided a basic and common understanding of the problem and its causes, shared by all concerned – scientists as well as local managers. It was clearly recognised by all participants that the model was not necessarily correct, but it was recognised as being useful.

Problem recognition does not guarantee that viable and acceptable solutions will be found; neither the researchers nor their community

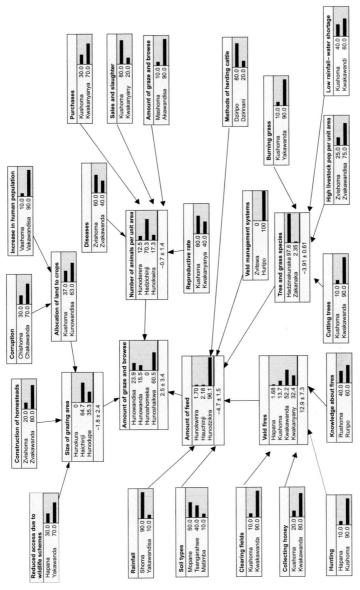

Fig. 5.3. Implementation of the Bayesian network indicating the factors affecting the supply of adequate graze and browse to livestock in Mahuwe Ward. Each box represents a variable with a number of states. Three factors were identified as being important: the area of grazing land, the number of livestock and the amount of feed per unit area. These are shown as the input nodes to the central node representing the amount of graze and browse per animal. The node titles are in English but the states are in Shona, the workshop participants' home language. (From Lynam *et al.*, 2002. See footnote 2.)

counterparts were that naïve. The development of the models described above was the first step in a lengthy process of identifying management strategies that were believed most likely to achieve the desired results. Once these were identified and tested in a modelling environment, the next step was to identify the organisational and institutional changes required for the successful implementation of such locally desirable changes. Again, this involved the local development of computer-based tools.

A key lesson from the work was the need for research to be adaptive if it was to benefit adaptive managers: the orientation of the project needed significant changes as stakeholder's needs were better understood. Participatory engagement with stakeholders is a time-consuming and relatively costly process where, in the case studies, most of the costs were born by the research projects themselves. The authors raise the concern that these activities may not be widely replicable if these costs are not reduced or if they have to be born by the stakeholders. It is all too easy to waste the time of local stakeholders in endless negotiation and data collection. There has to be a balance between the time investments required of local people and the tangible benefits that they derive from the project.

The focus of research such as this should be to use experimentation, observation and analyses to improve the capacity of local managers to manage their resources. This will, in all likelihood, be a slow process but one that stands a reasonable chance of having a sustainable impact on people's ability to manage their production system.

Knowledge management and negotiation support

Perhaps the more common view of models in formal systems analysis is in their role of representing current understanding of the system and thence being used in a predictive mode to identify key intervention points and key gaps in knowledge. Integrated modelling provides us with a means of comparing different scenarios. It provides us with the analytical framework to understand the consequences of changes in the components of a system in both the short and long term, at a range of scales. By holding some components constant, one can explore the impacts of changes in other specific components. However, complex systems models built for their predictive power probably have the least potential in the large-scale action research that we advocate. They can be very valuable in the understanding that they bring to a cross-scale complex problem (see Chapter 4); however, their data needs are often high and it can take a long time to build the model: many people would consider that it takes too long. In action research, the models are unlikely to be ready when needed. In addition, they are prone to the problem of becoming ends in themselves – driven to extremes of complexity by the curiosity of the modellers.

While complex models undoubtedly have their place, we are attracted by the concept of 'throw-away' models: working computer-implemented models that are built in a few days to solve a particular problem and are then discarded. Tim Lynam, of the Tropical Resource Ecology Programme in Zimbabwe, noted that 'We should build models but when they have satisfied our needs we should throw the wretched things away'. Building a simple model of a natural resource system can provide a valuable framework for a workshop. It helps people to communicate, opens their eyes to new ideas and can play a powerful role in building shared understanding amongst members of teams.

The definition we have used for integrated modelling specifically excludes management information systems that, while allowing human and biophysical data to be compared, generally do not support 'what if?' analyses. However, such systems may be usefully linked to an integrated model to provide the basis of a decision-support system (Box 5.1).[8]

Box 5.1. Decision support for water demand by agricultural households in Thailand

A team of researchers working on a catchment project in northern Thailand has built a decision-support system (DSS) that deals with increasing demand for water by agricultural households.[1] The boundary, scale and scope of the issues to be addressed, and the relevant management scenarios, are determined by the interaction among households, government agencies and other stakeholders and the underlying biological processes.

The DSS comprises data, analytical and integrative modelling tools and a user-friendly interface. It has the potential to help stakeholders to negotiate a consensus management regime. The DSS recognises the nested operational scales of stakeholders' interests with production decisions from the local level feeding through to the wider regional, national and international scales. In turn, the human and natural resource systems of these wider scales impact on the local level, commonly through changes in commodity prices or environmental conditions. Given the linkages of these scales, different analytical tools are used to accommodate the precision required at each scale, ranging from bio-economic models to computable general equilibrium models for assessment of

---

[8] Simonovic, S. P. Decision support systems for sustainable management of water resources: 2. Case studies. *Water International* **21** (1996), 233–244; Henderson-Sellers, B. Decision support systems for stored water quality: 1. The environmental decision support system. *Environment International* **17** (1991), 595–599.

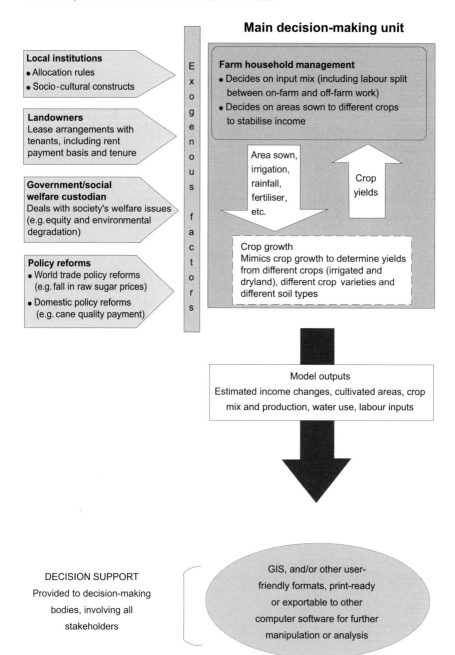

Fig. 5.4. Example of the structure of a decision support model. GIS, geographical information system. (From Lal *et al.*, 2001. See footnote 1 in this box.)

industry-wide impacts. Padma Lal, from the National Centre for Development Studies at the Australian National University, one of the researchers on the project, notes that this integration of disciplines and interests leads to immense complexities that are difficult to manage.

The biophysical and socio-economic data sets that form the data module of the DSS were collected from different sources and included indigenous knowledge. The DSS uses these data for three purposes: first, to provide information to users; second, for data inputs into the modelling tools; and, finally, to produce model outputs using the DSS. Data are both spatial and non-spatial, and qualitative and quantitative. Geographical information system (GIS) technologies underlie the data module, with the system capable of spatially depicting both characteristics of linked databases and the simulation and optimisation results of the model.

The major model within the DSS comprises a number of biophysical and socio-economic submodels. The model represents stakeholder groups as discrete modules, each with characteristic decision-making behaviours and patterns (Fig. 5.4). Much attention is devoted to the household component of the model. Households were classified into groups depending on ownership of high-quality paddy land and access to irrigation, the two most important factors that are thought to determine household decisions. Embedded in the farm household model is a crop model for analysing the bio-economic viability of various farming practices. This allows the decision-makers to assess the environmental feasibility of adopting best-practice farming methods and planting high-yielding crop varieties as farmers respond to challenges in their operational settings, brought about by policy and institutional changes or expected climatic conditions. The crop model considers a number of both perennial and annual crops grown in the catchment, under rainfed and irrigated conditions, on different soil types. Given the focus on dry-season demand for water, the crop model needed to determine the impact of irrigation on crop yields.

The stakeholder groups are interrelated to the extent that their production and consumption decisions affect each other, with the combined impact of the decisions that they make (or fail to make) determining the likelihood of achieving their envisioned future. As an example, one stakeholder is the weir management committee that allocates water from weirs to households. In periods of water shortage, the committee determines the mechanism for rationing. A series of charges and fines are levied on households who do not obey these rules. Weir management committees are responsible for the repair and maintenance of the weir, for which they draw upon household labour. Households often contribute labour according to the area of land irrigated or are required to pay an equivalent quantity of cash. In some cases, downstream committees also negotiate with upstream committees. A weir allocation module is included in the DSS, which mimics the current rules used for water allocation. Users of the DSS are able to manipulate the allocation rules by changing policy scenarios.

The DSS is characterised by a highly intuitive user interface to allow decision-makers to explore alternatives by changing values and data in the model. The interface guides a non-technical user through the stages of accessing and manipulating data and developing and assessing scenarios. Users can alter input data to reflect more up-to-date knowledge or expert opinions. Users are guided through the input data required for a particular scenario and can select the way in which they want to view the results from the scenario. Results from the model could be summarised in a tabular format, plotted or collated into an exportable text file. A variety of presentation tools can be used to reflect different stakeholder needs.

The DSS was used to assess many management scenarios during multi-stakeholder workshops. Examples include implementation of forestry regulations, introduction of crops through agricultural extension, construction of water-storage facilities and investment by households in more efficient irrigation. Scenarios were assessed through a range of indicators that captured the broad socio-economic and biophysical processes (e.g. water supply, water diverted, crop yields, gross margins, cash crop income, on- and off-farm income and shadow prices of constraining resources). The DSS was a key element in joint learning by multiple stakeholders and led to many positive development outcomes.

[1]Lal, P., Lim-Applegate, H. and Scoccimarro, M. The adaptive decision-making process as a tool for integrated natural resource management: focus, attitudes, and approach. *Conservation Ecology,* **5** (2001), 11. Online: http://www.consecol.org/vol5/iss2/art11.

Increasingly, integrated models are being linked to a variety of databases. Even when not linked in this manner, integrated natural resource management will invariably require that data from different sources be managed in some kind of database. Data can be of a spatial or non-spatial nature, and both qualitative and quantitative data can be included. Geographical information systems (GIS) are usually involved in such data-management systems. Peter Jones and Philip Thornton have demonstrated valuable applications of spatially explicit databases operating across various scales (Chapter 4). The focus in this chapter is on formal knowledge, but it is important to recognise that formal knowledge management may be less important than the management of the informal or tacit knowledge of local resource managers (see Chapters 2 and 7).

Decision-support systems are created to address different management scenarios. They usually:

- adopt a systems perspective to describe key processes and spatial and temporal interconnectedness within and between human and biophysical subsystems
- adopt a multi-disciplinary analytical approach to provide a definitive and rigorous representation of the system using logical and mathematical formulations and algorithms
- incorporate multiple management objectives within the evaluation framework identified by stakeholders.

Decision-support systems usually comprise a set of biophysical, social and economic databases; a set of individual discipline-based and/or integrated analytical, simulation and optimisation models; an output module of spatial and non-spatial depiction of expected future outcomes; and a user-friendly interface for relevant stakeholders to do 'what if' scenario analysis.

In the real world, human impact on natural resources derives from a large number of individual decisions. People usually take these decisions with different access to knowledge and information and with different means to exploit this knowledge. They may also have different objectives, constraints, priorities and strategies. The best that we can hope for is a process of negotiation among stakeholders that leads to a modification of the individual decisions and thus produces superior outcomes from the broader social perspective. The term 'decision support' suggests that a single entity will seek a solution that optimises the way multiple objectives can be achieved and then takes decisions that will be imposed on the various actors and stakeholders. This suggests an overtly top-down decision-making process. Meine van Noordwijk and his colleagues at the World Agroforestry Centre prefer the term negotiation support for constructs that help in obtaining a common perspective on the 'if this, then that' relations for a range of possible future landscapes (Box 5.2). To function adequately, the negotiation support system itself will have to be the subject of negotiation and shared development efforts among stakeholders.[9]

Box 5.2. Moving to negotiation support for catchment management in Sumatra

During the first two phases of the Alternatives to Slash and Burn Project facilitated by the World Agroforestry Centre, it became clear that catchment protection functions of forests and the way these functions change after forest conversion are a major source of conflict in Southeastern Asia.[1] There are challenging scale relations, involving distances beyond those under the influence of local institutions. As several hierarchical layers of stakeholders are involved, a complex negotiation process is likely to be necessary and a decision-support system based on a model of how real-world landscapes function may be

---

[9]Lal, P., Lin-Applegate, H. and Scoccimarro, M. The adaptive decision-making process as a tool for integrated natural resource management: focus, attitudes and approach. *Conservation Ecology*, **5** (2001), 11. Online: http://www.consecol.org/vol5/iss2/art11; van Noordwijk, M., Tomich, T. P. and Verbist, B. Negotiation support models for integrated natural resource management in tropical forest margins. *Conservation Ecology*, **5** (2001), 21. Online: http://www.consecol.org/vol5/iss2/art21; Hagmann, J. R., Chuma, E., Murwira, K., Connolly, M. and Ficarelli, P. Success factors in integrated natural resource management R&D: lessons from practice. *Conservation Ecology*, **5** (2002), 29. Online: http://www.consecol.org/vol5/iss2/art29.

a helpful tool in this process. To this end a stakeholder analysis was conducted at the site in Sumatra, Indonesia, to define the problem clearly, to set the boundaries and constraints of various alternatives, and to compile the perceived causal relationships. Different 'what if' scenarios, based on stakeholder inputs and feedback, allowed an exploration of various possible options. Scenarios needed to be developed for uncontrollable external parameters such as migration, world market prices or precipitation. The main objective of this model building is to put stakeholders on a more equal footing and thus help them in negotiating an acceptable agreement over future resource use and access rights. The modelling and social interaction are an iterative adaptive learning process, contributing to the stages of problem definition, evaluation of options, negotiation, and implementation and monitoring of agreed solutions.

[1] Tomich, T. P., van Noordwijk, M. and Thomas, D. E. (eds.) *ASB-Indonesia Report 10: Research Abstracts and Key Policy Questions on Environmental Services and Land Use Change, Bridging the Gap Between Policy and Research in Southeast Asia.* Bogor: World Agroforestry Centre, 1999.

As with systems models, negotiation support tools help in under-standing the problem, provide a mechanism whereby a range of possibilities can be compared and help to develop a shared vision. Negotiation-support tools encourage dialogue over possible misinterpretations of scenarios. Such discussion is necessary for a balanced consideration of the stakeholders' diverse interests. These models are powerful tools to help diverse stakeholders to negotiate trade-offs or arrive at a consensus.

Charting a way forward

A series of steps is envisaged in implementing an integrated modelling and negotiation support agenda. As with all 'steps' in integrated research pro-grammes, they are not neat steps taken in clear temporal sequence. For ex-ample, during the adaptive learning cycle, there would be constant returning to Step 3, as the 'throw-away' model is constantly adapted, with concomi-tant revision of problems, best bets, etc. There are similarities between the steps suggested here and summarised in Box 5.3 and those proposed by Brian Walker and colleagues of the Resilience Alliance in a recent paper in the online journal *Conservation Ecology*.[10]

[10] Walker, B., Carpenter, S., Andreis, A. *et al.* Resilience management in social–ecological systems: a working hypothesis for a participatory approach. *Conservation Ecology*, **6** (2002), 14. Online: http://www.consecol.org/vo16/iss1/art14.

Box 5.3. Summary of steps in a modelling approach

Step 1

1. Problem definition
2. Preliminary best bets
3. Defining a data management structure.

Step 2

1. Conceptual framework of causal links (across scales and stakeholders)
2. Problem further clarified
3. Bottlenecks to agricultural and natural resource production identified
4. Negative effects of resource development identified
5. Best bets further clarified
6. Selection of indicators to assess the results of the learning process
7. Data management structure finalised.

Step 3

1. Computer-based model developed (a throw-away model)
2. Various scenarios explored for their impacts and bottlenecks, with best bets being further refined
3. Data-management system populated with data (many best guesses included), including the collection of data on the selected indicators
4. Best bets implemented.

Step 4

Predictive models and/or negotiation support tools developed.

Step 1 Problem formulation, initial generation of alternatives and establishment of a knowledge management system

The first step would typically involve a multi-stakeholder process to define at least one problem and its boundaries, and understand how the different stakeholders approach the problem. An initial definition of some best bets or plausible solutions should also be attempted, though these may be rather preliminary. A framework for data collection and management would be set up at this step.

Step 2 Qualitative system design: conceptual modelling

In the second step, a causal relationship diagram, system diagram or conceptual framework will be produced. In this process, the focus is on identifying the key relationships among components of the particular system under study and on the constraints operating on the system. The framework would be expected to address issues of spatial and temporal scale. A conceptual framework could be viewed as a series of hypotheses about the processes operating. Consequently, variables in the model should be theoretically and logically linked. The process of developing a conceptual model clarifies the nature of the problem itself, the bottlenecks to agricultural and natural re-source production, the potential negative effects of resource development and the possible entry points for interventions. The conceptualisation should also identify the potential impacts of research and development, and thus guide the selection of indicators of the performance of the resource system. In this way, indicators can be selected that are causally and theoretically linked.

An example of a conceptual model is presented in Fig. 5.5, for a case study in Chivi, southern Zimbabwe.[11] This is a box-and-arrow conception of livelihoods within the area. The model reflects the diverse livelihood options of people, and some of the key 'external' variables, such as AIDS and climate (in particular drought). It was produced as a group effort by the dozen researchers involved. It was only used to consider which variables to focus on and how these might influence other variables of interest.

Step 3 Developing a computer-based model

In a number of cases, Step 2 may be the end of the modelling component of the project, with the conceptual framework guiding subsequent action. In other cases, it may be appropriate to develop a throwaway model. Such a model would be sure to capture some of the key processes but it will not be at the level of a complex predictive model. It could possibly incorporate 20–50 variables and would take no longer than 10–20 days to develop. It would assist stakeholders to clarify further the nature of the problem, to provide some level of quantitative assessment of various scenarios, to refine the selection of best bets, to assist in stakeholder negotiation, etc. Good facilitation of this process is essential, ensuring that stakeholders engage each other meaningfully.

[11] Campbell, B., Sayer, J. A., Frost, P. *et al.* Assessing the performance of natural resource systems. *Conservation Ecology*, **5** (2001), 22. Online: http://www.consecol.org/vol5/iss2/art22.

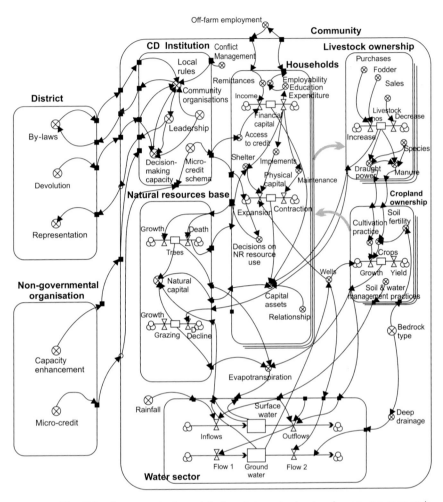

Fig. 5.5. A conceptual model of an integrated natural resource research and management site in Chivi, Zimbabwe. (From Campbell *et al.*, 2001. See footnote 11.)

Step 4 Moving to fully blown predictive models and/or decision-support systems

In many research and development contexts, step 4 will not be carried out because of the heavy demands on data and modelling skills. In addition, such models generally take so long to produce that they are of minimal value in the relatively rapid learning cycle that characterises natural resource management initiatives. An example of a fully developed decision support system was given in Box 5.1.

The keys to the use of models for natural resource management

New approaches to modelling provide novel means of engaging with multiple stakeholders, as has been illustrated by such diverse examples as Zimbabwean pasture lands and Thailand water management. However, models can also be demanding masters – modelling itself must never be allowed to become the objective.

- Natural resource system models are almost always wrong, in the sense that reality rarely conforms to their numerical projections, but they can be very useful in exploring options and testing scenarios.
- Models can be useful simply to do routine bookkeeping on large amounts of data from complex systems.
- Simple, throwaway models coupled with good facilitation can be valuable tools for team building and enhancing shared understanding amongst stakeholders.
- Models enhance adaptive capacity by making management interventions more explicit and, through simulations, extending the range of management experiments that are possible.
- Modelling should ideally be an interactive learning process, contributing to the stages of problem definition, evaluation of options, negotiation and evaluation.

Part II

Realities on the ground

6 Institutions for managing natural resources in African savannas

Zimbabwe has had a long and distinguished history of agricultural science, built on the classical transfer of technology model. A number of national and international research organisations have conducted excellent on-station technological research in the country. With hindsight, it is easy to find fault with much of this work, which has failed to address the realities of small-scale farmers. In this chapter, we first explore the component science and then describe a more integrated approach, drawing on a case study in southern Zimbabwe.

Component science in complex savanna environments

A good example is the Makoholi Research Station. It is part of the Division of Livestock and Pastures, one of the divisions in the national agricultural research service. This station is 150 km from Chivi, the area we return to later in this chapter. The work at Makoholi should serve the needs of smallholder farmers, the main stakeholders for work of the national research organisation. In 1993, the station housed six professional officers and six research technicians and 13 projects were being undertaken.[1] The work covered a large number of narrowly focussed projects. These included studies of cow performance in relation to use of cows for draught power; characterisation of goat production systems; performance of goats in relation to variety, feed supplementation, dipping and watering; sheep breed digestion studies; production characteristics of forage grasses and legumes; and digestibility studies of legume trees and shrubs. Some of the work was probably quite useful. For example, understanding the impact of using cows for draught power on productivity is important as small-scale farmers usually resort to using cows because of lack of oxen. There is, however, no indication how any useful results are disseminated to stakeholders. There were seven publications from the researchers in that year. While some scientists based at other research

---

[1]Department of Research and Specialists Services. *Annual Report of Division of Livestock and Pastures 1992–93*. Harare: Ministry of Agriculture, 1995.

stations in the division had published some articles in farmer magazines (not read by smallholder farmers), none of the staff at Makoholi had published such material in that year or in the two preceding years.

Most of the studies can be criticised for their lack of relevance to the smallholder. For instance, goats never receive supplementary feed and are never dipped; sheep are not important in the farming system (and it is unclear how studies on sheep digestion would be important even if sheep were part of the farming system); and forage grasses and legumes are never grown by smallholder farmers. In addition, the key issue of grazing areas being common pool resources was not researched. Detailed research was carried out on the optimum spacing of fodder grasses and the effect of cutting frequency on dry-matter production of fodder legumes and massive fodder species trials (using nearly 200 accessions) were conducted before there was any check as to whether smallholder farmers might grow such fodder plants. Lastly, maize–legume intercropping trials used fertiliser applications many times those used by smallholder farmers.

While it may be easy to criticise the officers at Makoholi, it should be noted that their work was carried out in conjunction with a number of other agencies, including the International Livestock Centre for Africa (ILRI), the World Agroforestry Centre (ICRAF) and International Crops Research Institute for the Semi-Arid Tropics (ICRISAT). And one of us (BC) was supervising one of the researchers. The more important point is that the incentive system for research did not make it responsive to the needs of smallholders.

Improving soils with woodland leaf litter

Farmers in the area use litter from the local miombo woodland to improve soil fertility. One of the studies conducted at Makoholi Research Station was on the impact of litter on soil fertility and growth of maize under dryland conditions. One of us (BC) supervised the researcher who was undertaking this work for a higher degree. By academic standards, the study was well done, with a Ph.D. awarded and four refereed publications. However, the utility of the work can be seriously questioned. For instance, farmers tend to use litter more in their irrigated garden farming than for dryland maize. Litter used for dryland fields does not go directly on the fields but rather to bulk the manure in the pens, and the commercial fertiliser and manure application rates that were used were many times those used by smallholder farmers. In addition, the experiment was conducted in a very dry period – one of the three seasons recorded the lowest rainfall in a century, and the other two seasons had lower than normal rainfall. To our knowledge, no extension messages have ever been developed from the work. This is not an isolated example. There is abundant evidence from many public sector research institutes throughout the developing world that the bulk of the work being conducted is not relevant to the needs of the clients.

Recreating farming systems

One of the more bizarre experiments at Makoholi Research Station was set up in the 1980s. Farming systems research ideas were sweeping through the country at that time. Independence had come in 1980 and for the first time the scientific community was moving to study smallholder agriculture (previously research had focussed on large-scale commercial agriculture). However, the scientists in question were probably unnerved by the prospects of entering the messy reality of the smallholder farmer. Therefore, a smallholder sector was established on the research station! Peasant households were relocated to the research station and became paid employees of the research service. They were employed to farm like peasants, but within a certain framework. A number of farmers were thus established and their cropping and livestock operations were monitored. This work was conducted for a number of years but does not appear to have been written up. One can probably trace this experiment to the training of the scientists in question: the need for controlled experiments had been driven home! As Thomas Kuhn has suggested, changing ways in the scientific community is not easy.

The research community's lack of connection to reality was the subject of an article on the ICRISAT research station in Southern Zimbabwe by Ian Scoones in the 1990s.[2] He described how peasant farmers were taken from nutrient-poor semi-arid environments in air-conditioned buses to the oasis of the ICRISAT research station, where they could view highly productive sorghum growing on irrigated and nutrient-rich soils behind six-foot fences. This was happening at a time when incentive structures had caused most of the peasant farmers to abandon small grains in favour of maize. The realities of the communal areas were far removed from what they saw at the research station.

Developing productive water points

The Centre for Ecology and Hydrology (UK) and its local partners in Zimbabwe have been involved in some excellent work on communally

[2]Scoones, I. A visit to ICRISAT. *Haramata Bulletin*, **12** (1991), 19.

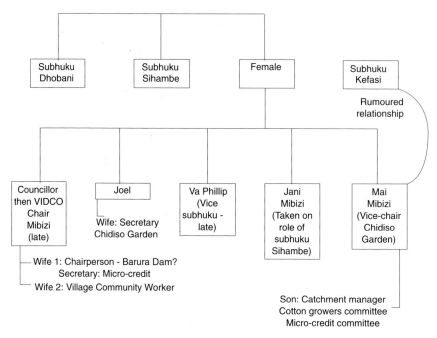

Fig. 6.1. The ruling elite in Romwe: together they control the village leadership and therefore the collector well and community garden, as well as most other village development. In this way, these 10 households exert influence over the activities of about 125 other households and capture a disproportionate share of the development initiatives. Sabhukas, village leaders; VIDCO, Village Development Committee Organisation.

managed water points in the area. These are designed to capture water that is surplus to domestic needs which may be used for economically productive purposes. In Romwe catchment in Chivi, a collector well was sunk in 1991. There were massive well failures throughout southern Zimbabwe in the early 1990s as a result of a series of droughts, but this well did not fail. The danger of not looking at social processes when doing technical research and development is illustrated by the information collected by Bevlyne Sithole and Witness Kozanayi, which showed that a few households control the collector well and the associated garden. Three villages, which had a total of 126 households, have implemented the garden scheme irrigated by the collector well. The garden has plots for 50 households. The family tree of the ruling elite (Fig. 6.1) suggests that a few households from the same or interrelated lineages have captured the leadership role for most projects in the area. Three of these households are those of the village leaders (*sabhukus*), who are very influential in decision making in the area. Another household is that of the councillor who later became the Village Development Committee Chairperson. One household contains the Catchment Manager, an employee of the project earning an income well above that of most households in the catchment. This manager also benefits through the power he wields in this position. He also holds a prominent position in the micro-credit scheme, another role that gives him power and influence.

So where are the problems?

Several problems have limited the impact of much of the past natural resource research in the area. There has been a consistent lack of connection between technology development and the real-life context of smallholder farmers. Scale issues were rarely considered and temporal risks and off-site effects were not taken into account. Above all, insufficient attention was given to social processes, especially local politics and common property resource management.

In many ways the problems have reflected the inappropriate manner in which the research and development system has been organised. Researchers are divorced from the system they attempt to influence, and farmers have little or no influence on the choice or development of technologies. Madondo, who was an extension officer for 25 years in Zimbabwe, came to the conclusion that the artificial division into a research and an extension department was at the core of the problem. The impact of the malfunctioning of the system is obvious; Hagmann writes that extension officers in Masvingo Province (where Chivi and Makoholi are located) hardly ever utilised any of the technologies that were developed by researchers.[3] Research results remained in a scientific form that was inaccessible to extension workers. Even if the technologies had been better communicated, it is doubtful whether they would have had practical value in the real world.

Readers may counter these arguments by saying that we have described a system from the past, citing the numerous innovative participatory research programmes that have been implemented in the 1990s. However, we return to this theme later in this chapter; it is easy to hide behind the words 'participation', 'action research', etc. but the examples of successful participatory and action research programmes are few, and in far too many

[3] Hagmann, J. *Learning Together for Change. Facilitating Innovation in Natural Resource Management Through Learning Process Approaches in Rural Livelihoods in Zimbabwe.* Weikersheim: Margraf Verlag, 1999.

cases technology-focussed research is still being pursued even where it is irrelevant to the needs of resource users.

Research and development in Chivi

The colonial heritage of Zimbabwe left a large part of the indigenous population concentrated on areas of low productivity land. Land pressures are manifest in shortages of fuelwood and water, and periodic famines occur when there are periods of low rainfall. This section explores the successes and failures of an innovative attempt to use an integrated approach to manage catchments in Chivi.

The 'Micro-catchment Management and Common Property Resources Project' involved a multi-disciplinary team of researchers and numerous stakeholders in developing and assessing management strategies for small catchments in this semi-arid region.[4] The project had two study micro-catchments: Romwe is 4.5 km^2 in area and Mutangi 5.9 km^2. The users of the woodland and water resources in the micro-catchments come from households in numerous surrounding villages, covering 32 km^2 in Romwe and 51 km^2 in Mutangi. Population densities are 60–90/km^2. This initiative set out right from the start to combine research with development and to emphasise stakeholder participation. The team included scientists from a full spectrum of disciplines (hydrology, ecology, sociology, economics and agriculture) and it was able to draw upon the expertise of leading national figures in action and participatory research.

While many of the outcomes have been well received by the international scientific community, some components of the project have been far from successful. In order to pinpoint reasons for success and failure of integrated projects, we explore the nature of this catchment management project.

Living in a complex world: the Kefasi family in Romwe

As argued in Chapter 2, reductionism in science has seen the partitioning of natural and social sciences into isolated units of study. Resource users themselves live their lives in a much more complex and interconnected world. Box 6.1 is a personal account by a farmer from the Romwe study area and shows how small-scale farmers are the ultimate integrators. They manage

---

[4]The main research organisations were the Institute of Environmental Studies (IES), the Centre for Ecology and Hydrology (CEH), the Center for International Forestry Research (CIFOR) and the Department of Research and Specialist Services, Zimbabwe Ministry of Agriculture.

social interactions at the local level and live in economically complex family units. They utilise woodlands whilst growing crops in an unpredictable environment. They have elaborate links into the urban and national economy, and they even maintain a healthy respect for witches.

Box 6.1. The integrated use of resources by a small-scale farmer

The following account was written by Witness Kozanayi, a research assistant living in the Romwe area.

Mr. Kefasi, his wife and his extended family arrived in the area in 1952 after having been evicted from land that was designated for white commercial farming. Kefasi, now in his seventies, has two wives, as a result of receiving a second wife from his in-laws when his first wife became mentally ill. Kefasi claimed that his first wife became mentally ill after she was severely beaten by the Rhodesian forces during the liberation war in the late 1970s for refusing to divulge information about the movements of the freedom fighters. Kefasi curses the day he was installed as a village head (*sabhuku*) in the 1960s for he then became a key target of both the freedom fighters and the government soldiers. The beating incident resulted in Kefasi vowing not to indulge in national politics, but the present unrest in the country has seen him back again in the political ring, throwing his considerable standing in the community behind an independent candidate, much to the displeasure of one of his daughter-in-laws who is campaign manager for a candidate from the ruling party.

Kefasi has five children by his first wife, all married now. By local standards and expectations this is very few. His pride has, however, been restored with the arrival of two children by the second wife. His married children do well by him. His three sons work in towns where they stay with their wives. They have built nice brick-walled and asbestos-roofed houses near their father but they hardly ever return to stay there. His one daughter stays in Gweru with her family while the younger one is married locally. Kefasi reminisces on the time when it was possible for sons and daughters to get jobs in the city and break away from the poverty of the communal area – he notes that the new generation is stuck in the communal area on ever-dwindling land resources. A major portion of his livelihood portfolio is satisfied by the money and goods that the sons send back to him, though in recent years he fears that this has diminished – his sons plead economic hardships (as the national economy stagnates and declines). The money and goods are critical as farming inputs – Kefasi realises that much of the small success he has had in farming are due to the commitments of his grown children – he can afford fertiliser and hired labour to work in his fields. Though there is no clear trend in the amount of money sent to him, his neighbours believe that Kefasi is never without money. In his happy moments Kefasi boasts of how his grown children pamper him with goods, including nappies for the new babies. He even claims that his sons hatched the idea of him getting a second wife.

In the late 1970s Mr Kefasi was a very productive farmer. But this was also partly a result of the links Kefasi had with the urban economy – his work as an earthmover driver gave him sufficient income to purchase a water pump. With the water pump he could grow vegetables all year round in his 0.25 hectare garden. He sold the farm produce from the garden locally and at times some customers would come from as far as 30 km away.

The neighbours believe there are other reasons behind his farming successes. It is rumoured that Kefasi has consulted a *n'anga* (witchdoctor) to get *divisi* (a charm to cause abundant grain). The charm that he got was so strong that it needed an additional person to work well, and thus he needed a second wife. Others, the jealous ones it is said, link the arrival of the mental illness with the *divisi*. Kefasi sometimes regrets that he is an important leader in the community, as the many interpretations of the facts and the under-currents of jealousies and witchcraft, make decisions difficult and he feels that he spends an inordinate amount of time on settling disputes and leading the community. Of late, he has been at loggerheads with his daughter-in-law, Mrs Mutadzi, a productive farmer with land near to the community dam. In an earlier community meeting, it was agreed that a hole in the dam be sealed so as to prevent wastage of water. Kefasi, as the chairperson of the dam committee, sealed the hole. The water from the hole flows to Mutadzi's garden. Many people in the community were upset as they sympathised with Mutadzi. Kefasi then found his left foot swollen, and he strongly suspected that Mutadzi had bewitched him. In the middle of the night he opened the outlet valve and released almost all the water in the dam.

The extended family is both a drain on resources and a means of achieving certain ends. One of Kefasi's brothers passed away in the 1960s forcing Kefasi to look after his six orphaned children. Two of his nephews joined the army but then died, so Kefasi, as head of the family, has also had to look after the widows. Kefasi talks of the widespread deaths in the area and the many changes that are being brought on social customs in the last decade [the AIDS pandemic]. According to Shona custom, Cep, a nephew, plays a very crucial role in the Kefasi clan. He is an arbitrator, a go-between in the Kefasi family and within the community. In fact all village meetings are held and all cases tried at Cep's homestead. Dus, Kefasi's younger brother, also plays a key role. He acts as *sabhuku* if Kefasi is absent and Kefasi delegates Dus to make decisions on his behalf, especially if the decision is tricky. Locally they say Kefasi is a shrewd strategist, always managing not to get entangled in controversy. When there are tricky decisions to be made, Dus will often make the decision. If people are incensed by the decision, Kefasi will quickly apologise and deride the decision claiming that it was a slip of the tongue by his junior.

Kefasi holds numerous positions in the organisations of the area. He is the Chairperson of the Chidiso garden, the Cotton Growers Association, the Catchment Management Committee, the Zimbabwe Farmers Union and the Barura Dam. In his Church, the Seventh Day Adventists, he is an elder. He has passed on his post of Chairperson in Chidiso to Ms Mibiza, a shrewd woman in her early sixties. Kefasi once had an affair with Mibiza before he married his second wife, resulting in a child. The gift of the chairmanship was an apparent attempt to appease her. This move has contributed to the decline in a once vibrant community project. Project members do not want Mibiza as the chairperson, but Mibiza has threatened that if members do not want to listen to her then that will be the end of the project. Mibiza is from a very powerful family in the catchment and, therefore, her position appears invincible. In addition she is rumoured to be a witch and therefore unchallengeable.

Kefasi's hold on power is said to be not only due to his power as a *sabhuku*. Through Mibiza he is connected to a powerful family, and in addition his close friend Bepe is locally known as a virulent witch. Together Kefasi and Bepe commanded much respect in the community garden.

Those who have known Kefasi since his heyday testify that he is now a shadow of his former self. Since the water pump broke down about 12 years ago, Kefasi believes that his life has been dogged by misfortunes. He recounts how in 1969 he lost more than 30 head of cattle after temperatures plummeted in winter. Then in 1992, the worst drought in living memory wiped out most of his herd. In that year there was no crop production and even the usually perennial well in his garden dried up. That year survival was through food handouts from the government and from his sons. He recognises that he was lucky as he got extra handouts from the local councillor through his relationship with Mibiza, the councillor's sister. In 1999 there was cyclone Eline. He had ploughed the fields early, had two of his grandchildren come to stay with him to help with labour and had bought inputs worth more than US$500. Then the cyclone came and flooded the crop fields. Twice he applied fertiliser to try and recover the crops, but this did not work. He had borrowed some of the money for the inputs from the micro-credit scheme and now it was said that defaulters would not get any further loans, so the impacts of cyclone Eline will affect him for a number of years.

Kefasi is happy that he lives in Romwe for one reason – unlike other communal areas, the widespread woodlands in the hills are a very important source of wood, thatching grass, medicinal plants and wild foods. The researchers have indicated to him that the woodlands may disappear one day as one of the important trees (*Brachystegia glaucescens*) does not have sufficient saplings. To him this seems a minor problem. There is plenty of woodland now, and there are many other problems to deal with. Anyway where would the community find alternative sources of wood?

Kefasi smiles ruefully as he thinks of the researchers that are trying to promote development in the area. From his discussions with them he can see that they still do not understand how the community functions, and what it requires to get the community to facilitate development themselves.

Modelling: fuzzy holistic approaches or rigorous pragmatism

Into this complex world came our interdisciplinary team of scientists. From the outset of the micro-catchment management project, the team embraced the principles and practices of systems thinking. This was reflected in the original logical framework (log-frame), all the annual planning meetings, the constant attempt to develop integrated models and the development of an integrated data-archiving system.

One of the models was a conceptual model: a box and arrow diagram of the key elements of the system (Fig. 5.5, p. 115). The major stakeholders in the system are regarded as being the local community, non-governmental organisations (NGOs) and district authorities. At the community level, household livelihoods are conceptualised as comprising off-farm employment, crop and livestock production subsystems and woodland use. In these semi-arid regions, water is a crucial component of livelihoods; therefore, one of the subsystems looks at water, both surface and groundwater. Institutional components of the system are captured at the community and district level, with NGOs playing a role in shaping these institutions. This kind of model was used to structure the research effort to see how the different components were related, where research from one component would likely be of use to other components and where the gaps in the research effort were.

A different kind of model was used to evaluate interventions under different management scenarios.[5] This has been a highly iterative process. An initial stakeholder consultation identified five issues that had to be tackled in model development.

1. The model should improve understanding of complex systems among important stakeholders so as to provide a common platform from which management decisions can be made.
2. The model should link information and analyses provided by different expert disciplines and other stakeholders.
3. The model should allow different stakeholder perspectives to be recognised in model development and analysis.
4. The model should be easily updated in response to new information and so support adaptive management.
5. The model should be able to deal with limited data availability in a way that does not inhibit analysis.

The initial model was subsequently built by a small group of project participants, shared with the larger group, used to evaluate the impacts of a micro-credit intervention (see Fig. 10.4, p. 224) and then discarded as having served its purpose. In the course of the adaptive management of the project, the emphasis moved away from technical interventions in dryland agriculture to institutional and water-related interventions; therefore, a second model was built for that purpose.

---

[5] Cain, J., Moriarty, P. and Lynam, T. *Designing Integrated Models for the Participatory Formulation of Water Management Strategies*. Unpublished document.

It was decided to develop these models within the framework of a Bayesian network, as this could cope with many of the design requirements.[6] Previous research showed that it was understandable by a wide range of stakeholders and could facilitate exploratory modelling. For the initial model, an integrated analysis was carried out with the Bayesian network by selecting each of the management plan options in turn and examining the effect they have on income, well-being and vulnerability. The model design allowed the impact of the plans to be studied from a holistic perspective and was explicit about the uncertainty associated with each decision. For example, examining the change in probabilities when the management plan was changed from one soil conservation method to another indicated that the chance of income being doubled was only a small percentage.

The Bayesian network itself was not seen as the entire integrated model. Rather, the integrated model was viewed as the sum of two things: the discipline-specific analytical tools used to examine parts of the whole environmental system plus the Bayesian network used as a means of achieving integration between them. The discipline-specific analyses included econometric and statistical analyses for household livelihood studies, hydrological simulation models, visioning on institutional arrangements, land-cover simulation models, etc. (Fig. 6.2). These analyses fed the Bayesian network with information about how a part of the system works (e.g. the social dynamics) and it also allowed the interactions between these parts of the system to be investigated.

The dangers of the systems approach are that the team loses its focus on the key issues or that the system becomes so complex as to defy understanding. The dangers of being lost in detail are real, as many of the Chivi project participants can attest. In the modelling, we generally focussed on three to five main drivers of change: rainfall, the state of the macro-economy, institutional effectiveness and the desire to improve livelihood status. However, the models soon became very complex and difficult to comprehend by all participants. There are still sceptics amongst the project team as to the value of the modelling. All participants in the modelling work filled in a questionnaire that assessed their thoughts on the role of modelling. In general, the report-back was positive, but one of the eight participants in the final model building exercise noted that 'I for one would have avoided punching in all those numbers and just interviewed people on what they think would better their lives'. Modelling does appear to be an essential and important part of an integrated project, but it is only one small part. In addition, modelling is only one way of organising data. When other essential

[6] Also see Chapter 5 and Fig. 5.3 for use of this tool.

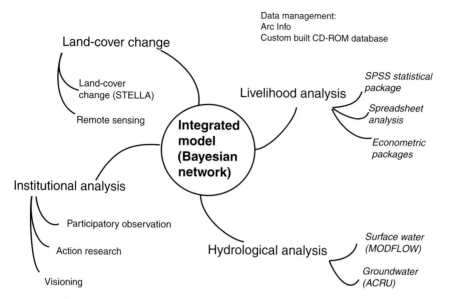

Fig. 6.2. The integrated model and its relationship to more disciplinary approaches.

parts of a project are missing, then the modelling becomes 'academic' (in the derogatory sense of the word). In retrospect, a greater focus on some key intervention possibilities – best bets or plausible promises – would have been appropriate. This would also have given greater focus to the modelling.

Integrating across disciplines

Work in Chivi clearly required close collaboration between scientists from a number of disciplines. Our movement between integrative work and detailed disciplinary work is illustrated by some of the aspects of the livelihoods component of the work. Our income analyses covered the full spectrum of activities: remittances, home industries, crop production, livestock production and forest gathering (poles, firewood, wild plant and animal foods). To capture such diverse activities was not easy. For example, the forest gathering activities of a male adult, female adult and child were ascertained by asking these respondents what they had gathered in the forest during the previous week; this was repeated for 15 weeks during the course of the year for the 200 households. The profiles of net income indicated the diverse nature of livelihoods, with different portfolios of activities for rich as opposed

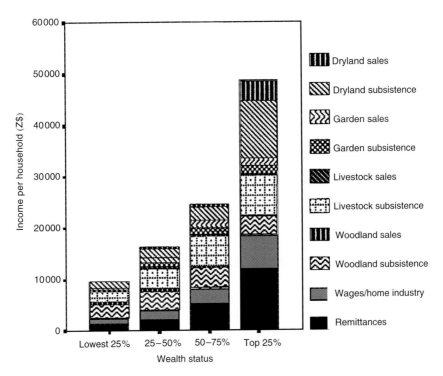

Fig. 6.3. Net income (cash and subsistence) sources for households of different wealth status in Chivi. US$1 = Z$39; wealth quartiles defined by total net income. Net income is calculated as the difference between gross income less all cash and in-kind expenses (e.g. draught power expenses are subtracted from crop income, but if they are supplied by own livestock then they are captured as livestock subsistence income). (From Campbell *et al.*, 2002. See footnote 7.)

to poor households (Fig. 6.3).[7] The 'wealthy' households were minimally dependent on woodlands and had high remittances, which were used to drive agricultural production. For all these 'farmers', farming rarely contributes more than 50% of total income.

   Time devoted to different activities was also assessed, but here the recall period was for the previous 24 hours. The time analysis shows how women spent considerable time on domestic activities, and somewhat more

[7]Campbell, B. M., Jeffrey, S., Kozanayi, W., Luckert, M., Mutamba, M. and Zindi, C. *Household Livelihoods in Semi-arid Regions: Options and Constraints.* Bogor: Center for International Forestry Research, 2002.

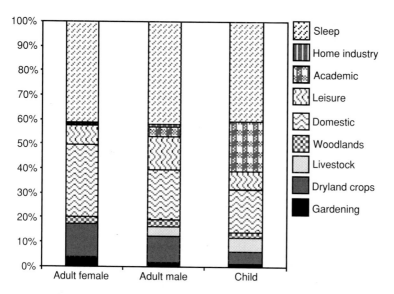

Fig. 6.4. Time allocation by different household members in Chivi: average allocation over a year.

time on dryland agriculture and gardening (Fig. 6.4). Men played a bigger role in livestock production and kept more time for academic pursuits and leisure! Getting a job in the outside world, a key source of cash income and a highly desired goal, is strongly dependent on having a minimum educational level, so these opportunities are mainly open to men. The seasonal profile shows that it is not true that the dry season is a period of labour inactivity, as is commonly assumed. This is the time to consolidate on household assets, such as home repairs, pen construction, fuelwood stockpiles, etc.; this is also the time for gardening, and the prime time to earn some money in off-farm activities.

Production of a document that would cover the multi-spectrum household portfolio, therefore, required the use of in-depth disciplinary skills. Several economists contributed to this component, but an ecologist also assisted in the design of the questionnaire. One economist also worked with sociologists on tenure issues, thus bringing household livelihood perspectives to that debate. As the livelihood data came from only one year, the work was extended through time by interacting with modellers of biophysical phenomena (e.g. modelling of dryland crop production). The livelihood data formed a central place in the integrated Bayesian network model, thus providing a core of the integrating activities in the research.

Integrating across scales

Given the importance of scale, and the concern about whether it is possible to extrapolate results from case studies, an early component of the Chivi study was to consider the scaling issues.[8] For several centuries before colonisation, the indigenous people were part of localised territorial groupings and natural resources were abundant in relation to population. Colonial land apportionment brought an abrupt change in tenure and settlement patterns. People were forced onto native reserves, mostly in parts of the country least favoured for agriculture. Romwe was resettled in the early 1950s as a result of seizure of land for commercial farming. All land is owned *de jure* by the state but, *de facto*, cropping land is owned by families under customary arrangements while grazing land, forests and water are being managed through common property arrangements or are open access.

Settlement occurred quickly but related environmental change accumulated over decades, while some environmental legislation put in place nearly a century ago has survived even to this day because the responsible institutions do not easily change.[9] Environmental concern goes back to the first half of the nineteenth century, driven by experiences with disasters elsewhere such as the American dust bowl. Since the early 1970s, there has been a widespread perception that land management in communal lands was leading to general desiccation of the environment. Work by the Centre for Ecology and Hydrology began in the early 1990s; one of its aims was to help to resolve the uncertainty about the changing status of water resources.[10] Through a combination of ground-truth studies, monitoring and modelling, it partitioned the cause of groundwater decline amongst rainfall pattern, land-use change and human abstraction. Rainfall in this region exhibits periods of above and below average levels. This means that areas such as Romwe actually fluctuate between being semi–arid and semi–humid. The implications for natural resource management are enormous. Figure 6.5 shows cumulative departure from mean annual rainfall recorded

[8]Lovell, C., Mandondo, A. and Moriarty, P. The question of scale in integrated natural resource management. *Conservation Ecology*, **5** (2002), 25. Online: http://www.consecol.org/vol5/iss2/art25.

[9]Mandondo, A. *Situating Zimbabwe's Natural Resource Governance Systems in History. Center for International Forestry Research Working Paper 32*: Bogor: Center for International Forestry Research, 2000. Online: http://www.cifor.cgiar.org/publications/pdf_files/OccPapers/OP-32.pdf; North, D.C.. *Institutions, Institutional Change and Economic Performance*. Cambridge: Cambridge University Press, 1990.

[10]Bromley, J. A., Butterworth, J. A., MacDonald, D. M. J., Lovell, C. J., Mharapara, I. and Batchelor, C. H. Hydrological processes and water resources management in a dryland environment I: an introduction to the Romwe catchment study in southern Zimbabwe. *Hydrology and Earth Sciences*, **3** (1999), 322–332.

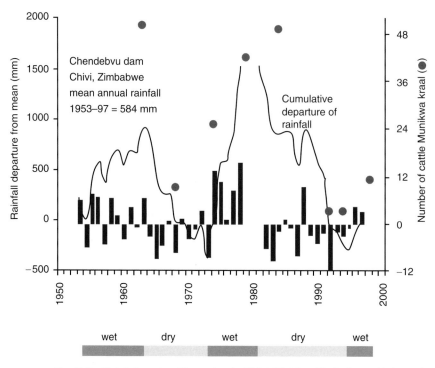

Fig. 6.5. Rainfall and cattle cycles in Chivi District, Zimbabwe. (Adapted from Moriarty, 2000. See footnote 11.)

since 1953.[11] It also shows oscillations in cattle numbers recalled by village elders. Similar oscillations may be expected in grain yield, vegetation cover, erosion and siltation. Certainly, modelling catchment hydrology for this period shows that rainfall is the driving process determining natural resource status. Long-term trends in groundwater reflect cumulative rainfall variation, and the main cause of water point failure in the early 1990s was the extended dry period from 1981 to 1992. Human impact through land-use change is secondary and human impact through groundwater abstraction is trivial. In similar environments to that of Chivi, the temporal scale of investigation must cover (or allow projection over) the full range of rainfall variability in order to take account of natural fluctuations in resource status.

It is not only rainfall that changes in these semi-arid systems. Smallholder farmers are also linked into the national economy through remittances and prices of agricultural inputs and products. In Fig. 6.6 we show

[11] Moriarty, P. B. Integrated Catchment Management and Sustainable Water Resource Development in Semi-arid Zimbabwe. Dissertation. University of Reading, UK, 2000.

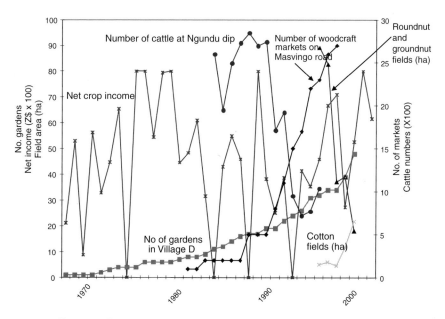

Fig. 6.6. Three decades of change in Chivi.

how four components of livelihoods changed: dryland agriculture, live-stock production, gardening and woodlands. Dryland crop output changed in relation to rainfall, resulting in a very unreliable food and cash income source. Over a five-year period, there were major changes in areas devoted to root crops and cotton, illustrating how rapidly farming systems can adapt. Livestock fluctuated in relation to droughts. Considerable time is needed to rebuild the herd after severe droughts. In an attempt to improve food security and cash income in this drought-prone area and as a result of the breakdown in the enforcement of regulations limiting cultivation near streams and wet-lands, gardening has shown a steady increase over the past three decades. Woodland-based cash income activities have increased in the last decade, as shown by the exponential rise in woodcraft markets on the Masvingo road in the 1990s. The changes illustrated indicate the danger of the 'snapshot' interpretations often arrived at by visiting teams of experts. Snapshots can easily lead to erroneous conclusions. Integrated research must invariably al-low for longer-term perspectives; it will generally involve historical analysis and making projections through simulation modelling.

The importance of biophysical scales can be illustrated from a con-sideration of groundwater. Groundwater processes are driven by the crys-talline basement geology. In contrast to sedimentary aquifers, where recharge can percolate to great depths and move over large distances underground, basement aquifers are localised in sump points. Storage takes place only in areas of relatively deep weathering rarely exceeding 40 m. The aquifers are relatively small in area, shallow, discontinuous and seldom match the boundaries of surface water catchments. The important implication for land management in this environment is that management does not have to be applied consistently over huge areas to have a measurable effect. This contrasts with, say, catchment management for surface water, where a beneficial effect often lies hundreds of kilometres from the point of intervention (e.g. headwaters managed to improve dam performance downstream). For groundwater in basement areas, decisions and actions that have a real impact on the *locally* available resource can be made at the *local* level. Such decisions include whether to adopt water-harvesting methods to enhance groundwater recharge or to focus on rain-fed crop production. Choices have also to be made on whether to develop woodlots on aquifers rather than irrigated gardens. The correct biophysical unit for management in each case is the groundwater micro-catchment. While this seldom, if ever, coincides with an existing institutional boundary, it does at least make micro-catchment management an appropriate strategy in this environment and is a scale conducive to working with small interest groups, typically numbered in tens of families rather than hundreds.

Spatial scale is often conceptualised from a geographical perspective. Most biophysical scientists in integrated projects would tend to focus on sets of nested catchments. There is also a need to deal explicitly with organisational scale. In the Romwe study, we have had a series of researchers looking at institutional issues from the very local to the national.[12] The lowest organisational level is within the household, where groupings along age and gender are apparent, with different activities undertaken by different household members. The livelihood data have provided information on this organisational level (Fig. 6.3). At the next level, there are a myriad of types of household grouping in Romwe and Mutangi, both informal (tree enthusiasts group, close friends that have strong reciprocal relationship, etc.) and formal (cotton growers group, church groups, micro-credit group, garden group, dam users, borehole users) (Fig. 6.7). These groups overlap and form complex relationships with the biophysical units. At the next broader level is the traditional village, led by a *sabhuku* and his advisors. Overlapping with the traditional village, and encompassing a number of these villages, are the

---

[12]Mandondo, Situating Zimbabwe's natural resource governance systems in history; Nemarundwe, N. and Kozanayi, W. Institutional arrangements for water for household use: a case study from Southern Zimbabwe. *Journal of Southern African Studies*, **29** (2003), 193–206.

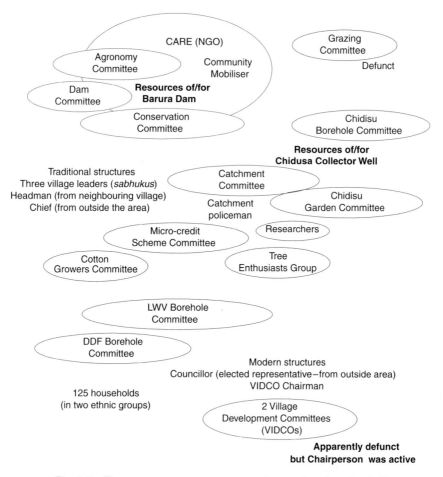

Fig. 6.7. The numerous user groups and committees active in Romwe catchment. (Data provided by Witness Kozanayi and Bevlyne Sithole.)

government-facilitated village development committees. These committees appear to have minimal power in Romwe and Mutangi and many people do not even know who the committee members are. However, in Romwe, the chairmen in one village wields considerable power. He is part of the traditional ruling elite and a former councillor. In the government-facilitated system, there are then wards and their Ward Development Committees, the chairmen of which are the elected councillors for the ward. The councillors are then represented at the next level, the Chivi Rural District Council, located some 70 km from Romwe and 20 km from Mutangi. On the traditional side, the *sabhukus* fall under *sadhunus* or headmen, encompassing a few traditional villages; they, in turn, report to the chief, there being two chiefs in Chivi Communal Land. The chiefs are also represented at the district council level. The districts, in turn, link up to provincial and then national structures.

Prior to the 1950s, local control was vested in traditional structures; after that, various functions were transferred to government agencies. After 1970, powers were returned to the chiefs, who were then discredited by the liberation movement during the war of independence in the 1970s. After independence in 1980, circumstances changed again, with the state vesting its power in the elected and newly created Village and Ward Development Committees. There are current moves to return some degree of control to traditional leaders. Therefore, the development of local institutions for managing natural resources is marked by confusion, alternating between empowerment and dis-empowerment of traditional structures.[13] This institutional confusion has in many areas led to struggles for power over resources, with certain sectors of the population aligning themselves with particular institutions, the result of which is the lack of legitimacy of any one institution.

Decentralisation is now high on the agenda of the state, inspired in part by the appeal of a 'back to the people' movement, which is seen to be more ethical and effective than centrally directed management of natural resources.[14] Of late, a new rural development thrust, coming with structural adjustment programmes, has also encouraged cash-strapped governments in many African countries to decentralise by shedding some of the roles to lower levels of government. In spite of the merits of decentralised natural resource management, experience in Zimbabwe generally suggests that the state is reluctant to relinquish control. The state view of appropriate management of resources still appears to extend to local communities through a centrally directed structure and process. Effective control is still

[13] Matose, F. and Wily, L. Institutional arrangements governing the use and management of miombo woodlands. In *The Miombo in Transition: Woodlands and Welfare in Africa*, ed. B. Campbell. Bogor: Center for International Forestry Research, 1996, pp. 195–219; Sithole, B. Access to and Use of Dambos in Communal Areas of Zimbabwe: Institutional Considerations. Ph.D. Thesis, Centre for Applied Social Sciences, University of Zimbabwe, Harare, 1999.

[14] Murombedzi, J. The need for appropriate local level common property resource management institutions in communal tenure regimes. In *CASS Occasional Paper Series – NRM 1990*. Harare: Center for Applied Social Sciences, University of Zimbabwe, 1990; Murphree, M. W. Decentralising the proprietorship of wildlife resources in Zimbabwe's Communal Lands. In *CASS Occasional Paper Series – NRM 1990*. Harare: Centre for Applied Social Sciences, University of Zimbabwe, 1990; Murphree, M. W. *Gatekeeper Series 36: Communities as Resource Management Institutions*. London: International Institute for Environment and Development, 1993, pp. 1–35.

largely vested in the state or bureaucracies under its direction, like the Rural District Councils. State regulation is, however, severely undermined by its inherent incapacity to assert effective control. Several major challenges associated with the quest for decentralised natural resource management still remain. One is the identification, design and empowerment of institutions to fit more closely with local forms of control. Another is defining the limits within which external and internal forms of authority are most effective. Finally, it is necessary to reverse the state's long-standing obsession with directing the process instead of facilitating it.

The complexities of establishing appropriate institutional arrangements are illustrated in the case of Romwe. Surface-water management must be catchment-wide, while for groundwater, smaller localised areas could be managed. Who could be the management authority for the entire catchment? It contains parts of three traditional villages, which fall into two Village Development Committees; these, in turn, fall in two different Wards (Fig. 6.8). In addition, Nontokozo Nemarundwe has shown that the resources of the physical catchment are currently used by many different traditional villages, with a different grouping of villages using different subsets of resources (different water points, grazing, mushrooms, fibre, poles, firewood).[15] There is no match between organisational boundaries (be they traditional or modern administrative ones) and biophysical boundaries, and for each woodland resource there is a different user group. Boundaries are generally porous, are open to individual interpretation and contestation, and are changeable. It is very difficult to see how boundaries can become more clearly defined. Any attempts to harden the boundaries, as envisaged in conventional responses to common property resource management problems, are likely to be frustrated by local people or user groups.

Integrating across stakeholders: why knowing the theory and having the best practitioners is not good enough

Let us introduce the field team in the Chivi micro-catchments. There is Edward Chuma; his work with Jürgen Hagmann in a neighbouring Ward to the Romwe Ward has received much attention in terms of its innovative participatory action and extension approach.[16] Then there is Nontokozo Nemarundwe, whose early work with Louise Fortmann led her to embrace

[15]Nemarundwe, N. Negotiating resource access: Institutional arrangements for woodlands and water use in southern Zimbabwe. Dissertation. Swedish Agricultural University, 2003.

[16]Hagmann, *Learning Together for Change.*

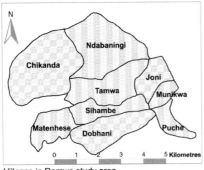

Villages in Romwe study area

Villages that use Mapande hills for grazing livestock

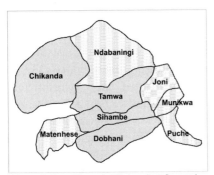

Villages that use Mapande hills to collect firewood

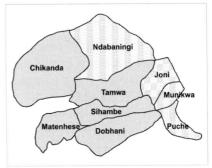

Villages that use Mapande hills to cut timber

Villages that use Mapande hills to collect fibre

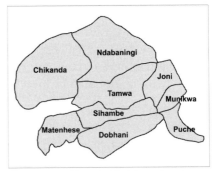

Villages that use Mapande hills to harvest mushrooms

Fig. 6.8. The relationship between traditional village and administrative boundaries and woodland resource use in Romwe. The physical catchment of interest covers much of the traditional villages of Sihambe and Dobhani and a very small portion of Tamwa. A Ward boundary separates Dobhani from Sihambe and Tamwa villages although in local terms the three villages are seen as constituting the core of the Romwe community. This boundary also coincides with a chiefdomship boundary. At another scale, both Sihambe and Tamwa villages are part VIDCO F, a local government administrative unit forming part of Ward 23. Dobhani village lies in VIDCO D of Ward 25. Numerous villages use the resources of the catchment, but the patterns differ according to resource type.

participatory rural appraisal.[17] Nontokozo is now regularly sought after by donor agencies, international NGOs and consulting companies to conduct participatory appraisal and training courses. And finally Witness Kozanayi, who in 1995 started as a research assistant in a participatory valuation exercise in his home area of Hot Springs,[18] went off to do an agriculture diploma, and returned as a full-time research assistant in 1998. He has lived in Romwe micro-catchment for three years. The Institute of Environmental Studies has conducted research and training exercises using participatory tools annually for six years; these have familiarised all staff with the tools and practice of participatory appraisal, as well as helping to develop an understanding of the strengths and weaknesses of these tools.[19]

Despite our understanding of the theory and practice of participatory work, the feeling at the end of the three-year Romwe project is that we never fully engaged with the stakeholders in action research. We were unable to influence, let alone meet, the key players in the water sector reform process that will lead to the introduction of catchment councils. This process is heavily top-down. The proposed catchment councils and the subunits thereof will cut across the current organisational structures and will be difficult to make operational. The specialists involved in the reform process, like our own project team, were overextended; they lacked the time to interact. In addition, there was no formal institutional mechanism by which interaction could be ensured. We have also had the feeling that we were unable to tackle the real needs of the local people. Needs assessments were conducted and priorities were developed mutually, but some of these were outside the mandate of the project or had insufficient resources to bring in expertise in newly identified areas. There was consequently insufficient

---

[17] Fortmann, L. and Nabane (Nemarundwe), N. *NRM Occasional Paper 7: The Fruits of their Labours: Gender, Property and Trees in Mhondoro District.* Harare: Centre for Applied Social Sciences, University of Zimbabwe, 1992; Nemarundwe, N. and Richards, M. Participatory methods for exploring livelihood values derived from forests: potential and limitation. In *Uncovering the Hidden Harvest. Valuation Methods for Woodland and Forest Resources,* ed. B. M. Campbell and M. Luckert, (People and Plants Conservation Series.) London: Earthscan, 2002, pp. 168–196.

[18] Hot Springs Working Group *Research Series 3: Local-level Economic Valuation of Savanna Woodland Resources: Village Cases from Zimbabwe.* London: International Institute for Environment and Development, 1995.

[19] For example: Campbell, B. M., Luckert, M. and Scoones, I. Local-level valuation of savanna: a case study from Zimbabwe. *Economic Botany* **51** (1997), 59–77; Adamowicz, W., Luckert, M. and Veeman, M. Issues in using valuation techniques cross-culturally: three cases in Zimbabwe using contingent valuation, observed behaviour and derived demand techniques. *Commonwealth Forestry Review,* **76** (1997), 194–7; Hot Springs Working Group, *Local-level Economic Valuation of Savanna Woodland Resources.*

room or resources for opportunism. A 'project' with narrow boundaries and set activities is not conducive to solving complex problems.

We did engage the local communities and the district officials in a series of meetings that have led to a new way of thinking about local governance for natural resources. Through a series of visioning exercises, through giving a voice to local people and through developing a close relationship with the Chief Executive Officer of the Chivi District Council, we were able to develop a progressive vision amongst members of the district council. The retrogressive bylaw legislation was analysed by the local stakeholders and top district officials and determined to be unworkable. We reached agreement on the need to overhaul the entire system in a series of test areas. In some ways, this exercise was opportunistic, in that we accessed separate funds for the series of meetings that led to the new vision. By the end of our project, the resource monitors for the bylaw system had been fired and the district officials had held consultations and training exercises for local leaders to implement a system that was more accountable to local people.

This project was more successful that most in engaging with local stakeholders in participatory appraisal and action, but the above discussion indicates that there were still some limitations. The structural problems in governments (such as the lack of sectoral integration), the problems associated with projects (such as not being able to go outside the initially conceived framework) and the complexities of the systems (such as the lack of fit between resources and management organisations) all go towards making engagement with multiple stakeholders difficult.

Conclusion and the key lessons from Chivi

Stakeholder engagement, participatory research and action research is not easy to achieve, even with good intentions and excellent facilitators. Natural resources are not just there to be managed – they represent a significant source of power for various stakeholders. Institutional change for appropriate management is at the core of natural resource management, but institutional change is slow, incremental and open to power politics and corruption. The problem of the 'project' as the mode of operation (as discussed in Chapter 1) is clearly revealed in the Chivi situation. Being outside the mainstream of government has the advantages that bureaucratic inertia is not an excessive obstacle, but the 'project' is too narrowly defined and is much more difficult to scale up even if it is locally successful.

Nonetheless, taking an integrated approach did have good pay-offs. Positive impacts at a range of scales were achieved as these examples indicate:

irrigated gardens were expanded, committee effectiveness was improved, the district bylaw system was overhauled.

- Objectives have to be realistic, especially regarding the speed and extent of change. The time span and resources available were really not adequate to the scale of the problems being addressed.
- Local politics proved a significant driver of change and were difficult to influence.
- Success took the form of creating conditions so that local people could innovate. Outside advisers and scientists enriched the pool of ideas and facilitated social learning but did not deliver technological packages.
- While it is easy for research and development officers to use the terms 'participatory', 'action research', etc., the realities on the ground make it very difficult to have really successful participatory processes or to match the good intentions of textbook action research or adaptive management.

7   Forest margins in Indonesian Borneo

The vast rainforests of the island of Borneo have excited the imagination of scientists and traders for centuries. Outsiders saw them as a wild and inhospitable wilderness inhabited by headhunting tribes of Dayaks. They were the home of new and exotic animals and plants and a source of scarce and valuable products: birds' nests, *gaharu*, rhinoceros horn, etc.[1] Until the latter half of the twentieth century, forests covered most of the island and small trading posts at the mouths of rivers were the main point of contact for the outside world with the sparse but significant populations of Dayaks who inhabited the hinterland. In the late 1960s, construction booms in Japan, Europe and North America and the availability of mobile chain saws and tracked vehicles led to the beginning of industrial-scale logging for international markets. This period also saw the strengthening of efforts by the Indonesian government to resettle people from the densely settled island of Java into the frontier areas of the outer islands of Indonesia.

The 1970s and 1980s saw major investments in opening up the remote forests of the Indonesian provinces of Kalimantan in Borneo. New roads were constructed for logging and to provide access to areas of planned agricultural settlement (transmigration). Central government institutions established footholds throughout the region. Significant commercial and public sector investments were made in the 'development' of the area. From the late 1970s onwards, there was increasing concern both locally and internationally at the potentially harmful social and environmental impacts of transmigration and logging. In response, the Indonesian government and a number of international development assistance agencies launched programmes to improve the sustainability of both transmigration and forestry.

---

[1] Two species of swiftlets (*Collocalia* spp.) make nests suspended from the roofs of caves from a secretion from their salivary glands. The nests are harvested and used by the Chinese to prepare soups. Eaglewood (*gaharu*) is the heartwood, modified by fungal infection, of species of *Aquilaria*. It is harvested in the wild and sold for the manufacture of incense, mainly to markets in south and west Asia, Japan and the Arabian Peninsula.

Throughout the 1980s and into the early 1990s, shifting agriculture was seen as the main threat to the environment in Kalimantan. Logging roads provided the opportunity for both Dayak and transmigrant 'shifted cultivators'[2] to move into logged-over forest areas and clear them for agriculture. The resulting fallows were often invaded by the fire-dependent grass *Imperata cylindrica* and the forests were progressively transformed into fire-climax grasslands. The conventional solution to these problems lay in improved agricultural planning and the introduction of higher-input agriculture that would be sustainable on the poor acid soils of the region (see Box 2.3, p. 44). The theory was that the population would then adopt stable sedentary agriculture and cease encroaching on the forest. Major investments were also made in improving logging practices so that the residual stands would be less susceptible to fire and to encourage the rapid regeneration of commercially valuable species. It was thought that this would add to the value of the forests and make people less inclined to clear them for temporary agriculture. Agricultural and forestry development activities were conducted by different government departments and tended to be geographically and functionally separated.

In the late 1980s, the Dayak communities began to be more assertive in defending their traditional rights to the land. At this time, international scientists and activists demonstrated and championed the ability and rights of Dayak communities to have much greater control over the forest and land resources of their traditional domains. Shifting agriculture began to be seen as a viable and sustainable technology in areas of poor soils and sparse populations. The harvesting of non-timber forest products was recognised as a profitable and sustainable use of the forests. The negative consequences of the investments in both transmigrant agriculture and industrial forestry became issues for international campaigns. Outside investors were both destroying the environment for short-term profit and disrupting the economies of the local inhabitants. The government and its international sponsors began to look for development pathways that were based upon better integration of a diversity of sustainable agriculture and forestry practices to maintain environmental services and biodiversity and provide for improved livelihoods for the resident populations.

In 1993 the Center for International Forestry Research (CIFOR) was established in Indonesia. Its mandate was to research more environmentally and socially sustainable management of forest lands. It gave particular

---

[2]The term 'shifted cultivators' seems first to have been used by Norman Myers to distinguish the destructive activities of farmers encroaching upon forest areas from the more sustainable practices of traditional 'shifting cultivators', who practised sustainable cycles of cultivation and fallow in a closed system.

emphasis to forest-based development that favoured the poor. As part of its host-country agreement with Indonesia, CIFOR was to be allocated a significant area – initially 100 000 ha – of forest for research purposes. The debate as to the location and nature of this research forest was itself an interesting reflection of attitudes of people with different perspectives on the role of science in natural resource management. Several scientists advocated the delimitation of an area of forest that could be subject to a variety of management regimes in a controlled experimental environment. Others preferred a more heterogeneous and ill-defined area where the interactions amongst different stakeholder groups could be studied.

The initial decision was to take a large forest area that had not yet been logged but was scheduled for logging in the medium term. The area selected was adjacent to a large national park, Kayan Menterang, on the assumption that the research forest would act as a buffer zone for the protected area and that research requiring access to extensive pristine forests could make use of the park. The area chosen was also subject to a variety of uses by different indigenous communities. On its western border, it abutted on active logging concessions. The area chosen was subject to a ministerial decree allocating it for research and it subsequently became known as the Bulungan Research Forest. The research forest included a number of different forest types, largely differentiated by topography. Subsequently, it transpired that the area would not be logged as soon as expected. In order not to delay experimental work directly related to logging, CIFOR began to conduct studies in adjacent logging concessions. As the research programme unfolded, it proved expedient to locate more and more of the work in areas outside, but adjacent to, the designated research forest. Eventually researchers were active in various parts of the administrative district in which the research forest was located; in fact more work was going on in the inhabited areas outside the forest than in the forest itself.

During the reforms that followed the collapse of the Suharto regime in 1998, the district was accorded a much larger degree of autonomy than it had hitherto enjoyed. The legal decree designating a limited area for research was never changed but CIFOR began to see the entire administrative unit, now known as Malinau District, as its study area. This district covered 43 000 km^2 and has a population of about 36 000 people. The western part of the area includes the town of Malinau with its ethnically diverse population of traders, civil servants and workers in the cash economy. Malinau town contains more than half the population of the district, leaving the rural areas with only 0.4 persons/km^2.

The changing face of the forest landscape

Households in the forest have seen many changes, as is illustrated by an account of one of the local residents, Mr. K. (Box 7.1).

Box 7.1. The changing nature of forest households

I was married in 1979 and came to the village of Long Loreh in 1982 when our people, the Dayak Punan, were transferred here by the local government. The government provided us with free supplies for five years, of sugar, rice, kitchen tools and medicines as part of the relocation programme. Our motivation to move was not merely to receive the free supplies, but mainly so that our children would receive good education, we would all be close to health facilities, we could be part of development generally, and we would be less dependent on nature for all our livelihood needs. In moving we had to make many adjustments, including getting familiar with a market economy, integrating with different social groups and adapting to the hotter weather, which left us frequently ill. Our family earns a living from planting upland rice, groundnuts and cassava, making handicrafts, hunting pigs and deer for special foods, fishing at the river and collecting *gaharu*. Although there are times of sufficiency and times of needs, we enjoy our simple life and the times of hardship are less than when we were in remote villages before 1979. Prior to the entrance of timber and coal companies in this area, the forest was undamaged, and animals that could be hunted were plentiful. There were also many fruit trees, sago palms and *gaharu* trees. The river water was not polluted. With the coming of the timber companies in the early 1980s and the coal company in the mid 1990s there have been many negative changes. Tree and animal resources are now less plentiful and *gaharu* gathering is difficult. The coal company has polluted the water. The companies did bring some important positive changes. There are now roads to remote upland areas, and easy transport is available to the district capital, Malinau. In the past we were lucky if we got to Malinau town in two days (by boat) but now it takes less than six hours. Farmers, who used to rely on boats to practise upland cultivation along the rivers, can now cultivate along the roads and use the company's vehicles for transport. After the dawn of national reform in 1998, people have been more vociferous in their demands of companies, and there have been numerous people's demonstrations. These demands have included provision for profit sharing, clean water and electricity. More outsiders have moved into the community (especially following the entrance of the coal company) and livelihood strategies have diversified as new economic activities have become available (selling of farm produce, small-scale trading, temporary employment, etc.). In general, the changes have resulted in improved standards of living.

The constitutional and financial crisis that hit Indonesia in 1997 and 1998 took everyone by surprise. The rapid depreciation of the exchange rate of the Indonesian rupiah against most other major currencies and the breakdown of the iron-fisted control hitherto exercised by the regime in

Jakarta had major impacts on economic and political activity in Bulungan. Currency depreciation increased the profitability of export crops, the production costs of which were mostly in local currency. The political crisis opened the way for a surge of uncontrolled exploitation of resources previously monopolised by companies linked to the ruling elite.

In the Bulungan area, the political crisis came at a time when forest depletion was causing a shortfall in the supply of logs for plywood and sawmills in other parts of Indonesia and adjacent states of Malaysia. The breakdown in existing control mechanisms and the high profits to be made by anyone who could deliver timber to the mills led to a rapid expansion of illegal logging in Bulungan. Anyone who had access to logging equipment and a truck or boat could make money, but quite a lot of the illegal logging was by employees of the state logging corporations moonlighting with government-owned equipment. An additional dimension was added to the problem when control over natural resources devolved to local people and provincial administrations. This occurred spontaneously as the authority of the central government declined and also in a more formal way when a governmental decree in January 2001 gave control over forest resources to local authorities. Traditional *Adat* rights had always been enshrined in the Indonesian constitution but local people had been unable to exert these rights in the face of the power of the big companies; after the fall of Suharto there were renewed efforts to exert these rights. *Adat* gives extensive rights over natural resources to local people.

Under these new laws, local Dayak communities were entitled to claim ownership of land, including forests in the vicinity of their village. The intention behind the law was to defuse the long-standing tensions between the Dayaks and the timber companies who arrived in the area with concessions allocated to them by the authorities in Jakarta. These concessions took no account of traditional land-uses or rights. It was hoped that communities might either manage these forest areas sustainably or clear the forest to plant estate crops such as rubber or oil palm. In reality, there was a rush to acquire these rights in order to sell them on to entrepreneurs for industrial-scale logging. In many cases, the local forests that were logged under these arrangements lay within existing concessions. The result was a breakdown of any semblance of sustainable forestry with a free-for-all developing as various operators competed to log all the most accessible sites (Fig. 7.1). This was understandable given that the local people had little confidence that the central government would guarantee their rights in the longer term.

In general tropical rainforests are protected by the fact that it is not profitable to log any but the best specimens of the most valuable species.

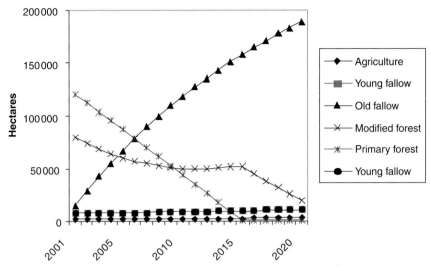

Fig. 7.1. Projection of the land cover classes in a 250 000 ha area along the Malinau river. The projection is based on current patterns of land-use, and assumes the present levels of logging continue into the future. The landscape changes from a largely forested landscape to a largely unforested landscape within 15 years as primary forest is converted to modified forest by large-scale concessionaires and from modified forest to 'old fallow' by small-scale concessionaires. Local people have little direct impact. Such models have the classic weakness of the 'Club of Rome' model, they extrapolate present trends. They are not predictive as they do not incorporate people's responses to changing situations.

The relatively high costs of extraction and transport and the low value of tropical timbers has, in many parts of the world, proved more effective in protecting the forests than have plans for sustainable forestry. Even this form of *de facto* protection shows signs of breaking down in Bulungan. So much over-capacity has been built up in the logging industries that concessionaires are pushing into more and more rugged and remote country in the search for logs. Topography and access are still the limiting factors, but entrepreneurs are pushing extraction to the absolute limits of what is physically possible.

The plantations established to provide wood for a large new pulp mill on the coast downstream from Bulungan failed to produce wood in time. The mill, therefore, operated on mixed tropical hardwoods salvaged from the logged-over natural forests in the area. One of the major costs of logging in remote areas in the tropics is that of fuel. In Indonesia, the government had fixed fuel prices in local currency on the basis of pre-crisis exchange rates. Devaluation resulted in fuel becoming extremely cheap and the cost of moving mixed tropical hardwoods to the mill was correspondingly low. The combination of opportunistic logging of good-quality timber for plywood and sawmills followed by salvage logging of the remaining trees for the pulp mill was very destructive.

Chris Barr and colleagues from CIFOR have shown that the natural resource arena in Malinau is marked by institutional complexity and confusion, partly as a result of all the changes that are occurring. The large scale-concessionaires (HPHs) received their permits for operation from the Forestry Department from the late 1970s up to the early 1990s. Concession allocation was essentially a Jakarta-based process. Much of the area allocated went to state timber corporations. The concession boundaries do not correspond to the current district boundaries. The agency overseeing local operations and enforcing regulations is the provincial government's forestry department. Two branch offices administer Malinau's five subdistricts. These also have jurisdiction in those parts of the concessions that extend beyond the district. This has the curious consequence that the areas for which statistics are collected do not correspond to areas subject to district-planning processes.

Malinau Kabupaten (District) came into existence in late 1999, following partition of the former Bulungan Kabupaten. In the 11-month period from April 2000, Malinau District allocated some 39 small-scale conversion permits, representing a major income source for the district (and informally for those controlling the process). In the following 12 months, it was estimated that 10 000 ha of the 250 000 ha area in the Malinau catchment was logged through large-scale concessions, while perhaps as much as 30 000 ha was logged by the small-scale operators. The district has no capacity to monitor the small-scale operators, and the provincial branch office has only a single officer in Malinau. The small-scale concessions have been allocated on forests already allocated to large-scale concessions and are ostensibly for conversion of forest to agricultural or tree crops. There is no evidence that this conversion is occurring; rather, the permits are used to extract the maximum volume of timber.

The large-scale concession holders in the Malinau catchment have made some attempt to apply the principles of sustainable forestry. However, roads are poorly constructed, skidding is very destructive and the employees of the company hunt and poison wildlife. The logging operations have also been very destructive of aquatic resources. Notwithstanding this, underharvesting is more frequent than overharvesting because the machine operators are paid by logs delivered to the landings and they will often ignore those in less-accessible sites. However, under the current conditions, there is little incentive to practise sustainable harvesting, as any timber left by the large-scale concession holder will be removed by others. The large-scale concessionaires have remained aloof from local communities and have provided few local economic benefits. The communities have, therefore, aligned themselves with the small-scale operators, who promise an array of benefits and provide some employment.

Some informants in the study of Chris Barr have suggested that district authorities have transgressed the limits of their legal authority in allocating small-scale concessions within the boundaries of existing large-scale ones.[3] Some see the small-scale allocations as a deliberate attempt by the districts to send a political message to large-scale concessionaires that their access to timber is now dependent on the district government and not on political backing from Jakarta. In this way, the large-scale operators would become more responsive to district regulations and to periodic requests by local officials for informal payments. The timber business in Indonesia has always been notably corrupt: under the reforms, the locus of corruption is moving from Jakarta to the provinces and districts.

A holistic study of the changing landscape

CIFOR's experiences of trying to orchestrate an integrated approach to the study of a large complex forest system merit reflection, both because of the partial success that we achieved and because of the significant difficulties that were encountered. CIFOR has a number of global programmes, each dealing with a research theme of importance for forests and forest-based livelihoods. Each programme has a research team working on a coherent set of research activities throughout the tropics in a highly decentralised mode. From the beginning, CIFOR management was clear that it did not want to establish a free-standing team of scientists to work independently on the Bulungan area. It was decided that several of CIFOR's global programmes should have some level of activity in Bulungan. Bulungan was to be the place where a number of the research teams would intersect in the hope that this would spontaneously yield synergies and insights that the teams working in isolation would not have achieved. In principle, the scientists were given a lot of space to develop their research activities as they saw fit – both in Bulungan and elsewhere – but management constantly encouraged the different groups to exchange information and seek areas of collaboration.

---

[3] Barr, C., Wollenberg, E., Limberg, G. *et al.* Case study 3: The impacts of decentralisation on forests and forest-dependent communities in Malinau District, East Kalimantan. In *Case Studies on Decentralisation and Forests in Indonesia*, Bogor; Center for International Forestry Research, 2001, p. 48.

Facilitated workshops, informal meetings and shared field visits were used to maximise interactions amongst the scientists.

A major problem emerged, however, as an increasingly large proportion of the research budget began to be targeted to priorities of individual donors. Scientists were subject to pressures to deliver 'component' products to meet specific donor targets and time frames. Donors did not want to buy-into a large complex programme; they wanted to be able to identify with a defined product. This made it difficult for the different scientists to collaborate optimally. Even with good intentions and generally good interpersonal relations, it was simply not efficient for the different groups to work together and to meet donor expectations. This situation was further complicated by the inevitable fact that different disciplines and different research problems often require different methods, locations and facilities.

Even the choice of a location for a field headquarters presented problems. Silvicultural researchers needed to be located near to the zones of active logging. Studies of traditional management systems for non-timber forest products were easier in remote unlogged areas. Some biodiversity studies required areas with minimal levels of disturbance. The initial intention had been to build a single permanent field station and significant money was raised for this purpose. Finally, and with hindsight fortunately, we opted for a number of more temporary field locations. The researchers stayed in temporary camps near the areas of active logging, in villages or in the district capital. It was important for everyone to be near to the areas or resource users that were to be the object of their studies. This was itself a major departure from the approach of other large international projects that also sought to take a broad holistic approach to forest issues. Almost invariably, these projects made heavy up-front investments in fixed infrastructure and in so doing they obliged their scientists and technicians to work in the same locality; this precluded much of the flexibility that subsequently proved of great value to CIFOR researchers.

The opportunistic selection of research locations in the study area had at least two significant and unintended impacts on the research programme. First our scientists were much more dispersed over the entire area than they would otherwise have been. We, therefore, observed the full complexity of the system much more than if we had all operated out of a single location. Second, since our scientists were often living close to the local communities or logging companies amongst whom they worked, they became much more sensitive to local perspectives than would have been the case if a large monolithic residential research facility had been the focus of all of the work.

The Bulungan programme was criticised for being insufficiently integrated. Visitors observed that scientists were not always fully aware of what their colleagues were doing. In some cases, different groups of scientists were approaching the same or closely related problems in different ways. There was only a rather weak shared knowledge base. Most observers saw this as inefficient. However, this inefficiency also yielded unintended benefits. We did not have a single uniform view of the problems of the area. The facts that scientists were working in partial isolation from their colleagues and were in general spending as much, or more, time with local people as with their scientific peers meant that collectively we had a pluralism of views about the problems and the role of research in finding solutions. At various times, some tensions emerged between different groups of scientists as their understandings of the dynamics of land-use change and human well-being diverged.

CIFOR did not, therefore, evolve a simple, rigid perspective on the area and its problems. There was constant discussion and uncertainty that involved both scientists and other stakeholders, and the group as a whole was constantly revising its understanding and knowledge of the issues (Box 7.2). At the time many people saw this as a weakness – manifest for instance in the difficulty of fitting everyone's perspectives into a single model or logical framework for the research programme. With hindsight, we conclude that the collective knowledge that we now have for the area is much richer and more pluralistic than it would have been if a uniformity of vision had been more actively sought at an earlier stage in the process. The very detailed planning and predefinition of milestones and outputs that came into play as more targeted donor funding was sought had major impacts on the cohesiveness of the overall programme. Donor requirements for rigid log-frames led to greater efficiency and ease of understanding to outsiders but to a programme that provided fewer insights and innovations. This is not necessarily an argument against formalised research management systems such as log-frames, but any management system used must encourage pluralism and flexibility.

Box 7.2. Developing a conceptual model of the key problems and issues in Bulungan

While the intention has always been for the research in Bulungan to bring CIFOR's inter-disciplinary strengths to work on priority problems, this has proven difficult.[1] Silvicultural research has focussed on industrial logging, while social science research concentrated on local communities. Conceptually, there was a link between these activities but few synergies emerged. In late 1999, Ken MacDicken the Research Director at CIFOR, initiated the process of developing a conceptual framework, leading to shared understanding and improved research integration in Bulungan. The process involved all stakeholders through a series of meetings. Participants included representatives from local and regional government, local communities, the university, CIFOR and timber concessions. The group tried to define the framework, including problem definition, research areas, desired future land-uses and stakeholders.

The resulting framework was problem based, with four levels:

level 1: the central problem

level 2: 'conceptual cornerstones' (important components of the central problem)

level 3: elements (explaining the causes of the problems identified in the cornerstones)

level 4: causes (of the problems described in the elements).

The central problem and conceptual cornerstones are given in Figure 7.2.

The initial purpose of the conceptual framework was to organise and communicate the key problems related to forests and people in the Bulungan Research Forest. It served as an organisational tool and helped to communicate the complexity to outsiders; it included the views of most of the local and outside stakeholders, and it established links between commonly observed problems and their causes. The more difficult linkage – the

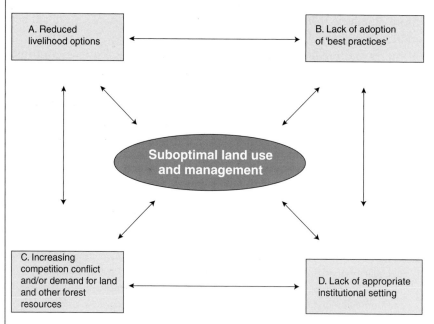

Fig. 7.2. The central part of the conceptual framework.

interaction between causes – has not been attempted, although one could argue that these interactions should be critical research questions.

The value of the framework is illustrated by the changes that have been made in our understanding of the relation between research components dealing with timber-harvesting practices and those addressing local needs. Prior to the development of the framework, researchers were investigating forest uses by indigenous communities independently of those studying reduced impact harvesting by an industrial timber concessionaire. Even though there is a general recognition that industrial timber harvesting and swidden agriculture, hunting, gathering and fishing are interrelated, the critical research required to make industrial logging and community forest uses more compatible was not explicitly addressed. Social science research is still perceived by the concessionaire as a threat to as yet unlogged timber resources, and timber-harvest research is seen by communities as a contributing factor to expanded logging (and as a threat to their way of life). Significant convergence between these research activities has occurred as the programme has evolved.

The framework has improved the shared understanding of problems among CIFOR researchers and our partners and demonstrates clearly that most of the key problems in the Bulungan Research Forest are too multi-faceted to be dealt with solely on a component basis. It has identified a range of causal links between key problems faced by stakeholders and provides a forum for continued refinement in our understanding of key intervention points that might be suited to research. It does not yet allow us to demonstrate linkages between causes, nor does it provide a framework for understanding the relative impacts of interventions on problems. It is in a sense an intermediate tool: it assists integration by relating research on interrelated problems but does not provide an analysis of the nature of potential change as problems are solved or modified.

About a year later, researchers from the Bulungan group convened again in a series of small meetings and attempted to re-evaluate their conceptual understanding of the key issues within the Bulungan system. The group of researchers set out a visual framework, focussing on scales (biophysical and institutional), key elements within the system and plausible innovations that research might yield: those aspects of the system that researchers and their collaborators may be able to change (Fig. 7.3). Also identified (but not shown here) were systems indicators, these being a minimum set of variables that could be used to track the trajectory of the system. This conceptual framework, produced in 2001, was considered as a tool for promoting dialogue amongst researchers and for identifying points of overlap and possible synergies amongst the different research teams. A next step is to include the other stakeholders in the discussions. This will be initiated through a discussion of the systems' indicators that stakeholders would like to see measured.

[1] Much of the first part of the box is taken from text by Belcher, B., Colfer, C. and MacDicken, K. Towards INRM: three paths through the forest. In *Proceedings of a Workshop on Integrated Natural Resource Management in the CGIAR: Approaches and Lessons* 21–25, April 2000. Penang: ICLARM. Online: http://www.inrm.cgiar.org/documents/workshop_2000.htm.

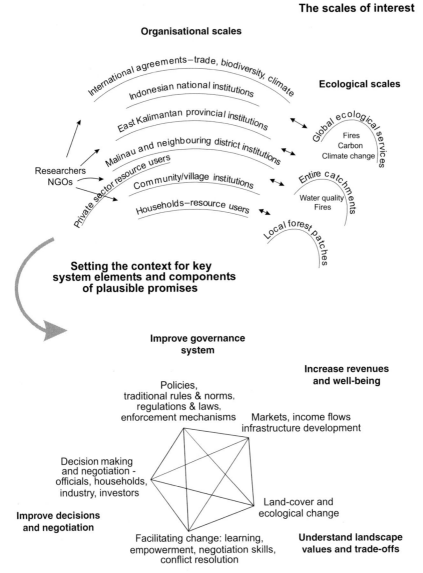

Fig. 7.3. Scales of interest in the Bulungan forest and plausible promises for interventions. (NGOs, non-governmental organisations.)

Tacit and explicit knowledge

It may appear from the above that we are attempting to justify a somewhat anarchic and opportunistic approach to a major research endeavour. However, the real lesson that we are trying to draw from our Bulungan experience is that the over-planning and excessively restrictive management imposed by donor-driven projects (see Chapter 1) on a complex research endeavour will be counter-productive. In addition to these institutional constraints, the research approach is further limited by assumptions that the researchers bring with them from their past work and disciplinary backgrounds. Researchers will attempt to collect and manage data to fit the analytical models with which they are familiar. They will focus on the explicit knowledge of science and will draw selectively on their observations and the tacit knowledge of local resource managers to feed their explicit models.

The tacit knowledge of resource users, in this case the Dayak communities who inhabit the Bulungan forest, has been accumulated over generations and finely honed by the harsh realities of struggling for survival in a hostile environment. This knowledge draws on multiple sources and is enriched by infrequent and unusual events. Much natural resource management research consists of fitting the existing knowledge of resource users into predetermined models – of translating the rich and tested resource of tacit knowledge into a more easily communicated and manipulated body of explicit scientific knowledge. In Bulungan, some of CIFOR's early work, and much of the work of other institutions that preceded us in the area, consisted of compiling inventories of different natural resources: lists of plants and animals, maps of different soil categories or estimates of the volume of timber in different forest types. Quite a large body of this explicit knowledge now exists, but it is seldom used, except by outsiders. Local people's day-to-day decisions about natural resource management often do not require such explicit 'scientific' knowledge.

Several examples serve to illustrate this point. A lot of effort is invested in pre-logging inventories of harvestable timber. However, our observations suggest that the patterns of timber harvesting are determined by the tacit knowledge of the fellers and equipment operators. Their decisions are influenced more by considerations of safety, ease of access and their experience of where in the landscape they are likely to find concentrations of high-value trees than by maps and tables from inventories. Similarly, in other parts of Indonesia, transmigration planners have a surprisingly low rate of success in mapping areas that will ultimately prove amenable to sustained exploitation by small farmers. The indigenous farmers themselves have a higher success rate when they base their choices on their accumulated knowledge of the potential returns to their labour from the cultivation of different sites. The biodiversity inventories conducted by visiting taxonomic specialists in support of protected area programmes in many tropical areas are extremely costly and yet this information appears to be little used in taking practical management decisions.

Our conclusion is that in the early stages of integrated natural resource management programmes it is important to invest in exploiting and strengthening the body of pluralistic tacit knowledge. We believe that many natural resource management programmes in less-developed countries invest in establishing new 'scientific' databases that are not connected to, and do not use, the rich tacit knowledge of local resource users. Moving too quickly into conventional mapping and inventories precludes options and limits the scope of investigation. It can create false realities that then come to dominate the thinking of outside scientists. Scott, in his book *Seeing Like a State* has described the way in which maps create 'official' versions of reality that are often only one of a number of possible portrayals of the situation as it relates to the lives of different resource users.[4] Scott argues that maps reflect assumptions and predetermined positions of the people who make the maps. Kain and Baigent have written the following about cadastral maps.[5]

> The Cadastral map is an instrument of control which both reflects and consolidates the power of those who commission it . . . the cadastral map is partisan: where knowledge is power, it provides comprehensive information to be used to the advantage of some and the detriment of others, . . . Finally the cadastral map is active: in portraying one reality, as in the settlement of the new world or in India, it helps obliterate the old.

This seems to us to be a particular problem in development projects where mapping from remote-sensed data often precedes any significant fieldwork. The maps that are thus established are just one of a potentially large number of ways in which the landscape can be categorised. Local resource users might have divided up the landscape in totally different ways.

Teamwork to exploit opportunities

Our intention when we began work in Bulungan was for our scientists to work as an interdisciplinary team. We assumed that it would be possible for scientists from different disciplinary backgrounds to work together to formulate hypotheses and design data collection and analysis in a fully integrated, holistic way. This was the melting-pot scenario whereby tools are drawn as appropriate from different disciplines to solve a complex problem. This proved very difficult to achieve in practice. With hindsight, this may have been an unrealistic expectation. Scientists ultimately have to focus on

---

[4]Scott, J. C. *Seeing Like a State; How Certain Schemes to Improve the Human Condition Have Failed.* Newhaven, CT: Yale University Press, 1998.

[5]Kain, R. J. P. and Baigent, E. *The Cadastral Map in the Service of the State.* Chicago, IL: Chicago University Press, 1992.

the specific component problems that their own disciplinary backgrounds enabled them to address. Advocates of large-scale interdisciplinary holistic research on natural resource problems may be pursuing a chimera. It will often be impossible to formulate a single big problem or large-scale hypothesis that an interdisciplinary team could reasonably tackle. Natural resources problems will normally have to be disaggregated into discipline-based components whose outcomes will feed into the holistic understanding upon which management decisions are based. Thus discipline-based scientists must provide the problem-solving focus that feeds into the broad vision of holistic management. In Bulungan, we found it expedient to work in a multi-disciplinary mode. The scientists did not pool their skills in a melting pot but rather worked in smaller teams on the elements of a mosaic. The result was a number of smaller groups of scientists moving forward in parallel on independent but interrelated research questions. The work of each of the smaller teams gradually evolved over time as they received feedback from the other teams and from the resource users with whom they were in daily contact.

With hindsight, we also now believe that this was a better strategy for learning and building-up a knowledge base than the purer approach of beginning with a single interdisciplinary model. At one point in the early development of work in Bulungan, we did decide to use a simulation model as a tool for achieving the integration of all of the different aspects of our research. It was surprising how quickly the needs and perspectives of the modellers began to drive the process. Reality had to be adapted to the model rather than the model adapting to correspond with reality. The problems began to be defined in terms of the things that the model – and the modellers – could cope with rather than by a dispassionate view of what the problems were. Eventually the modellers shifted the geographic focus of their work to locations that were 'easier to model'. At this stage, it was obvious to all that the model had taken on a life of its own and had ceased to be a tool to help to solve problems. At a later date, we returned to modelling but at that stage the emphasis turned to a more demand-driven 'throw-away' model (Box 7.3).

Box 7.3. Using systems modelling as a tool for communication amongst researchers

In developing a conceptual model of the Bulungan research in 2001 (Box 7.2), one of the subsidiary aims was to explore the role of systems modelling as a tool for negotiation amongst researchers in terms of setting research objectives and providing an integrating framework. In this setting, systems modelling is not being used as a predictive tool; rather, the models are 'throw-away' models – models that are produced rapidly to help to build consensus and clarify debate but are subsequently discarded.

From a series of meetings on the conceptual framework for Bulungan, we produced a graphical summary. The summary tended to focus on the elements of the discussion that could be modelled using an ecological – economic simulation model. This framework was not embraced enthusiastically by the Bulungan researchers as it was felt that its focus

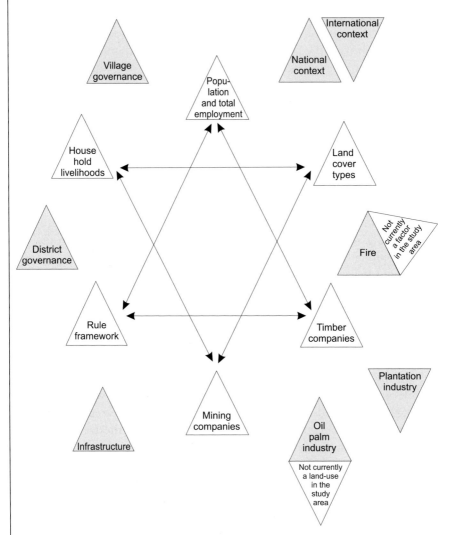

Fig. 7.4. Proposed components of the integrated model for Bulungan. Only those with arrows have been elaborated at this stage. Even at this early stage of model building, the model was producing results of interest to the researchers.

was too narrow, illustrating how simulation modelling frameworks can become restrictive: the modelling tool brought the danger of predetermining the direction of the conceptual understanding.

After the conceptual model was completed (Fig. 7.3), we returned to the systems model, working with different subgroups of researchers to fill in the model with details of different components of a simulation model (using the STELLA package). A first step was to map in the broad components of the systems that should be included. This covered the full spectrum of issues raised in the conceptual model, including components that would not be simple to model: village governance, district governance, etc. The next step was to produce the detailed linkages and parameter values for each component. The simple ones were tackled first: land-cover change, household livelihoods, population growth and employment in local industries (mining, logging). Relationships and parameter values were best estimates by researchers on the specific topics. The current version of the model took 10 hours to build and provided insights into land-cover change and changing livelihood status (Fig. 7.4).

It became apparent very soon that a simulation model cannot be transparent to all researchers, let alone other non-research stakeholders. Because of limited time available, researchers will not have the time to build the entire model, and they do not generally even have the time to build the component that they are tackling in their research. Building a model demonstrates the components of the research that are weak, where data are missing and what components of the system need more attention. If modellers build the model, rather than the researchers, then the integrative systems understanding is limited to the modellers, thus limiting the role of the model in promoting dialogue amongst researchers and in providing the desired conceptual framework.[1]

[1] The problems of big-system modelling were already apparent in the era of the International Biological Program in the 1970s, but they continue to be pitfalls to integrative science.

As our work in Bulungan evolved, a series of unexpected developments created opportunities for the work of the different research teams to coalesce around specific problems. The first of these came when we needed to strengthen the concepts underlying criteria and indicators for assessing the sustainability of forest management. This was clearly an issue where the divergent perspectives of the different research teams could all be brought together. CIFOR's criteria and indicator studies drew on work from many localities around the world but the pluralism of approaches exemplified by the work in Bulungan led to us challenging some of the entrenched conventional wisdom of the forestry community. It exposed the need to escape from the notion of a single universally applicable set of criteria and indicators – the fallacy of the 'one size fits all' vision of forestry.

It became obvious that every forest situation was different and this led us to develop a toolbox of criteria and indicators that could be used to design criteria and indicator sets to match any particular combination of local conditions.[6]

A more dramatic opportunity to draw the diverse aspects of our work together came as a result of the political changes in Indonesia in 1997–98. When we first began work in Bulungan, we were criticised for having chosen an area that was isolated and would be unlikely to change significantly in the lifespan of CIFOR's research. This argument was particularly attractive to those who believed that the development trajectory for the Bulungan area was more or less predetermined and would reflect the spatial plans and associated maps developed for the area by the government. Nothing was further from the truth, as was illustrated above in our description of the spectacular changes in the area.

The totally unexpected combination of circumstances raised interesting issues relative to CIFOR's research agenda. Our initial forest management research had aimed at testing techniques for reducing the environmental damage caused by logging. The research was based upon the assumption that the state timber corporations and some private concessionaires would remain the only significant timber operators in the area and we, therefore, focussed on developing techniques that these loggers could use. When the breakdown in formal control of logging occurred, our reduced-impact logging research became largely redundant. The environmental damage caused by the opportunistic logging by multiple operators dwarfed that caused by the corporations. In addition, it was difficult to imagine that anyone could oblige the operators to adopt better logging practices in the prevailing conditions. Reducing environmental damage became much more of a social and political issue. The key was to develop a widely shared agreement on logging rights.

This crisis occurred after CIFOR had already been operating in the area for about five years. We already had good contacts with most of the parties concerned. We were able to convene a meeting of local political leaders, village representatives, employees of logging companies and of conservation non-governmental organisations to review the issues related to the management of forests under the new decentralised arrangements. CIFOR could draw upon scientists working across the range of spatial scales from global to local. We also covered a range of disciplines and research themes from forest management, local community organisation, community-based

---

[6]CIFOR C&I Team. *The CIFOR Criteria and Indicators Generic Template*. Bogor: Center for International Forestry Research, 1999.

mapping, management of non-timber products and broader policy issues at the national level; these combined to enable us to deal with the full range of perspectives on these complex issues. We were not able to present any simple short-term solutions to the problems of natural resource degradation under the new decentralised regime. But we were able to contribute to the debate and try to steer the process towards equitable and environmentally benign outcomes. We provided information and analysis and our models helped to facilitate a debate on the likely outcomes of certain courses of action. It now appears that the preferred longer-term option is likely to be based upon some sort of negotiated agreement on logging rights between timber corporations and local people, with local people taking a much larger role in overseeing best practices by operators. It is too soon to know if we will be successful in this. However, it is certain that had our research been locked into a single vision of a desired outcome it would have been irrelevant to the local reality as it unfolded in response to the political crisis.

Almost no opportunities have occurred in Bulungan for large-scale experimental manipulation of any parts of the agro-ecological system. This was never the intention and the nearest we have come to this is in the establishment of plots of a few hectares in extent where we have experimented with reduced-impact logging technologies. Most of our knowledge has been acquired through observing the response of the forests to management and the changes in household and village well-being. We have also tapped the very extensive knowledge of local people. There has, however, been one valuable form of experimentation: the elaboration and modification of policies. As Kai Lee exhorts us, 'policies are experiments; learn from them'.[7] Monitoring the response to any action or policy yields knowledge, even when what occurs is different from what was expected. Kai Lee continues 'adaptive managers plan for unanticipated outcomes by collecting information'. Our presence in the area allowed us to monitor the impacts of decentralisation policies on local forestry practices and hence on the livelihoods of local people.

In retrospect, our objectives would have been better met if we had started the entire exercise with a good process facilitator interested in synthesis and integration. A small amount of time devoted to bringing the research team together, with other stakeholders, and planning for integrative products would probably have resulted in more synergies amongst team members. We would conclude that such process facilitation should be a

---

[7]Lee, K. L. *Compass and Gyroscope: Integrating Science and Politics for the Environment.* Washington DC: Island Press, 1993.

fundamental part of any long-term integrated natural resource management programme.

The role of research: understanding development trajectories

Our experience in Bulungan leads us to conclude that in dealing with large complex areas with relatively weak institutions one has to have modest expectations of the ability of research to make an impact on large-scale development trajectories. However, if the research effort is sustained, if it is pluralistic in its approach and if the researchers become integrated into the institutions and knowledge systems that govern development, then research probably can have positive influences. The nature of these influences may be hard to predict at the time that research is initiated. Rather, opportunities will unfold that will enable researchers to help other actors to nudge the system in the direction of sustainability and improved human well-being. This message may be unpalatable to those in the development assistance community who seek to make major impacts on entire economic systems within the three to five year time spans of their projects. However, we would contend that the record of development assistance in achieving impacts on large-scale development trajectories is poor. We are not claiming that investments in development assistance and associated research should be abandoned. On the contrary, we believe that our research presence in Bulungan is contributing to incremental improvements in the decisions that are being made on the sustainability of resource management. Yet these contributions are modest, and the larger and more complex the resource management system that is being managed, the more limited the potential for significant impact will be. Those who seek major impacts quickly will need to restrict their attentions to smaller, simpler natural resource systems that are more isolated from broad development trends.

We have developed these arguments at some length because they are central to making decisions on the allocation of resources for research and development on natural resource management systems. Many integrated natural resource management initiatives have sought to make major changes in the development trajectories of large ecological systems. Integrated catchment management projects and integrated conservation and development projects are good examples. Many of these projects have sought to use technical advice and relatively modest financial contributions to change the way of life of hundreds of thousands, or even millions, of people. There is now a widely held view that such projects have failed to deliver the benefits that were expected.

Significant, short-term impacts in Bulungan could probably have been achieved if we had applied our entire resources to a small, circumscribed area with a narrow objective: a modest-sized nature reserve or logging concession, for example. However, short-term impacts would easily have been reversed by the political and economic changes that occurred in Indonesia in the late 1990s. Our present strategy of working from within the system to make small, incremental impacts on natural resource management decisions may have an influence that is more sustainable and could affect a far larger resource domain.

It is, however, important to note that we are not arguing for undirected programmes of 'blue sky' research in the hope that they will yield opportunistic and incremental improvements in decision making. Rather we are arguing for a dual approach to research in support of natural resource management. Single-factor research will always be needed. Protection against new pests, improvement of important crops and so on may continue to be the 'bread and butter' of research institutions. We are arguing that the probability of being able to focus research on the right component and the critical problem, and the chances of the research solution proving appropriate to local conditions and thus adoptable, are much greater if the research emerges from a system where science is more fully integrated with management. These arguments resonate with similar debates that are occurring in the corporate sector on the relationship between research and practice. Roussel, Saad and Erickson have described three generations in the relationships between research and development and corporate organisation.[8] The first generation is where a corporation funds a research facility, provides it with some general guidance and then hopes that something useful will emerge. The second generation is where the corporation identifies problems or opportunities requiring research and allocates grant funding to carry out that research. The third generation is where the scientists and managers sit together to determine overall corporate strategy and where research is a fully integrated part of that strategy. Roussel and his colleagues argue that '. . . because third generation R&D management plans do not stand alone but are integral to corporate and business plan, flexibility and adaptability must also characterize the R&D component of corporate plans'. A more recent book describes a fourth generation of R&D in which knowledge and the ability to generate and manage it become even more central to corporate competitiveness.[9] This equates to the ideal where all

[8]Roussel, P. A., Saad, K. N. and Erickson, T. J. *Third Generation R&D: Managing the Link to Corporate Strategy*. Boston, MA: Harvard Business School Press, 1991.
[9]Miller, W. L. and Morris, L. *Fourth Generation R&D: Managing Knowledge, Technology, and Innovation*. New York: John Wiley, 1999.

management is experimental and all research is aimed at understanding real-world phenomena.

We do not wish to imply that the relationship between research and management in Bulungan has achieved the level of integration that Roussel and others advocate for corporations. However, as our programmes have evolved, we have involved more local scientists, developed closer relationships with local stakeholders and become far better attuned to local realities. The level of trust and information exchange between local resource managers and scientists has increased and our research agenda has become much more attuned to, and responsive to, local realities. The fact that we began work in the area with a flexible and pluralistic approach has made it much easier for us to break down the barriers that often separate scientists and managers in other large-scale natural resource management programmes.

A number of the research activities in Bulungan produced results that found applications quite different to those anticipated when the work was initiated. Research on traditional types of social organisation found unexpectedly valuable applications when the government suddenly and unexpectedly devolved management of natural resources to local communities. Similarly, it was possible to mobilise our 'installed scientific capacity' to respond to emerging needs. Decentralisation created a need for maps of community lands. CIFOR's scientists were well placed to help communities to produce such maps rapidly using techniques not otherwise readily available to local people (Box 7.4).

It is worth examining the way in which research has its impacts on natural resource management in the industrialised world. In developed countries, scientists rarely manage large natural resource systems, nor do they even make plans for such management on their own. However, scientists normally contribute to decision making. Kai Lee's account of scientists working with other stakeholders to integrate the management of salmon fisheries and forests in the Pacific northwest of the USA is exemplary.[10] The relationship of the scientists with resource managers that Kai Lee describes will be difficult to emulate in many developing countries, especially if the scientists all come from different cultures and only stay for a few years. However, this only strengthens our view that the achievement of science-based natural resource management in developing countries must be seen as a long-term endeavour. Its likelihood of success will increase to the extent that at least some of the scientists are drawn from local society.

---

[10]Lee, *Compass and Gyroscope.*

Box 7.4. Learning cycles in the Bulungan research forest

Lini Wollenberg, leading the research in the Adaptive Collaborative Management (ACM) programme in Bulungan, has outlined the learning cycles that have occurred in the work of the team (Fig. 7.5). By adopting a learning process, the ACM team was able to adapt to the rapidly changing circumstances. The learning cycle was rapid, allowing for several cycles in a few years, and the major learning cycle gave rise to additional cycles within cycles, as illustrated for the 1999–2001 cycle.

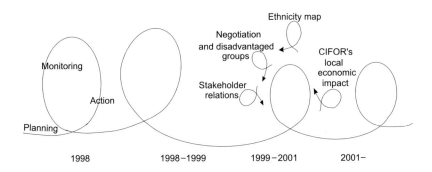

Scenarios

- Develop learning tools for villagers
- Literature review, partner discussions
- Focus on two villages: 1 person in the field
- Methods guide, article

Mapping training

- Increase capacity to claim traditional lands
- Training
- Focus on two villages
- Demand for more training; process too fast, communities needed more preparation

Boundary disputes & mapping

- Increase negotiation skills among villages and capacity to claim land
- Needs assessment, major workshop and training, conflict facilitation, field mapping, meetings with local government, next major workshop (negotiation training, legal awareness), newsletters, monitoring
- 27 villages, 7 NGOs, 9 persons in the field

Principles of community governance under multi-stakeholder conditions

- Stimulate debate and action
- Intensive case study, training, community and multi-stakeholder workshops, policy
- Focus on 10 villages, engage partner NGO, 7 persons in the field; 2 policy persons; follow-up work with original 27 villages

Fig. 7.5. The learning cycles and their characteristics. (NGO, non-governmental organisation.)

The challenges of solving the resource management problems of areas as complex and extensive as Bulungan will not be met by the delivery of technological packages produced by teams of visiting scientists or even concocted on research stations or in university laboratories and then delivered to local resource users. These challenges are of a scale that requires that science is a respected and integral part of society. Integration in this context is not just integration amongst disciplines, but the integration of scientists with the people who manage resources on a daily basis.

Conclusions and key lessons

The main conclusion of the seven years of research that we have conducted in the Bulungan area is that our ability to influence outcomes favourably has been greater because we did not go into the area with a rigid predetermined agenda. We did not isolate ourselves in an ivory tower and do research only to promote particular outcomes or solve specific technological problems. We went in with the more general objective of exploring and seeking to understand what determined the sustainability of the forest resources and how this related to the well-being of local people. As we acquired more knowledge, we adapted our programmes. We were opportunistic in encouraging scientists from partner institutions to join us to work on issues that appeared to be relevant to our general objectives. We sought to get to know the communities in the area, both local villagers and the political leaders of the administrative districts in which we were working. To the extent of our limited ability, we sought to respond to requests for our assistance in addressing local needs for information. We intend to continue to invest in strengthening our integration and acceptance into local society.

It is interesting to speculate as to whether we might have done things differently over the past six years and had higher impact with lower costs. The answer is probably that with the benefit of hindsight we could have done better. The flexibility, pluralism and adaptability that we have described in this chapter could have been more explicit and deliberate components of our original strategy. We could have benefited by achieving greater integration and more synergies by giving more attention to process facilitation. However, had we opted for a more structured approach when we first began work in the area in 1995 it is almost certain that we would have reduced our ability for flexibility and adaptation by confining ourselves more to our perceptions of the problems as they existed at that time.

A number of major conservation and development projects funded by international donors have been operating in similar situations in Indonesia during the period that we have been working in Bulungan. Without exception, they have had far higher budgets than we had. They were all planned in very great detail with outputs and milestones defined in advance. Significant proportions of their budgets were invested in facilities for the international advisers who ran the projects. Almost all of these projects have run into serious difficulties. They operated outside the system, and they were unprepared for and unable to adapt to the changes that occurred in Indonesia in recent years. They all found themselves pursuing visions for their areas that were at variance with those of important local stakeholders.

CIFOR's work in Bulungan has not solved either the conservation or the development problems of the area – far from it – but at least we now have a better understanding of what these problems are. However, we may have made as much contribution as was reasonable given the time and resources available and the inherent problems confronting the area. By proceeding slowly and hesitantly we may have established a better basis for future influence than we might have achieved had we focussed on short-term impacts. We believe that there are elements of our experience in Bulungan that merit serious reflection by those scientists who are confronted with similar situations elsewhere. Several key lessons have emerged.

- In dealing with large complex dynamic systems, it is essential to begin research in an open exploratory mode.
- Initial work must focus on learning and listening. Formal 'characterisation', mapping and planning approaches will often themselves limit flexibility.
- The main benefit from research may be to reduce uncertainties and inform choices, thus providing an improved ability to adapt. This will enhance the resilience of the system.
- A continuing process of learning and adaptation needs to be a feature of programmes such as that in Bulungan.
- Major unanticipated changes may be common in dealing with large complex natural resource systems.

8 Learning by doing on tropical American hillsides

The natural forests of the hillsides of the Andean Mountains in central and northern South America are reputed to contain higher diversities of flora and fauna than any other forests in the world. They also protect the watersheds of the rivers that provide water for the countries of the region. However, these same hillsides are also major producers of food: 40% of the food produced in the Andean countries comes from hillside agriculture.[1] They provide for the livelihoods of most of the rural poor of the countries from Peru to El Salvador. Hillside agro-ecosystems cover 96 million hectares in the region and similar land types extend into Brazil; 25 million hectares are already highly degraded and an additional 53 million hectares are experiencing rapid rates of erosion and deforestation. Some degree of erosion is seen on 50% of the hillsides of Colombia and 83% of the Andean region as a whole.[2] Central America is said to have the region's highest proportion of its land with moderate to extreme erosion. And the situation is getting worse. The large farmers in the valleys are expanding their holdings and peasant farmers – the *campesinos* – are forced into the hills. The associated evils of drug production and trafficking and politically motivated banditry further erode the security of the lives of the people of this region.

Forests, watersheds and poor farmers

David Kaimowitz of the Center for International Forestry Research (CIFOR) has reviewed the 'useful myths and intractable truths' relating to watersheds and hillside agriculture in Central America.[3] He traced the

---

[1] Lopez Cordovez, L. Trends and recent changes in Latin American agriculture: a cross country analysis. *Cepal Review*, **16** (1982), 7–42.

[2] This chapter is based upon the work of Jacqueline Ashby and colleagues from the International Center for Tropical Agronomy Cali, Colombia. See particularly Amezquita, E., Ashby, J., Knapp, E. K. *et al. CIAT's Strategic Research for Sustainable Land Management on the Steep Hillsides of Latin America*. Cali: Unpublished document, CIAT, undated.

[3] Kaimowitz, D. Useful myths and intractable truths: the politics of the link between forests and water in Central America. In *Forests–Water–People in the Humid Tropics*. Cambridge: Cambridge University Press, 2003.

concerns about soil erosion, sedimentation and the hydrological impacts of forest clearing in Central America back to the 1920s. However, he shows that it took alarmist reports about the sedimentation of the watershed of the Panama Canal and some of the region's other main hydroelectric dams to put watersheds on the political agenda. In the late 1970s, Wadsworth and Larson both warned that degradation of the Panama Canal watershed could seriously affect the Canal's operations within a few decades.[4] The Harza Engineering Company International claimed that sedimentation had reduced the original capacity of the El Salvador's '5 de Noviembre' reservoir by almost two-thirds. The US Agency for International Development issued reports asserting that siltation of the region's hydroelectric dam reservoirs would greatly decrease their lifespan and cause hundreds of millions of dollars in damages. Two scientists from the prestigious Smithsonian Institute released a study purporting to show that deforestation had reduced rainfall in the Panama Canal watershed and in northwest Costa Rica. Kaimowitz concluded that, by the time Jeffrey Leonard published his influential assessment of natural resource degradation in Central America in 1985,[5] it had become conventional wisdom that deforestation seriously endangered the region's energy supplies and navigation routes and probably contributed to flooding and droughts.

These findings resonated among certain key international agencies and policy-makers. Costa Rica, El Salvador, Guatemala, Honduras and Panama depend heavily on hydroelectric energy, and hydroelectric dams account for a major share of their foreign debt. The canal is central to Panama's economy and the reports about siltation problems came out at about the time that Panama and the USA were negotiating the future ownership of the canal. The fact that US government agencies issued several of the more alarming reports and followed up by funding a regional and several national watershed management projects lent credibility to some of the sensationalist findings, thus causing even greater concern.

The 1990s witnessed the rapid expansion of environmental activities by non-governmental agencies (NGOs). Foreign assistance agencies shifted support from public sector agencies to NGOs and gave the environment higher priority. Many NGOs wished to convince local farmers and

[4]Wadsworth, F. Deforestation: death to the Panama Canal. *United States Strategic Conference on Tropical Deforestation*. Washington, DC: US State Department and United States Agency for International Development, 1976, pp. 22–24; Larson, C. Erosion and sediment yield as affected by land use and slope in the Panama Canal watershed. In *Proceedings of the Second World Congress on Water and Resources of the International Water Resources Association*, Mexico, 1979, pp. 1086–1095.

[5]Leonard, H. J. *Natural Resources and Economic Development in Central America*. New Brunswick, NJ: Transactions Books, 1985.

communities that environmental problems directly affected their well-being and used watershed degradation as a case in point. These groups told farmers that if they cleared additional forest and failed to protect their soils, their water sources would dry up, their yields would decline and their crops would receive less rain. Numerous press reports echoed their message, which was consistent with the popular perception that deforestation was drying up the region's rivers and streams.

In 1997, when the El Niño phenomenon caused serious droughts throughout the region, the link between drought and deforestation reappeared as a frequent topic of conversation and press reports. The droughts provided optimal conditions for forest fires to proliferate and the region experienced some of the worst fires in its history. Much of the public and the media attributed the drought and the fires to environmental degradation brought on by deforestation and logging.

In spite of all this, Kaimowitz goes on to show that there is little hard empirical evidence for the ways in which deforestation affects rainfall. Simulation models predict that massive deforestation will decrease rainfall in some areas and increase it in others. Scientists anticipate larger effects in regions where a large portion of the rain that falls comes from evaporation within the region itself. This holds for the Amazon, but not so much for regions such as Central America and Southeast Asia. Modellers have concentrated on simulating the effects of total forest conversion over very large areas. Whether the climate changes resulting from land-cover changes in Central America would be large enough to have major impacts remains uncertain.

Kaimowitz concluded that there is little evidence to show that landuse changes involving only a few thousand square kilometres, as typically occur in Central America, significantly affect rainfall, although recent work in northern Costa Rica suggests that the patterns of cloud formation above forested and cleared areas differ. Careful scrutiny of studies that make such claims has generally found that they used poor methodologies or that other plausible explanations may account for their findings. For the moment, one cannot discard the possibility that land-use changes in Central America have caused rainfall to decline. Still, many researchers believe this is unlikely, particularly given that Central America is a narrow isthmus where climate is heavily influenced by the surrounding oceans.[6]

[6]Bruijnzeel, S. Hydrology of montane cloud forests: a re-evaluation. In *Second International Colloquium on Hydrology and Water Management in the Humid Tropics*, Panama, 22–24 March, 1999; Calder, I. R. *The Blue Revolution, Land Use and Integrated Water Resources Management*. London: Earthscan, 1999.

Tropical montane cloud forests constitute a partial exception. These forests are known to intercept clouds or fog and channel some of the water to the forest floor as canopy drip. Thus, even though strictly speaking they may not affect rainfall, they do influence the amount of water that moves from clouds to the forest floor. As a result, removing cloud forests may well reduce the amount of water available for crops and human use.

A similar story applies to flood control. Research shows that land-use affects the infiltration of water into the soils and land-use changes that compact the soil or diminish porosity will increase run-off and peak flows, and arguably, flooding. At the same time, contrary to popular wisdom, the removal of tree cover tends to increase annual water yields, since more water evaporates from trees than from shorter crops.[7]

Nonetheless, these results hold mostly for small areas. At larger scales, local effects average out and any storm long and intensive enough to cause major floods is likely to overwhelm rapidly the soil's capacity to absorb the rainfall. In such circumstances, land-use is unlikely to affect greatly how much flooding occurs. Most studies of large-scale flooding find no relation between land-use and flood intensity.[8] Hence, whether farmers deforest their watersheds almost certainly does not greatly affect the intensity of major floods, such as those associated with Hurricane Mitch.

Kaimowitz recognised that the issue of dry season flows is less clear. On the one hand, forest vegetation usually reduces annual water yields, leaving less total water available. On the other hand, any land-use that improves water infiltration should help to replenish groundwater reserves. Greater groundwater reserves imply more available water in the dry season. Whether the negative evapo-transpiration effect or the positive infiltration effect dominates depends largely on the rainfall regime, soil type and the land-uses involved. Burning, overgrazing and completely eliminating scrub vegetation typically reduces water infiltration into the soil. Certain soil conservation measures have the opposite effect. One cannot assume that planting trees on soils degraded by erosion will automatically re-establish or improve dry season flows in the medium term. In the initial years, forest plantations have

[7] Bruijnzeel, S. *Hydrology of Moist Tropical Forests and Conversion: A State of Knowledge Review.* Paris: UNESCO International Hydrological Programme, 1990; Hamilton, L. S. and King, P. N. *Tropical Forested Watersheds, Hydrological and Soils Response to Major Uses or Conversions.* Boulder, CO: Westview Press, 1983.

[8] Anderson Jr, R. J., Da Franca Ribeiro dos Santos, N. and Diaz, H. F. *LATEN Dissemination Note 5: An Analysis of Flooding in the Parana/Paraguay River Basin.* Washington DC: World Bank, 1993; Chomitz, K. M. and Kumari, K. The domestic benefits of tropical forests, a critical review. *World Bank Research Observer,* **13** (1998), 13–35; Enters, T. *Methods for the Economic Assessment of the On and Off-site Impacts of Soils Erosion,* 2nd edn. Bangkok: International Board for Soil Research and Management, 2000.

high evapo-transpiration rates, whereas the positive effects of the trees on soil infiltration capacity remain limited. It is only several decades after tree planting that the rainfall absorption capacity of a once degraded soil starts to come anywhere near its former value under natural forest conditions.[9] In the special case of tropical montane cloud forests, there is apparently some reduction in dry season flows following conversion to agriculture. However, it is not clear whether this is primarily a consequence of the loss of cloud water inputs after forest removal or reduced infiltration.[10]

The constituency supporting measures to conserve the upland forests of Central America was reinforced by conservation biologists from developed countries. The forests of Central America are not only very rich in biodiversity, they are also the most accessible tropical forests for North American scientists and naturalists. Added to this was the fact that in politically stable Costa Rica foreigners were allowed to purchase forestland and establish private nature reserves and eco-tourism enterprises. Large numbers of students and concerned citizens from North America have taken an interest in the ecology of these mountain forests and added their voices to those supporting upland conservation. Well orchestrated fund-raising campaigns to pay for forest conservation and restoration at La Selva and in Guanacaste in Costa Rica have reinforced public concern for Central American forests. A major recent conservation initiative aims to establish a Meso-American biological corridor. This will be a ribbon-like protected forest area running the length of the Central American isthmus. It is supposed to provide continuity in the habitats of some of the region's endangered animals and plants. Like the watershed conservation efforts, this initiative has proved attractive to funding agencies and the public. However, like the watershed campaigns, there is little empirical evidence to suggest that it will be the most effective way of achieving biodiversity conservation goals.[11]

Throughout the region, the poorer farmers who cleared forests on the hillsides to cultivate their crops were seen as the cause of these problems. However, in many cases, these *campesinos* were being forced to move to areas that were more and more marginal for agriculture, as land elsewhere was consolidated into large holdings by rich entrepreneurs. In Colombia in 1983, ownership of 11 million hectares of pasture was concentrated in the hands of large- or medium-scale cattle ranchers. Poor farmers, unable to purchase this land, move into the hills and deforest more land, migrate to the cities, seek

[9] Gilmour, D. A., Bonell, M. and Cassells, D. S. The effects of forestation on soil hydraulic properties in the middle hills of Nepal: a preliminary assessment. *Mountain Resources Development*, **7** (1987), 239–249.

[10] Bruijnzeel. *Hydrology of Moist Tropical Forests and Conversion*.

[11] Simberloff, D., Farr, J. A., Cox, J. and Mehlman, D. W. Movement corridors: conservation bargains or poor investments. *Conservation Biology*, **6** (1992), 493–504.

employment on larger farms or may get drawn into drug production and trafficking. This erodes family and community viability and drives a vicious circle of degradation and violence. The problem of hillside conservation in the Americas is more than just an environmental problem, it has become a major social problem with profound consequences for the stability of the region. In the Andean countries, cocaine cultivation in remote areas has become the only viable option for many of the marginalised people. Despite decades of well-funded efforts to eradicate drug cultivation, the dangers and uncertainty of this illegal trade are still more attractive to many poor people than any of the other options available to them.

The steady degradation of these tropical hillside soils and their vegetation is a fundamental development problem. It is robbing small farmers of their best hope of giving themselves and their children a better future. Crops and livestock may survive on these eroded slopes, but they cannot thrive. People's incomes are low, welfare indicators are declining and population growth is rapid. The hillsides are the scene of endemic social conflict over access to, and control of, resources.

Seeking technological solutions: moving to farmers as owners of the research

The International Center for Tropical Agriculture (CIAT) in Cali, Colombia, has been trying for three decades to improve the productivity and sustainability of hillside agriculture. The focus of the work has been on hillsides at elevations between 800 and 2000 m above sea level. The soils are acid and the areas receive between 1500 and 1800 mm of rainfall. The farms in these areas are characterised by highly integrated smallholdings of coffee, pastures and annual crops of maize, beans and cassava. Jacqueline Ashby and her colleagues have shown how farmers' decisions are driven by considerations of survival more than any real attempt to sustain the natural resource base. Increasing population, decreasing farm size, declining labour productivity all combine to lead farmers to take decisions that result in soil erosion, fertility decline, deforestation, pesticide abuse, surface and groundwater contamination and eventual desertification.[12] One significant conclusion of Ashby's work is that the rate of deforestation in the hillside areas of the Americas is significantly higher than that of lower-lying areas.

[12] Ashby, J., Estrada, R. D. and Pachico, D. An evaluation of strategies for reducing natural resource degradation in the hillsides of tropical America. Paper presented at the *Annual Meeting of the International Association of Impact Assessment*, Quebec, Canada, 1994, http://www.ciat.cgiar.org/inrm/workshop2001/docs/titles/8-1BPaperJABeltran.

This deforestation leads inevitably to loss of biodiversity. Montane forests have very high levels of species' diversity, notably of herbs and shrubs occurring between 600 and 3000 m above sea level.[13] This is of particular concern because the wild relatives of many important cultivated crops occur in these forests.

CIAT's core business in the 1970s and 1980s was to develop improved technologies for Andean hillside farmers. Considerable resources were invested in developing improved germplasm. Legumes were produced with highly branched root systems that were efficient in taking up soil nutrients. Long-term plots were already established in 1987 to improve understanding of soil erosion processes. Experiments were conducted with minimum tillage, contour ridges and contour strips of grass to find optimal systems for reducing soil loss to acceptable levels. Different combinations of cassava, maize and beans were tried and leguminous trees and mulching systems all contributed to better soil retention. One interesting discovery was that leaving land fallow was not necessarily the best way of restoring fertility and reducing erosion. Under continuous cropping, it was possible to maintain soil conditions provided soil biomass was managed properly. The application of chicken manure as fertiliser could yield significant gains in soil quality whereas the use of nitrogen-fixing cover crops did not necessarily improve yields although it was good for long-term soil fertility enhancement. In the short term, the legume cover crop *Arachis pintoi* reduced maize yields, presumably through competition for water and nutrients.

The controlled experimental work on improved agricultural technologies yielded many new insights and techniques that had potential to improve the performance of small hillside farms. The problem was that every farm was unique and highly complex. The options for widespread adoption of simple technological 'fixes' were limited. Farmers needed a package of solutions that could be tailor made to address their specific needs. In most cases, the technologies developed on the research station needed to be adapted to the needs of each individual farm.

In the late 1980s, CIAT launched an ambitious programme of on-farm research at a number of so-called 'benchmark' sites intended to be representative of the major agro-ecosystems of the hillsides of Central America and northern South America. The intention was to take a more holistic view of farming systems and to work more closely with farming communities. Each benchmark area was intended to be representative of

[13]Bronson Knapp, E., Ashby, J. A., Ravnborg, H. M. and Bell, W. C. A landscape that unites: community led management of Andean watershed resources. In *Integrated Watershed Management in the Global Ecosystem. Soil and Water Conservation Society*, ed. L. Rattan. New York: CRC Press, 2000.

an 'application domain' where its results would be communicated to local farmers through extension programmes. The hillsides work was in the vanguard of the eco-regional initiatives launched by the Consultative Group for International Agricultural Research (CGIAR) in response to criticisms of the on-station, technologically driven, 'green revolution' research paradigm.

The early days of the hillsides programme were far from easy and reflected the numerous problems of multi-stakeholder collaboration, with the high transaction costs associated with changing the practices of large numbers of widely dispersed farmers (Box 8.1). Competition occurred between the technical agencies involved in the programme even though the intention had been to foster partnerships. In the haste to get programmes started, local people were often not consulted until after the research agenda had been set. They were, therefore, immediately marginalised. Part of the cause of the early problems was that donor agencies and researchers preferred to invest in simple short-term projects with highly predictable outcomes, and to avoid the complex problems of the real world that required longer-term investment.

The difficulties of the early attempts to improve hillside agriculture were instrumental in provoking critical evaluations of the overall approach. Technical innovation alone was recognised as being only one part of the problem. Much more attention began to be given to the relationship of the researchers with the farmers, the processes by which farmers adapted their resource management practices and issues relating to the regulation of resource use and to conflict resolution. Recognition was also given to the fact that individual farmers could not resolve many of the natural resource management problems. Those farmers who shared the same watershed could achieve this through collective action. In many cases, the costs of resource management interventions were not being born by the beneficiaries. Reaching consensus on the extent and distribution of costs and benefits of alternative solutions amongst different constituencies became one of the most contentious issues in the programme.

These realisations led to a gradual and significant change in the relationship between the CIAT scientists and their erstwhile clients. Much more of the research began to be conducted by the farmers themselves with the scientists as partners or advisers. The farmers themselves selected and developed new crop varieties. Plant breeders monitored the process and provided advice and technical inputs but they only exercised rather loose control of the process. One has the impression that this led to a much more egalitarian relationship between the farmers and the scientists, with the scientists showing more respect for the extensive implicit knowledge that governs the

---

Box 8.1. The difficult early days of the Hillsides Programme in Central America

The following description is based on an interview with David Kaimowitz.

The origins of work in the hillsides of Central America can be traced back to initiatives taken by the Consultative Group for International Agricultural Research (CGIAR), and the Director Generals of its key research organisations. The first on-the-ground activity was in the early 1990s when a conference was convened to initiate interagency collaboration on hillside problems. All the major international and regional stakeholders attended and a series of presentations demonstrated the competencies of the various stakeholders. After the conference, the planning began, but without much input from national stakeholders, let alone small farmers.

There was never an explicitly recognised set of problems driving this planning, but it was generally assumed that soil and water conservation would form part of the research agenda. Some time was taken to select a case study watershed, but eventually a most improbable watershed in Honduras was selected, probably the result of the personal interest of key researchers. At this point, national players began to get involved, but only those who were part of the research community. A marginally useful descriptive diagnosis followed, driven strongly by disciplinary and organisational interests.

A further large meeting was convened about a year after work commenced. This was a more positive meeting with new players being involved, and effective networking initiated. The writing of grant proposals began at this stage, but it soon became apparent that potential donors favoured only one of the partner institutions, and many of the others then lost interest in the programme. The proposals covered the full period of the proposed programme even though local partners were yet to be identified let alone consulted. Stakeholder meetings were required by the donor to discuss the proposal but these proved confrontational, with local players angry at being bulldozed by the main stakeholder. This stakeholder also initiated a period of internal reorganisation, such that it was only by the mid-1990s that effective fieldwork could begin. Somewhere in this period, the original watershed was abandoned, so the early diagnosis there proved of no value. At this time, accusations of data 'piracy' emerged, with some of the original members of the consortium unhappy at the use of their data by the other organisations.

Eventually these problems were sorted out. New management selected new sites, and negotiations between all the interest groups – international and national researchers and local interest groups – led to a stage where a stable institutional basis for the programme was established. Under these arrangements, the farmers moved to centre stage and took the leading role in guiding all research and development activities – a total reversal of the original situation.

---

farmers' day-to-day lives and the farmers coming to recognise and respect the fact that the scientists had access to knowledge and technologies that would otherwise be unavailable locally. What emerged was a new paradigm of participatory plant breeding that is now being widely replicated.

Organisational and resource management problems in the Rio Cabuyal

Most successful examples of collective action to improve natural resource management appear to have involved the work of local NGOs. An interesting case emerged from the work of CIAT in the Cauca valley of the inter-montane plateaux of southern Colombia.[14]

The Rio Ovejas is a tributary of the Rio Cauca, an important source of water and hydroelectric power for the city of Cali. The water quality of the Rio Ovejas was deteriorating, supposedly as a result of erosion caused by upstream land clearing and deforestation. Pollution by agro-chemicals, waste products from artesanal coffee processing and the run-off of excessive levels of organic fertiliser from the upper watershed all contributed to poor water quality. Upstream erosion was believed to be a major cause of annual flooding in lower-lying areas.

The Rio Cabuyal catchment at an altitude of 1200–2200 m was selected as a pilot area within the Rio Ovejas basin because it was representative of the soil, agro-climatic and demographic characteristics of the larger watershed. Small-scale farming and casual labouring were the principal sources of income for the population. Coffee, cassava, maize and beans and, in the upper watershed, fruits were the main crops. Livestock was of minor importance. The lower and mid-altitude areas had quite good access to markets. Standard techniques were used to improve the quality and quantity of downstream water. For instance, areas along riverbanks and around springs were fenced to allow natural vegetation to get established. Contour barriers were established to control soil erosion. However, there was little incentive for upland farmers to adopt these practices since all the benefits accrued to people further downstream. While external agencies concerned with natural resource management saw bad soil management as the major problem, the local farmers were much more concerned about lack of credit to buy fertilisers.

Stakeholders had divergent perceptions of the problems. Inhabitants of the lower and mid-altitude communities were concerned about the seasonal scarcity of piped water, the disappearance of streams and the decreasing

---

[14]We have drawn on a number of papers by Jacqueline Ashby and colleagues from CIAT in preparing this section. An especially good account of the issues is given in Bronson Knapp, E. *et al*. A landscape that unites.

flows in the river. They attributed this to deforestation by the inhabitants of the upper watershed. The agencies responsible to downstream users were concerned about water quality in the Cauca valley. The upper-watershed communities saw their own problems as lack of schools, electricity, all-weather roads and health services.

Different watershed resources were managed by independent organisations with different objectives. The piped water supply drawn from the headwaters of the tributary watersheds was managed by a local organisation, the *Junta del acueducto*, while an external agency was responsible for the conservation of forest reserves around the aqueduct intakes. There were no formal mechanisms for joint decision making or coordination among the local and non-local entities. In addition, there were other external agencies active in the catchment area with competing agricultural or conservation objectives. There were no incentives for these agencies to coordinate with each other or with local communities. Agricultural development programmes promoted credit, technical assistance and marketing outlets. They provided incentives to upland farmers to clear and burn secondary bush fallow and forests to plant cassava, notorious locally for causing soil degradation.

Watershed management agencies helped local people to organise themselves to tackle these problems. A coordinating committee was formed with representatives of the public sector, NGOs and grower associations. Its role was to collate all available information and make a joint diagnosis of the problems. This was the committee that selected the Rio Cabuyal as the pilot area. The boundaries of the watershed were defined to include the 1000 families in 22 communities who influenced the water regime of the Rio Cabuyal.

At the same time, in early 1993, community leaders began to visit different areas of the watershed to motivate people to collaborate in improving watershed management. They focussed their campaign on the issue of decreasing water availability. They organised a number of commissions to visit the communities in the upper watershed. They found that tracks were impassable; there were no schools; houses were of poor quality; crops were poor and there were large areas of degraded, unproductive fallow. There was much more poverty in these areas than at lower altitudes. The local farmers explained that cutting trees for charcoal around the water sources provided almost their only source of cash income.

In response, the community leaders began to seek support from outside organisations for activities to improve the quality of life in the upper watersheds. Such support was to be an explicit reward for the farmers to stop clearing the forests. Local leaders also formulated plans for lower-watershed farmers to teach the upland farmers how to improve their crops and to form marketing cooperatives.

At the same time, the external organisations in the coordinating committee began to develop a common set of activities to support the initiatives of the community leaders. A planning workshop was held and the 12 participating agencies committed themselves to a common agenda linked by formal agreements. They formed a watershed-based organisation called the *Consorcio Interinstitucional para la Agricultura Sostenible en Laderas (CIPALSA)*.

An important objective of CIPALSA was to provide a forum where local inhabitants could define, monitor and enforce their own regulations and determine the distribution of benefits to different stakeholders. As a result, a Watershed Users Association was formed. Members included schools, cooperatives, women's groups and village governments. By mid-1993, CIPALSA had acquired a substantial budget from outside grants and local participants. The watershed users group shared these grants and funds began to flow to activities to protect the upper watershed.

Locally negotiated measures to protect the upper watershed began to replace the ineffective regulations previously imposed from outside. Conservation areas were defined in the upper watershed. The Watershed Users Association was able to forge agreements and mobilise labour to plant trees and enclose critical watershed areas. Almost 4000 person days of labour were mobilised, 135 ha of land were enclosed and 150 000 trees were planted. The motivation for working together was explained in terms of making an investment in the future of their children. In addition, piped water was cut-off from families that did not contribute labour. The farmers at the lower elevation, who were the beneficiaries of these measures, also had to contribute labour. Subsequently, it was shown that small catchments throughout the watershed were just as important as the upper watershed areas in influencing stream flow, and conservation measures were extended to these areas.

In 1994, forest fires partly destroyed a buffer zone created by the Watershed Users Association. Slash and burn farmers who colonised the upper watershed had lit the fire. This highlighted the failure to identify these colonisers, who had no legal title to land as stakeholders in the watershed, and to consider them an interest group needing representation in the association. These groups were henceforth included in negotiations. A stakeholder analysis, facilitated by outsiders, was used to identify the conflicting interests and reasons for burning. A set of norms was developed specifying how and when burning should be conducted. Some communities formed groups to ensure compliance. Most farmers adopted these norms and introduced measures such as the making of firebreaks before burning. These approaches were more successful in controlling burning than previous measures because the farmers themselves developed them. Rather than simply condemning all burning, they acknowledged that burning was the only feasible means of land preparation in some circumstances. The development of these local controls illustrates the role of local organisation in providing a forum to analyse and negotiate interests.[15]

Box 8.2. Changing farming practices: the case of Mr Sanchez

Mr Sanchez was born in the hills of the Rio Cabuyal watershed. His household used to survive on the production of charcoal, with severe impacts on the forest. With the coming of the research committees, he has seen a major change in livelihood status and better protection of the forest. When the research committees were started, 12 families participated but now the whole community has been taking part. As part of the process of development driven by the research committee, Mr Sanchez has seen the introduction of electricity and the upgrading of schools. Forests that were previously being overexploited are now important as sources of litter to improve soils. Many new income-generating options have become available. Mr Sanchez now grows blackberries and produced 1 tonne last year. He sells the product to middlemen who supply both consumers and agribusinesses. He has heard of the move to certification and hopes that he can achieve this in order to get better markets in developed countries. Apart from the berries, he also produces beans, peas and many other crops, and also maintains a few cows.

His main worries concern issues beyond his control: the state of the national economy and climate change. However, some changes are definitely for the good: the use of soil conservation measures and soil fertility improvement techniques mean that the soils are slowly improving, to the point where future labour inputs will be reduced. This situation is most welcome, as it will ease the burden of farming for his children, who will take over the farm one day.

He knows that others worry about the sustainability of the research committees once the key partners withdraw at the end of their project. There are some concrete benefits to remaining in the research committees but these benefits will disappear – will the research committees survive if their only role is to stimulate collective action; and will they be strong enough to negotiate changed conditions for the farmers?

The area still needed technical innovation to promote conservation and enhance productivity. Local agricultural research committees were, therefore, formed to bring together groups of four or more farmers, elected by the community, to test and adapt technologies in the local environment

[15] Ravnborg, H. M. and Ashby, J. *AGREN Network Paper 65: Organising for Local Watershed Management: Lessons from the Rio Cabuyal Watershed, Colombia.* London Overseas Development Institute, 1996.

(Box 8.2). They worked on topics chosen by the community and combined local knowledge with technologies from outside. These committees identified new crops for upland farming and they formed producer groups. They received funds, specialised training and technical advice from outside agencies through CIPALSA. CIPALSA also provided the impetus for the development of small-scale dairy farming and this began to stimulate changes in land-use. Cut-and-carry pastures were planted to replace annual crops and milk producers' cooperatives were established. The Watershed Users Association used its influence to improve roads into the upper catchments to facilitate transport and marketing. Middlemen began to appear in the upper watershed to purchase dairy products, providing weekly cash income for farmers. The introduction of commercial production was linked to the adoption of the hitherto-rejected contour barriers, live fences, tree plantations and buffer zones, just as the community leaders had visualised.

Lessons learned

There have now been several decades of international investments in protecting watersheds and improving *campesino* agriculture in the hillsides of South America. Inspite of this, these areas still contain the greatest concentrations of poor people, and the environmental catastrophes to which the area is subject seem to occur with greater frequency. In the final days of October 1998, Hurricane Mitch unleashed an apocalyptic rampage of floods and mudslides that wreaked havoc on Honduras, Nicaragua, Guatemala and El Salvador, causing thousands of deaths and billions of dollars in damages.[16] Once the floods subsided, people throughout the region began asking why the storm had sown such great destruction and how they could prevent future catastrophes. David Kaimowitz reviewed the reactions of the press, public officials, environmentalists and international agencies;[17] they all claimed deforestation had greatly magnified the damage. To make the region less vulnerable to disasters, they proposed greater support for reforestation, soil conservation and civil defence. 'Watershed management' and 'vulnerability' became watchwords. The agencies practically fell over one another to see who could invent more initiatives with those words in their titles.

Kaimowitz pointed out that, prior to Hurricane Mitch, natural resource specialists in Central America paid scant attention to landslides

[16]Smyle, J. *Disaster Mitigation and Vulnerability Reduction: Perspectives on the Prospects for* Vertiver *Grass Technology (VGT).* San Jose, Costa Rica: Regional Unit for Technical Assistance (RUTA), World Bank, 1999.

[17]Kaimowitz, Useful myths and intractable truths.

and mass wasting. Discussions of 'soil erosion' focussed mostly on gradual and continuous soil loss (so-called 'sheet', 'laminar', or 'rill and inter-rill' erosion). However, Hurricane Mitch demonstrated the huge destructive potential of massive soil movements and the importance of occasional extreme events. Vegetation with deep and extensive root systems frequently provides greater soil stability and protects against soil slippage. However, geology, topography and extreme natural events play a greater role in major landslides than forest cover or its absence.[18]

Kaimowitz concluded that even if one decides to curtail sediment flows, research suggests that the planting of trees and introduction of mechanical soil conservation measures in agricultural fields are rarely the most cost-effective way to do so. In some instances, rural roads and construction activities and mass wasting contribute most to siltation, and frequently the channel system or flood plains already store massive amounts of sediment awaiting transport to the reservoir.[19] Soils often erode more under teak plantations than under well-kept pastures or scrub vegetation.[20] Most projects designed to control sedimentation from agricultural sources end up working where farmers express the greatest interest in participating, rather than where the greatest sources of sediment exist.[21] In many fragile areas that have already lost their original forest cover, natural regeneration and fire control might be the most cost-effective means of reducing sediment flows, but few watershed management projects concentrate on those issues.

To sum up, a good basic principle is that if the current land-use provides the quantity and quality of water the population demands with an acceptable intra- and interannual distribution, any alteration will increase the risk of that situation changing. This is a strong argument for maintaining natural forest cover in many contexts. That being said, the evidence suggests that many of the claims about deforestation leading to reduced rainfall and dry season flows, greater flooding and sediment flows that endanger dams and waterways in the medium term are exaggerated. Long-term gradual

[18]Cassells, D. S., Bonell, M., Hamilton, L. S. and Gilmour, D. A. The protective role of tropical forests: a state of knowledge review. In *Agroforestry in the Humid Tropics: Its Protective and Ameoliorative Roles to Enhance Productivity and Sustainability*, ed. N. T. Vergari and N. D. Briories. Honolulu: East–West Center, 1985, pp. 111–129. Smyle, *Disaster Mitigation and Vulnerability Reduction*.

[19]Nagle, G. N., Fahey, T. J. and Lassoie, J. P. Management of sedimentation in tropical watersheds. *Environmental Management*, **23** (1999), 441–452.

[20]Calder, *The Blue Revolution*.

[21]Agudelo, L. A. and Kaimowitz, D. *Serie Documentos de Discusión Sobre Agricultura Sostenible y Recursos Naturales, 3: Tecnología agrícola sostenible: retos institucionales y metodológicos, dos estudios de caso en Colombia.* [*Sustainable Agricultural Technology: Institutional and Methodological Challenges, Two Case Studies from Colombia.*] San Jose, Costa Rica: IICA/GTZ, 1997.

sedimentation problems deserve serious attention even though conventional cost–benefit approaches suggest that it might be better to let them persist. However, one needs to look to more creative and systematic approaches that have the clear objective of reducing sediment flows and focus more on controlling rural road construction activities and encouraging natural regeneration. As Kaimowitz demonstrated, even if the aid agencies had fundamentally misread the problem, the results of their investments have, at least in some cases, led to real benefits for the poor populations of the hillside areas.

The most notable success results from the work of Jacqueline Ashby and the CIAT scientists in the hillsides of the Andes. Their work, at least partially motivated by watershed concerns, has brought real benefits to many upland farmers. It has demonstrated how technological innovation must go hand in hand with the development of social organisation and of 'social learning' to improve the performance of the whole agro-ecological system of which the watershed functions are just one part. It has also illustrated the need for analysis and intervention across a range of scales. Farmers, community leaders, scientists and merchants have to learn and negotiate together on an equal footing. Farmers have to be empowered to experiment and innovate. Progress takes the form of a whole series of linked innovations spanning the range from norms, market access and technology through to improved planting materials. This provides a much more powerful impetus for change than the opportunistic introduction of new technologies in isolation. Outside funding can help these processes and protect farmers against the risks inherent in experimentation. Outside technical help needs the platform provided by local organisations in order to find appropriate entry points. The Andean hillsides' experience shares some features with the Australian Landcare experience, where the extent of resource degradation and the imperative for action had reached a stage where collective action was becoming essential for the well-being of local people. These were not problems perceived by outside aid agencies; they were real problems that the people were facing in their day-to-day lives. The time was ripe for action and the interventions from outside probably accelerated and strengthened changes and innovations that might have taken place anyway.

This experience of development assistance to hillside agriculture in Central America and northern South America carries a number of lessons for natural resource managers. Interventions sponsored by central governments and development assistance agencies have persisted for more than two decades even though they were based on flawed perceptions of the problems. Aid agencies have been unwilling to challenge conventional wisdom or perhaps unwilling to take a stand against the simplistic diagnoses of problems promoted by the media and NGOs. Meanwhile, scientists working in close association with upland farmers have been quietly experimenting and learning. Whether these efforts have had an impact on floods and water quality is uncertain. But these investments have yielded significant benefits in terms of the social and natural capital of the *campesinos*. The *campesinos* are now better organised and they use a greater variety of crops and technologies. Even more importantly, they have been empowered. They now have knowledge of the land that they farm and they also know more about the downstream problems. They have the ability to adapt their farming practices and are able to negotiate with downstream landowners. They can negotiate to secure benefits in exchange for improving the watershed functions of their land. Uncertainty still exists about the optimal upland land cover for watershed protection. It seems reasonable to assume that any stable and well-managed upland agriculture will be better than unstable and opportunistic resource exploitation. If it is eventually shown that certain dispositions of forests, perennial and annual crops are better for watersheds, then the upland farmers will be in a good position to seek compensation or incentives from lowlanders. The overall conclusion is that policies and programmes imposed from outside, and especially those put in place to respond to emergencies, have attracted most of the money but yielded few benefits. Meanwhile, long-term participatory research by *campesinos* and scientists from CIAT has not produced any magic bullets or dramatic breakthroughs but it has gradually established the foundations for better lives for the upland poor. It also provides a promising basis for addressing the problems of upstream–downstream linkages. Although we have mentioned CIAT throughout this account, the work initiated in the 1980s on hillside agriculture has been a shared venture amongst a number of international and national research organisations in the region. A new culture of large-scale action research and of constructive partnerships between farmers and scientists is now widespread in the region. Farmers and scientists show mutual respect and innovations are as likely to occur in the farmers' fields as they are on the research stations.

The keys to the success of the Andean hillside initiatives

Much of the early motivation for hillside conservation programmes was based on false assumptions about the links between upland land-use and downstream hydrological impacts. The early days of the programme were over-planned and based excessively on the sponsors' vision of technological solutions to problems. A more cautious start-up period with far more participation and negotiation should have been used.

- Successes began to be achieved when farmers and local organisations began to take genuine control of the programme and scientists became the partners in, rather than the drivers of, the process.
- Technical innovations and the building of social capital and learning all need to move forward in parallel. A portfolio of social and technical innovations will be needed and the balance of this portfolio can easily be predicted.
- Development initiatives of this sort must be sustained for decades; they are extremely unlikely to achieve significant and sustained results within the three to five year time frame of conventional development assistance projects.

Part III

The research–management continuum

9   The spread of innovations

Research on integrated natural resource management should aim to help large numbers of people explore the full range of options that are available for dealing with their local resource management problems. This means creating an environment where science and knowledge help people to develop a diversity of locally appropriate resource management solutions. Integrated natural resource management research should emphatically not be about the discovery of single technological solutions, produced on research stations and made available for widespread application. Consequently, the problems of getting uptake of the results of integrated natural resource management research are quite different to those associated with promoting the adoption of a new technology produced in the research laboratory. Widespread adoption of integrated management techniques may involve changing entire farming, forestry and fishery systems. There are rarely any silver bullets; what is required is often the synchronised change of policies, institutions and technologies: the entire production system has to evolve.

In the past, scientists often blamed farmers for not adopting the latest technological innovations. Farmers were said to be excessively conservative or even insufficiently educated. Some scientists tacitly assumed that the poor in developing countries were simply not smart enough. Most people now accept that in many cases the farmers were very wise not to accept the unproven technologies that were on offer. The life of a poor farmer is fraught with risk and many of the products of research laboratories are ill-adapted to the vagaries of weather and pests that farmers have to deal with in their daily lives. Farmers have to be cautious; they cannot afford to make mistakes. There are too many examples of innovations conceived by distant technocrats that have failed spectacularly when attempted in real-life conditions. Scientists and agricultural planners have tended to overlook the fragile safety net separating the poor farmer from starvation or destitution. Yet when a new technology does meet a real need, the rate of spontaneous adoption can be very rapid. Improved rice varieties and the fertilisers and pesticides that go with them spread very rapidly through Southeast Asia.

When an innovation meets a real need, the policy context is right and farmers can readily adapt their systems to incorporate it, there may be little need for promotion or extension.

If solutions to most resource management problems are really locality specific, how can research contribute to wide-scale improvements? Critics of natural resource management research have argued that scientists will not be able to produce technological packages that have wide application. This may be true, but it assumes that natural resources research will be organised in the same way as conventional on-station agricultural research. We argue for a radically different approach, where the role of the researcher is to work with farmers to experiment and learn. The key to solving the resource management problems that afflict hundreds of millions of poor people living in marginal agricultural areas in the developing world may be to increase the scientific literacy of the farmers. It may require a far greater use of science within natural resource management institutions at the local level. This has already happened in the developed world and it may not be such an improbable proposition for the developing world as it may at first appear.

Many countries already have extension services with considerable outreach into rural areas. However, most tend to promote a few well-tried remedies. They communicate and perpetuate the 'conventional wisdom' of the civil servants and scientists who constitute the agricultural elite. A first step might be encouraging fundamental change in the nature of the extension workers' job. We argue that they must change from being deliverers of ready-made technologies to being experimenters, facilitators and negotiators. In reality, good extension workers have always operated in this mode. The proliferation in developing countries of local non-governmental organisations (NGOs), often staffed by scientists and often employing some of the negotiating and learning approaches suggested in this book, has been a response to the real needs of farmers. For several years, the informal NGO movement has been having more impact than the public sector extension services. For instance, most of the advances in developing options for small-scale forestry in recent years have come from NGO projects and not from the forest research institutes. NGOs are filling the niche of bringing science to small farmers; they are acting as 'barefoot scientists'. This does not mean that specialised high-technology research institutes are no longer required but it does mean that the relationship of the extension worker to the research laboratory must be changed. It means that scientists, NGOs and extension workers must accept that innovation can occur anywhere and is not a monopoly of the advanced research institute. NGOs and extension workers must not only be aware of technological options but, just as important, must also be aware of farmer experimentation and communicate this and local problems and opportunities to the researchers. Information and ideas must flow in both directions. Extension must evolve to become a form of action research at real-life scales. In much of the developed world, this is already the case.

There is a great deal that has been learned from some of the innovative projects reviewed in this book which does merit much wider application. However, widespread adoption of science-based natural resource management will depend more on changes in the culture and organisation of science (discussed in Chapter 11) than on further refinement of the traditional communication and dissemination skills of the extension worker. Nonetheless, there remains a challenge of fully exploiting the potential of cutting edge science to help very large numbers of widely dispersed small farmers and resource managers.

The challenge is to achieve a 'vertical integration' between the cutting edge scientist in the laboratory and the adaptable small farmer in the field. The replication, dissemination and adaptation of technologies, practices or approaches, no matter where they originate, are challenges for natural resource management research. The products of research, both in the laboratory and on the farm, may include ideas, adaptable prototypes or well-tested technologies. If these products are not adopted on a wide scale, then we will have failed in our purpose of contributing to poverty alleviation, food security and environmental protection.

Integrated natural resource management research can be organised to meet this challenge. However, effective supportive institutions are needed in order to ensure widespread adoption of innovations. There are a number of fundamental principles:

- policies, organisations and rules affect the behaviour of communities and individual resource-managing families
- individual and group behaviour determines the selection and adoption of resource management practices
- use of new resource management practices affects plant and animal growth and biophysical processes
- feedback loops enable individuals and groups to manage biophysical processes to produce more at lower cost and to conserve their resource base.

Uptake and community empowerment

We must move away from the conventional paradigm that says that adoption and dissemination of improved resource management is simply a question of replication of the improved technology in other places. Rather, the emphasis must shift to community empowerment, experimentation and learning. A recent report from the NGO committee that advises the Consultative Group for International Agricultural Research (CGIAR) describes this well.[1]

> It is not technologies that are scaled up, but processes and principles behind the technologies/ innovations. This is consistent with the belief that scaling out is not just replication but adaptation and learning that is flexible and interactive. . . . Scaling-out is really about people – of communicating options to people, of a balance between introducing options and involving farmers' ability to adapt to changing contexts . . . Scaling-out as a development process rejects the cookie-cutter approach. [It] . . . achieves large numbers and wide area coverage through multiplication with adaptation . . .

Farmer experimentation and local initiatives are fundamental to the successful spread of improved resource management practices. The task of the research and development institute is to enrich the choice of options available to resource managers and then to ensure that the knowledge generated by individual farmer's experimentation is widely shared. Experience suggests that farmer experimenters are interested in trying out exciting practices developed by other farmers facing similar problems.

Farm-family empowerment in Bangladesh

Participatory approaches are powerful tools for achieving effective extension, especially those that respect the knowledge and integrity of the farm family. A good example comes from Bangladesh where scaling-out of seed management practices in rice–wheat-based systems has been remarkably successful. Much of the success can be attributed to what is called the 'Whole Family Training' programme. The design of this programme was based on the recognition that all family members typically take part in and are affected by agriculture. However, families have different ways of allocating labour to farming. Therefore, the programme was designed so that families learn, explore and adapt new practices together. This approach respects families' internal arrangements, rather than making assumptions about the gender- or

[1] Gonsalves, J. For the CGIAR NGO Committee. *Highlights of the Workshop Going to Scale: Can We Bring More Benefits to More People More Quickly?* Presented by the CGIAR–NGO Committee and the Global Forum for Agricultural Research with BMZ, MISEREOR, Rockefeller Foundation, IRRI and IIRR. 10–14 April, 2000. Silang, Philippines: International Institute of Rural Reconstruction, 2000.

task-specific frameworks for learning.[2] Women field workers were recruited from an NGO and were trained to facilitate the process. They conducted participatory seminars using informal methods with families invited from their working areas. In the first year alone, nearly 6000 people from more than 1200 families in eight districts attended. Families received personalised invitation cards, making them feel honoured; attendance was nearly 100%. Learning focussed on seed management (germination testing, selection, rates and storage for grain and seed) with some coverage of irrigation and water management practices and soil fertility management. Not surprisingly, farm families were a rich source of ideas for adapting and further improving the practices being discussed. For example, farmers provided useful alternative suggestions on testing seed germination, involving wet gunnysacks, stalks from banana plants or hot water. Follow-up studies show that families attending the seminars have taken up most of the practices discussed (adapted in one way or another to their own circumstances), with an increase in direct and indirect on-farm benefits roughly equivalent to a third of annual family incomes! The whole-family approach has spread to other institutions in Bangladesh, including other NGOs.

Landcare in Australia

Landcare is a mass movement of independent self-organised local groups who collaborate to address land degradation issues across Australia. Each group defines its own agenda and raises its own funds. Much of the on-the-ground work is carried out voluntarily. However, there are now many sources of public and philanthropic funds to support these local groups. At the end of the 1990s, the federal government was putting US$ 1 billion a year into Landcare but this made up only about 25% of the total expenditure under the programme. All major political parties back Landcare and even urban people now support and sponsor Landcare activities. The Landcare magazine is mailed to 36 000 readers – although it is heavily subsidised. Landcare claims many successes although even its strongest advocates acknowledge that much remains to be done. What is really interesting about Landcare is the way that it all began.

The movement emerged in the 1980s after several decades of rapid expansion of agriculture in Australia. Australia is a relatively flat continent

[2]Meisner, C., Sufian, A., Smith, M., O'Donoghue, M., Razzaque, M. and Shaha, N. Non-gender biased, innovative approaches for accelerated adoption of agricultural technologies, especially for wheat seed production and preservation. In *Proceedings of the POWER-Sponsored Workshop on Women in Seed*, May 2000.

and drainage is slow. Over vast areas, the soils have high salt content. The clearance of natural woodlands led to changes in drainage patterns and the emergence of salinisation as a major problem. The proliferation of domestic livestock caused widespread degradation of vegetation that had evolved to deal with the hopping marsupial grazers and browsers. During the late 1970s and early 1980s, concern about land degradation began to emerge on the national agenda, particularly among farmers themselves.

The official beginnings of the Landcare movement are attributed to a group of cattle ranchers in central Queensland who realised that the extent of the problems went beyond their individual properties. They agreed to collaborate to address shared natural resource degradation problems. It appears that at about this time there were quite large numbers of local groups forming throughout Australia to take collective action to address land degradation.

The first use of the term Landcare is attributed to Jock Douglas, the President of the Queensland Cattlemen's Council. However the movement seems to have entered the national consciousness when erstwhile adversaries Philip Toyne, the Director of the Australian Conservation Foundation, and Rick Farley, the Director of the National Farmers Federation, formed an alliance to promote better land husbandry. In 1985, an Australian phil-anthropic foundation, the Potter Foundation, put up the money to hire Andrew Campbell as national Landcare coordinator and the movement took off. Accounts of the early days of Landcare suggest that it was not the bright idea of an individual or small group of people but rather an emerging pop-ular concern whose time had come. Landcare, or something like it, was destined to emerge from multiple self-organised initiatives to address widely shared problems.[3] Landcare is one of the best examples of collaborative ac-tion to address major integrated natural resource management problems. It is significant that it was not designed by technocrats nor was it a government initiative.

Principles for achieving dissemination and uptake

Many scientists in the CGIAR network have long experience of working at the interface between the research institute and the farmer. A consensus is emerging amongst them that a number of principles are key to achiev-ing uptake of innovative resource management practices. Here are some

---

[3]Based upon interviews with people concerned with the Landcare programme in Australia and on information on the Landcare website http://www.affa.gov.au/docs/nrm/landcare/nlp.html.

suggestions from Larry Harrington and his colleagues at CIMMYT.[4] Many of these deal with improvements in human and social capital.

Generate more attractive products. Uptake is more probable when practices are less risky, more profitable and meet a range of objectives for resource managers. Products are more likely to be attractive if the 'customers' are involved in product development. It has repeatedly been shown that farmer participation in research increases the chances that attractive options will be identified (see Box 3.5, p. 74).

Balance supply-driven approaches with resource user demands. Demands from resource users must influence the research agenda and hence the kinds of option to be produced. Yet farmers cannot express a demand for practices of which they are totally unaware. Ways must be found for users to become aware of new options; these must be sufficiently plausible and realistic to motivate farmers to want to experiment with them under local conditions.

Use feedback to redefine the research agenda. As information accumulates on technology, performance and attractiveness, and on how policies and institutions influence these, resource management research can and should be adjusted. Researchers must be attentive to, and show respect for, the knowledge and opinions of farmers.

Encourage support groups and networks for information sharing. Community groups, cross-community networks, alliances of networks, study tours and scientific exchanges can all help resource users as well as scientists to understand the performance of alternative options under different conditions.

Facilitate negotiation among stakeholders. Natural resource systems managed by multiple users for multiple functions will inevitably entail trade-offs. This will often lead to conflicts among stakeholders. Facilitated negotiation and conflict management among interested parties will often be needed to resolve conflicts and allow equitable resource use practices to emerge.

---

[4]CIMMYT: Centro Internacional de Mejoramiento de Maíz y Trigo (International Maize and Wheat Improvement Centre); Harrington, L., White, J., Grace, P. *et al.* Delivering the goods: scaling out results of natural resource management research. *Conservation Ecology*, **5** (2001), 19. Online: http://www.consecol.org/vol5/iss2/art19.

Provide information to encourage policy change and institutional development. Self-interest and resistance to change of organisations can be a major barrier to improved resource management. Institutional and policy reform will often be the key to innovation. Scientists can provide information helpful in the process of policy formulation and institutional development. Policy-makers must be provided with research-based information on how resource management practices can help them to meet economic and social goals. New policies and institutions can influence human behaviour and increase the likelihood of technology adoption.

Make use of information management tools such as geographical information systems (GIS) and modelling. When practices are developed that raise productivity, improve quality and protect the environment, there is an understandable interest in seeing these practices used more widely. It is obvious that such practices will be attractive to other farmers or farming communities who face similar problems, with similar underlying causes. Modern spatial analysis tools can inform farmers' decisions. For example, in a certain community a green manure cover crop may be successful in smothering weeds, freeing up labour, improving water-use efficiency, reducing the need for external inputs, raising yields and improving farm family livelihoods. Research may suggest that this practice works best where the cover crop is climatically adapted, where soil fertility is in a certain range and where land-use intensity is low (allowing a cover crop–grain crop rotation). It may also succeed where marketing margins are high and the use of expensive external inputs unprofitable. Spatial analysis combining climate, soils, population density, crop distribution and transport infrastructure data can identify large areas in other communities where the practice holds promise. This outcome can be shared with NGOs, research and extension institutions, farmer groups and policy-makers for use as they see fit. This may encourage NGOs or farmer groups to foster experimentation and adaptation of the practice. It can also help to avoid the danger of over-enthusiastic promotion of new technologies and attempts to get them promoted in unsuitable places.

Information management tools for achieving uptake

Information management technologies can help to make the sharing process smarter and better focussed, so that research can indeed demonstrate its ability to benefit large numbers of poor across large areas within sensible time frames. The following sections provide examples of information management tools useful in the process of scaling-out of resource management practices. Most examples are drawn from the work of Larry Harrington and colleagues at CIMMYT.[5] Harrington and his team have collaborated with a wide range of partners in South Asia, southern Africa and Mesoamerica in developing their approach. The methods and tools used include site similarity analysis through GIS, linking of simulation models with GIS, use of farmer and land type categories, and 'whole family training'.

Site similarity analysis

A recurring problem in efforts to disseminate promising interventions is knowing how a practice developed at one location will perform over a broader range of environments? GIS can address such concerns, allowing scientists to share relevant results with colleagues elsewhere, find new sites for testing and adapting discoveries, and design more effective research programmes. One simple GIS-based approach is to identify areas that are similar, using criteria relevant to the problem at hand.[6]

To identify regions for introducing and adapting wheat production practices that might show promise for particular conditions in Bolivia, site similarity analysis was applied to key research sites in the country's two major wheat-growing environments.[7] In the highlands, wheat is grown on summer rains in numerous valleys and small plateaux. In the eastern lowlands, the crop is sown on residual soil moisture as temperatures drop and become more favourable for wheat.

Zones of similarity were defined using a GIS-based spatial characterization tool[8] by specifying the latitude and longitude of a given research site and then selecting criteria for similarity based on ranges of precipitation, potential evapo-transpiration and temperature. For the highlands, zones were based on the favourable five-month growing period, and for the lowlands, the coolest quarter was used.

[5] Harrington *et al.* Delivering the goods.

[6] Corbett, J. D., Collis, S., Bush, B. *et al.* USAID's African country almanac. Version 2.0.1. *Blackland Research Center Report No. 99–06.* Houston, TX: Texas Agricultural Research Station, Texas A&M University, 1999.

[7] Hodson, D., Corbett, J. D., Wall, P. C. and White, J. W. *NRG–GIS Paper 98–01: An Agro–Climatological Overview of Wheat Production Regions of Bolivia.* Mexico, DF: CIMMYT, 1998.

[8] Corbett, J. D. and O'Brien, R. F. The spatial characterization tool – Africa v 1.0. *Blackland Research Center Report* No. 97–03. [CD-ROM Publication.] Houston, TX: Texas Agricultural Experimental Station, Texas A&M University, 1997.

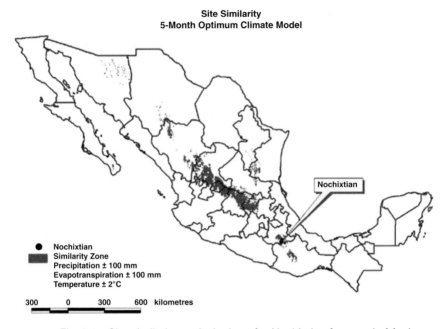

Fig. 9.1. Site similarity analysis done for Nochixtian farmers in Mexico to plan a study tour. (From Harrington *et al.* 2001. See footnote 4.)

The highland sites showed widely scattered zones of similarity in Bolivia, Peru, Colombia and Venezuela. Extending the analysis to Mexico, Central America and Africa identified additional areas with similar climates, notably in Mexico and Ethiopia. For the lowland sites, the largest regions outside of Bolivia were in two substantial but distinct areas of eastern and southwestern Brazil.

This specific analysis has yet to be used for the purposes of dissemination of research innovations. Yet it has now become clear that researchers and farmer experimenters in the widely dispersed areas of Bolivia, Brazil, Mexico and Ethiopia are addressing similar problems with similar interventions and would benefit from greater sharing of information.

In a different application and at a different scale, farmer experimenters from the extremely poor Mixteca region of southern Mexico used site similarity analysis to identify areas elsewhere in Mexico with climate and soil conditions similar to their own (Fig. 9.1).[9] This information was then used to plan a study tour of research and farmer experimentation in these other areas. The farmers returned home with new ideas about crop

[9]Harrington *et al.* Delivering the goods.

residue mulches and drip irrigation for fruits and vegetables that they have now begun to test.

Interfacing simulation models with GIS

Some situations can benefit from more complex comparisons. Stakeholders may want to examine trade-offs for different scenarios. For example, are the productivity gains from conservation tillage using crop residues likely to entirely offset the value of those crop residues if used for animal feed? How will system performance vary over time, particularly in extreme dry or wet years?

Process-based simulation models can simulate the 'growth' of a virtual cropping system over many seasons, quickly and inexpensively. The output, in effect, extends the reach of science beyond the practicable time horizons of most research programmes. It allows the examination of variables difficult or costly to monitor at the field level, for example, nitrogen leaching and volatilisation. By interfacing GIS with simulation models, researchers can develop simulated performance surfaces that portray the likely biophysical performance of a technology over space and over time.[10]

Outputs from simulations are compared with experimental results and with researchers' own experience. Using the resulting maps, researchers and decision-makers have been able to assess the simulated effects of conservation tillage on run-off and erosion, organic matter, soil structure and moisture conservation. For each soil type, maps produced using the simulations show differences across the region in the biophysical performance of the practice. Impacts can be expressed in terms of various factors, including yield, stability, biomass and soil organic carbon and nitrogen use efficiency. The methodology shows promise for providing information for a range of stakeholders: the maps and other outputs can guide NGOs, farmer groups and researchers on where conservation tillage may be most apt for farmer experimentation and adaptation.

Of course, data availability and quality can often constrain effective modelling. Calibration of models for multiple cropping system scenarios is a time-consuming exercise. Therefore, the decision on whether to use models interfaced to GIS will depend on the availability of appropriate data and models for the locality and cropping system of interest.

---

[10]Hartkamp, A. D., White, J. W. and Hoogenboom, G. Interfacing geographic information systems with agronomic modeling: a review. *Agronomy Journal*, **91** (1999), 761–772.

Land type and farmer categories

The GIS-based applications described above emphasise regional, national or international comparisons to guide dissemination. However, more modest tools and methods that feature comparisons across farms can be used for the same purpose.

It has long been known that many farmers recognise different land types within a farm. When problems, causes and management practices are specific to land types, then dissemination can be guided by such typologies. When land types are replicated across large areas of the landscape, efficiencies in dissemination can be considerable. Often, of course, farmers with different resource endowments use different management practices for the same land type. So, measures to foster dissemination must be sensitive to farmer categories as well as land types.

In the rice–wheat systems of the Indo-Gangetic plains, rainfall, water control and soil texture tend to follow an east–west gradient. Water control and soil texture in specific locations, however, are also influenced by land type (i.e. lower, middle and upper terraces) within a toposequence. Though a land type may be known by different local names in different parts of the Indo-Gangetic plains, its characteristics, uses and management are often similar and known to all farmers.[11] Lower terraces are characterised by heavier soils and relatively poor drainage and are more likely to be devoted to long-duration traditional rice cultivars. Middle terraces have somewhat lighter soils and fewer drainage problems; these typically are sown to modern varieties of rice and wheat, at times mixed with other crops. Upper terraces have the lightest soils of all and tend to have greater crop diversity. Here rice and wheat are sown, but also pigeon pea, sugarcane and vegetables.

There are many recurrent problems in rice–wheat rotations in the Indo-Gangetic plains. They include high costs for tillage and establishment, low water and nutrient use efficiency, soil fertility decline, salinity and sodicity and waterlogging. They all unfold differently in each land type. Similarly, remedies change according to land types – but also according to farmers' land category.

Farmers in southern Zimbabwe distinguish among *dambo* bottoms (wetter areas where rainfall accumulates through natural drainage), homestead gardens (with soils that benefit from crop residues, leaf litter, household

[11]Harrington, L., Fujisaka, S., Hobbs, P., Adhikary, C., Giri, G. S. and Cassaday, K. *Rice–Wheat Cropping Systems in Rupandehi District of the Nepal Terai: Diagnostic Surveys of Farmers' Practices and Problems, and Needs for Further Research*. Nepal and Mexico City: International Maize and Wheat Improvement Center (CIMMYT) and Agricultural Research Council/International Rice Research Institute, 1993.

waste and farmyard manure) and toplands (with soils of low fertility and low water-holding capacity, relatively distant from the household). These land types are managed very differently. Farmers use different strategies for crop selection and rotation, organic and inorganic fertiliser application, soil fertility management, and so on. In addition, farmers with many draft animals manage land types differently to farmers with few draft animals. Yet these land types and farmer categories are replicated across much of southern Zimbabwe and adjoining areas of South Africa and Mozambique. Forest-dwelling Dayaks in Kalimantan have sophisticated typologies for forest types that help them in choosing sites for shifting agriculture, hunting and gathering non-timber forest products.

Exciting practices for addressing problems of land type and farmer category can be widely shared with farmer groups, NGOs, researchers and other stakeholders working in similar areas. The intent is to make these practices available as new options to be introduced into local learning processes – not just for 'cookie-cutter replication'.

One challenge is to use GIS to improve linkages between biophysical determinants of land types and categories recognised by farmers. This will entail having relatively simple and robust tools for spatial analysis that come pre-loaded with relevant spatial data. The Country Almanac series for Africa shows considerable promise for such work.[12] The software works well with high-resolution (1:25 000 scale) data sets. Experiences with use of the Almanacs for training representatives of national research institutes, NGOs and the private sector suggest that a two-day workshop is sufficient to allow users to manipulate data efficiently. The main challenge is to obtain field data for topography, soils, land use or other variables at an appropriate resolution. Recent improvements in the accuracy of hand-held global positioning systems (as low as 6 m) and in availability of satellite imagery with grid sizes as low as 1 m offer prospects for overcoming these data constraints.

Bridging local to national and global scales: the experience of community watershed management

Certain forms of innovation in natural resource management require the simultaneous adoption of change amongst all of the participants operating in a large system. This applies especially to attempts to improve the performance of hydrological functions of a watershed subject to common property or common pool management. An essential part of achieving uptake in such

[12]Corbett *et al.* USAID's African country almanac.

situations lies in relationship building. In broad terms, it requires incentives for community participation, which, in turn, depends on the existence or creation of an enabling environment. Chris Lovell and partners have investigated the preconditions for success, drawing on the significant body of experience that has come from attempts at integrated catchment management, common property resource management and devolution of control for natural resource management.[13]

The weakness of delivery mechanisms was identified as the main failing with first attempts to implement integrated catchment management in both Australia and South Africa.[14] The importance of community participation and local development to the success of these national programmes was not at first fully appreciated. A recent survey by Hinchcliffe and colleagues of community-based projects considered the implications of using the catchment as the unit of analysis for integrated natural resource management.[15]

> Contrary to common viewpoints, the catchment . . . is not always the most rational unit for all activities . . . Because neither catchments nor the groups who live among them are homogeneous, the nature of their problems and the possible solutions are varied and complex. Prescriptive external solutions have little chance of fitting . . . and may be inappropriate or unacceptable to the majority of farmers. Nevertheless, working with common interest groups on contiguous areas of land, whose boundaries may be administrative, social or physical, enables agency staff to provide assistance more efficiently than where individual farms are scattered . . . Thus it is not 'catchment management' as such that results in improvements in agriculture and livelihoods. Insistence on such a framework may run contrary to communities' needs and priorities . . . Rather it is the integration of improved husbandry of land, of crops and of livestock with better interpersonal relations in the context of catchments that produces tangible benefits.

---

[13]Gibbs, C. J. N. Institutional and organizational concerns in upper watershed management. In *Watershed Resources Management: An Integrated Framework with Studies from Asia and the Pacific*, ed. K. W. Easter, J. A. Dixon and M. M. Hufschmidt. Boulder, CO: Westview Press 1986, pp. 145–156; Ravnborg, H. M. and Ashby, J. A. *AGREN Network Paper 65: Organizing for Local-Level Watershed Management: lessons from Rio Cabuyal Watershed, Colombia*. London: Overseas Development Institute, 1996; Rhoades, R. E. *Gatekeeper Series SA81: Participatory Watershed Research and Management: Where the Shadow Falls*. London: International Institute for Environment and Development, 1998.

[14]Blackmore, D. J. Murray–Darling basin commission: a case study in integrated catchment management. *Water Science and Technology*, **32** (1995), 15–25; van Zyl, F. C. Integrated catchment management: is it wishful thinking or can it succeed?' *Water Science and Technology*, **32** (1995), 27–35.

[15]Hinchcliffe, F., Thompson, J., Pretty, J., Guijt, I. and Shah, P. (eds.) *Fertile Ground: the Impacts of Participatory Watershed Management*. London: Intermediate Technology, 1999.

Hinchcliffe and colleagues reported on 23 case studies that present a rich and complex picture of the problems, achievements and continuing challenges faced by conservation professionals and farmers around the world. They concluded that the following features are common to successful adaptive management schemes at the community level.

> *Small scale.* They operate at the scale of small micro-catchments, recognising that boundaries cannot be precisely defined and are rarely hydrological.
>
> *Shared problems.* Planning units are collective (i.e. at the scale of community-based organisations rather than individual farmers), the emphasis being on working with people with something important in common (e.g. caste, blood, class, common dependence, common priority).
>
> *Social organisation.* They are rooted in a reasonable degree of social organisation through which the necessary critical mass of collective action can be organised. Where this social reality does not exist, it has to be created, requiring significant trust development and platform building. The social units most appropriate for participation need to be tailored to the particular setting, and the approach may not work where 'community' is not the norm and people are organised differently, for instance according to tribal groups, under the influence of absentee landlords or they are landless.
>
> *Flexibility.* They allow for flexibility — a thoroughly pre-designed and pre-planned project is not a good project. Indicators of success focus on adaptation rather than adoption.
>
> *Clear institutional roles.* The roles of the different organisations are clearly defined: government, NGOs and community-based organisations have complementary but different roles to play.
>
> *Integrated and holistic vision of officials.* Government personnel are familiar with and believe in participatory farmer-to-farmer extension. They are prepared to reorientate projects and extension approaches away from 'treatment' of soil and water conservation problems towards whole catchment management focussed on livelihood priorities.
>
> *Quick results.* Tangible benefits accrue to participants early in the process.

Credit available. Groups have access to finance through credit or other means.

Local people receive payments for downstream benefits. The most successful schemes are highly subsidised by government and donors, with local residents contributing only a small percentage of the value of the development works in cash or as labour. Adequate financial and institutional support is critical where authorities are handing responsibility for complex, costly and conflict-ridden problems back to local people.

However, almost without exception, successful interventions have been NGO-led projects that are small in scale and can be disseminated only by repeating the same slow, costly, in-depth techniques in successive villages. Farrington and Boyd identify three features important to replication over wide areas.[16]

Balance local leadership and outside technical inputs. Community leadership in local development is essential: this generates ownership of the process and enhances the prospects of effective and sustainable joint action. However, entirely 'bottom-up' initiatives limited to the possibilities already known to rural people will not suffice. The process must be open to the wider possibilities known to outsiders and in a procedure for planning, implementing and monitoring that allows outside agencies to verify that public funds have been spent properly.

Outside investment must not undermine local ownership. Support agency roles must allow the necessary degree of local participation and ownership for interventions to be planned and to function adequately, but the possibility for rapid replication must be fostered. A criticism of World Bank-supported watershed development projects, for example, is that, despite large amounts of funding for infrastructure, institutional arrangements are rarely adequate for continued maintenance. By comparison, long-term empowering approaches adopted by some NGOs achieve institutional sustainability in individual villages at the cost of extremely slow replication. A balance is required.

Local NGO solutions may fail to spread. There must be a clear strategy for dissemination of change; NGOs often fail to plan for

[16]Farrington, J. and Boyd, C. Scaling-up the participatory management of common pool resources. *Development Policy Review*, **15** (1997), 371–391.

wider-scale uptake. Certain types of technology – largely those that can be implemented individually – can spread laterally by farmer-to-farmer extension, but lateral spread that requires collective action is far more difficult to achieve.

Farrington and Boyd concluded that joint action and participation are central to successful management of natural resources; replication at any scale larger than a few villages has to occur within a structured programme and has to be based on multi-agency partnerships. The slow, long-term empowering approach cannot be handled by local NGOs alone, so the public sector has to play a significant role.

In only one setting, the Indo-German Watershed Development Programme (IGWDP) in Maharashtra State, India, did they find these preconditions for scaling-up thought through at the programme design phase (Box 9.1). This led to what they considered to be best practice in ensuring the spread of innovations. Farrington and Lobo discuss the institutional arrangements that have involved all stakeholders.[17] They concluded that the programme had generated a technically sound participatory watershed planning methodology, a coherent transition from capacity building to full-scale implementation, and a practical framework for field-level collaboration among NGOs, community-based organisations and government departments.

Box 9.1. The Indo-German Watershed Development Programme in India

The preconditions for scaling-up fell into five groups.

1. The setting of appropriate criteria for the selection of watersheds, villages and local-level NGO partners, and the design of local level collaborative mechanisms

Technical criteria included notable erosion, land degradation or water scarcity problems; villages located in the upper part of drainage systems; watershed size around $10\,\text{km}^2$; and village boundaries corresponding closely with those of the watershed. Socio-economic criteria included villages poorer than average with no wide disparities in size of land holding and villages that have concern for resource conservation and have a known history of working together for common causes. As a condition for support, villagers had

---

[17] Farrington, J. and Lobo, C. *Natural Resource Perspectives 17: Scaling-up Participatory Catchment Development in India: Lessons from the Indo-German Watershed Development Programme.* London: Overseas Development Institute, 1997.

to commit themselves to banning the felling of trees, banning free grazing, undertaking social fencing to protect vegetation, reducing excess populations of livestock, and limiting water-intensive crops. They also had to contribute voluntary labour to a value of 16% of the unskilled labour costs of the project (land-less and single-parent households were exempt), start a maintenance fund and set up a village watershed committee.

2. The design of village-level mechanisms for participatory planning, learning and implementation

Planning based on externally produced maps failed. The approach subsequently developed relied on consultations with farmers in their own fields, i.e. community mapping in partnership with external support agencies such as the Forestry Department. A capacity building phase of up to one year was undertaken in which a small segment of the watershed (typically 100 ha) was rehabilitated. Funds for this phase (up to US$16 000) were provided by the IGWDP through their technical support NGO.

3. Design of a sustainable mechanism for screening and funding individual proposals submitted for watershed rehabilitation

The IGWDP created mechanisms that channelled funds to local organisations with as few intermediate steps as possible. It established a project-sanctioning committee headed by the National Bank for Agricultural and Rural Development. The central role played by this respected national organisation in assessing and channelling finance to donor-supported projects was a cornerstone of replicability. Also, local currency could be channelled through this mechanism once foreign funds have dried up.

4. Mobilisation of administrative and political support from the early stages

The IGWDP focussed on obtaining political support, first by inviting members of the Legislative Assembly to visit successfully rehabilitated pilot watersheds, then by obtaining a Cabinet resolution implementing this devolution of control to village level through joint forest management arrangements with the state.

5. Establishment of channels for drawing on technical expertise in the post-rehabilitation period

The demand from communities for information and assistance to build on their initial success and to start a range of new projects was facilitated in the IGWDP by a Watershed Organisation Trust. This was a body of 29 staff covering a wide range of social and physical subjects that helped to put NGOs and community-based organisations in touch with relevant state departments. These links and the go-between role of the Trust are vital. (The Trust acts as a sort of 'help desk' during and in the follow-up to the project.)

Improvements in production formed only part of the vision of the IGWDP. In many respects, a more important part was the strengthening of local people's capacity to act collectively. Natural resource management involves essentially political questions within and between villages and with various levels of the administration. Progress cannot be made through local-level initiatives alone. Governments provide technical support services and also much of the fabric necessary in the form of legal and administrative systems. Local organisations have to be able to engage with government in order to draw on these services and systems in ways that meet their needs.

The NGO perception of scaling-up recognises that it is about relationship building, not just replication of technologies or approaches but expansion of principles and knowledge, such that people build capacity to make better decisions and influence the decision making of others.[18] However, the 'learning process' approach generally proceeds through three slow stages: learning to be effective (with emphasis on building interpersonal relationships), learning to be efficient (withdrawal from individual sites) and learning to expand (but focussed on local organisational development rather than policy and institutional arrangements). The NGO bottom-up way of thinking tends to be try a project, have success and only then think about scaling-up. It is often only at this point that NGOs start to develop relations with government agencies and start to form strategies for sustaining the momentum. For local success to have a high chance of widescale uptake, collaborative planning from the outset between NGOs and the government is necessary. Only through this can social change and people empowerment occur in a meaningful and lasting way.

The keys to widespread uptake

- Recognise that widespread uptake requires building relationships between local actors and national or regional actors.
- Innovation is not the exclusive prerogative of the on-station researcher. New technologies and even crops are likely to be developed in farmers' fields. Capturing this potential has to be seen as part of a knowledge management framework extending to all actors in a natural resource management system.
- The building of relationships of trust and mutual respect between scientists, political and social institutions, communities and the individual resource manager is fundamental to the spread of innovation.

---

[18] Gonsalves, *Highlights of the Workshop Going to Scale.*

- The spread of innovations will rarely be achieved by actions at a single level of organisation. Community NGOs, government agencies and international development NGOs and research institutes will have differing but complementary roles to play.
- Information management tools, especially GIS, can help to identify opportunities, avoid errors and generally lead to a better understanding of options for the spread of innovation.
- Experimenting, learning and adaptation by individual resource managers is an essential and fundamental part of the process of achieving widespread adoption.
- Planning for dissemination and widespread adoption has to be initiated in the design of projects.

10   Measuring the performance of natural resource systems

Researchers have finite resources and will seek to allocate these most efficiently. Therefore, they need to identify and assess priorities for research, monitor the progress of on-going research and evaluate the impacts of completed research. This is a difficult enough process in highly focussed technological research projects, but it is even more of a challenge for complex natural resource systems. The scale and complexity of assessment expands with the complexity of the system. Impact assessment for natural resources research requires quite different approaches to those used for technology improvement research.[1] In this chapter we argue for a different vision of the role and nature of impact assessment. We suggest that impact assessment should be an integral feature of natural resources research. We show how various approaches to impact assessment can be fundamental tools for adaptation, learning and performance enhancement, providing data for further negotiation amongst stakeholders as well as for resource allocation decisions.

Our review of approaches to impact assessment in natural resources research has major implications for the way such research is organised. It strengthens the case for viewing research and management as part of a continuum with effective flows of information and ideas along a chain from the 'hi-tech' laboratory to the resource manager (Chapter 11). We find the ideas of Roussel and colleagues on *Third Generation R&D* very relevant to the natural resource management situation.[2] They argue that research should not be an independent service that delivers ready-made technologies to resource managers; instead researchers should work with the resource managers to broaden the range of options open to them and enhance their ability to make decisions and to innovate. For natural resources research, this implies that instead of focussing on a simple analysis of how one technological change impacts on one factor of production, the focus should be on

[1] Campbell, B., Sayer, J. A., Frost, P. *et al*. Assessing the performance of natural resource systems. *Conservation Ecology*, **5** (2001), 22. Online: http://www.consecol.org/vol5/iss2/art22.

[2] Roussel, P. P., Saad, K. N. and Erickson, T. J. *Third Generation R&D: Managing the Link to Corporate Strategy*. Boston, MA: Harvard Business School Press, 1991.

Table 10.1. *Key problems faced in impact assessment for natural resource management research*

Problem/characteristic	Way forward	Comments
1. Natural resource management systems are complex (multi-scales, multi-stakeholders, multi-sectoral; they are subject to feedbacks, time delays and non-linearity)	Clarify the objectives, scale of the research and particular intervention possibilities. Recognise that most natural resource systems are not isolated entities and cannot be rigidly controlled	While any reference to 'clarification of objectives' is self-evident, it does stress the fact that impact assessment is an integral part of the whole research and learning cycle
	Develop a conceptual model that simplifies the system and makes explicit the key components and interactions	This conceptual model would be at the level of the particular system being studied (e.g. it could be based on a site like Chivi; Fig. 5.5, p. 115)
	Ensure careful indicator selection – covering different scales; basing selection on the sustainable livelihoods approach	There is a need to strike the balance between simplicity and complexity
2. Feedback, time delays and non-linearity mean that impact measurement within the project duration is often not possible	Develop simulation models as part of the impact assessment procedure; develop post-project back-up (e.g. the help desk described in Box 9.1, p. 207)	Simulation modelling may be the only way to explore the impact of research in some natural resource management systems
3. Participation is central to natural resource management, but external actors may have very different objectives from local stakeholders	Incorporate participatory impact assessment as well as more conventional systems	The participatory component is an ingredient in a feedback or learning process that is likely to increase the effectiveness of natural resource management
4. Natural resource management is context specific and yet for general lessons cross-site comparability is needed	Situate natural resource management sites within a landscape or resource management domain typology	
5. Remaining integrated in the face of numerous indicators is a challenge	Use techniques that can synthesise the numerous indicators that may have been measured: multivariate statistics, radar diagrams	

From Campbell *et al.* See footnote 1.

organising research so that it contributes to innovation and decision making throughout the natural resource system. Impact assessment should not focus on the delivery of a technological package but should examine the pathways[3] through which innovations influence the different actors who are managing the resource. The nature of these impact pathways and of the changes in the resource system that research hopes to promote must be central to the research process from the moment that the researchers first begin to contact the resource users or decision makers who are their clients. Impact assessment is thus part of the learning cycle that research is aiming to strengthen (Box 10.1). Some key problems that have to be tackled in this approach are summarised in Table 10.1.

Box 10.1. Learning together for improved conservation tillage in Zimbabwe

In the work of Jürgen Hagmann and colleagues, the goal of improving farmers' livelihoods was the 'guiding star' for steering the process.[1] This 'impact orientation' made the researchers develop an explicit strategy on how to achieve impact. The strategy, and accordingly the approaches, methods and activities, was adapted regularly in response to feedback from the researchers and the resource users. This was based on farmers' assessment of their own achievements, the farmers' assessment of the researchers' performance and the researchers' own self-evaluation. So, in this case, 'impact' monitoring and assessment was an internalised process for learning, reflecting and adjusting in order to improve both the researchers' and the farmers' performance. It was not an external assessment of the research impacts. The focus was on learning; therefore, monitoring and self-evaluation was an integral part of the action research loop at different levels. The guiding question to design impact monitoring was: 'Who wants to learn what and at what level?' Therefore, farmers monitored their activities and experiments and their social implications whilst researchers monitored the effectiveness of their intervention in enhancing these processes among farmers. For each of the superimposed learning loops of different actors and objectives, a set of performance criteria was defined.

The impact monitoring and assessment consisted of two elements: process monitoring and outcome monitoring. 'Mid-season evaluations' were conducted in the field where farmers and researchers together evaluated activities and technologies. In addition, annual reviews and self-evaluation exercises were conducted in the communities and also amongst members of the research and development team. The self-evaluation led to the readjustment of the strategy and the replanning of activities.

---

[3]Spilsbury, M. J. CIFOR: using a 'systems' approach to research evaluation. In *The Future of Impact Assessment in the CGIAR: Needs, Constraints and Options. A Workshop of the Standing Panel on Impact Assessment (SPIA) of the Technical Advisory Committee*, 3–5 May. Rome: Food and Agriculture Organization of the United Nations, 2001, pp. 11–17. Online: http://www.cgiar.org/tac/spia0500/cifor.pdf.

Process documentation ('writing the journal') was central to the researchers' own learning. It made their decisions transparent and helped external project evaluators to monitor their activities while giving the researchers the freedom to change continuously the planning framework. In an evaluation in 1995, the reviewers came to the conclusion that it was fortunate that the researchers had not rigidly followed the log-frame that had been developed at the beginning of the project. The team had responded to unforeseen opportunities and problems and had generated substantial impact. However, if they had not documented the process well, the danger of being derailed by external evaluations would have been high.

In the same evaluation, the reviewers were most impressed by the confidence, creativity, adaptability, commitment and social energy displayed by farmers when articulating and demonstrating the results of the project. Although there were numerous technologies developed and tested, the human capital was the strongest factor in convincing outsiders (research managers, policy-makers, etc.) of the success of the approach.

The performance indicators for processes were measures of human values such as empathy, confidence, self-esteem, creativity and social energy. Ultimately, it is the human dimension that makes the wheels of resource management turn.

This framework for assessing performance leaves many questions unanswered. How can one make an independent evaluation of the quality of a strategy or of process implementation? The external assessor will have to exercise judgement on the plausibility of strategies for dissemination of results, the effectiveness of coordination and convening processes and ultimately the legitimacy of the value systems employed. This approach to impact assessment implies a shift in emphasis from technology adoption or yield increases to assessment of changes in people's behaviour and their ability to learn and adapt.

[1] Hagmann, J. R., Chuma, E., Murwira, K., Connolly, M. and Ficarelli, P. Success factors in integrated natural resource management R&D: lessons from practice. *Conservation Ecology*, **5** (2002), 29. Online: http://www.consecol.org/vol5/iss2/art29.

Conceptualising the system: dealing with connectivity

Even when management objectives are relatively clear (e.g. 'sustainability' or 'equitable distribution' of benefits), the choice of impact indicators will depend upon the scale at which management takes place and the scale at which prevailing social and economic processes operate. Impacts may manifest at a higher spatial or longer temporal scale from that primarily being targeted. Additionally, impacts might be assessed as being negative at one scale but positive at another. For example, plantation managers may have to choose to reduce short-term yields at the scale of the management unit in order to obtain positive impacts at a larger scale over longer periods by reducing runoff and erosion or by enhancing biodiversity at a landscape scale. What, then, is the most appropriate level at which to judge the overall benefits? The answer depends on what types of impact are anticipated, the objectives of a specific assessment, the time scale used and the level of accuracy required. Ultimately, the value system that is chosen will add a dimension of subjectivity. Our conclusion is that research planning must go beyond the production of the research outputs and consider, from the outset, strategies to optimise impacts across the entire set of potential scales.

The use of impact assessment to focus research and allocate research resources is only possible in terms of clearly stated objectives, a well-reasoned definition of spatial and temporal scales and clear identification of particular intervention possibilities. The key to bounding of the problem lies once again in the strength of the conceptual model.[4] Using impact assessment as a tool for learning and innovation does not require that precise objectives be determined in advance. It simply requires that changes in important attributes of the system can be tracked and the causes of these changes understood. The selection of important attributes and of the sorts of changes that are desirable must be the subject of negotiation amongst stakeholders.

Selecting indicators

The literature indicates that there is no shortage of different indicators; in fact, the wealth of indicators is likely to mystify rather than enlighten. Consequently, the process of selection of indicators is a key step to be initiated early in the research process. One promising option is to base impact assessment on the sustainable livelihood concept. The concept integrates social, economic and ecological dimensions.[5] Robert Chambers and Gordon Conway regard sustainable livelihoods as comprising (i) the capabilities of individuals, (ii) the assets (including both material and social resources) that can be used by those individuals and households, and (iii) the resulting activities that are carried out. Five capital assets are often recognised: physical, financial, social, natural and human (Fig. 10.1).[6] However, some authors argue that financial and social capital should not be considered; for instance, they argue that financial capital reflects the values of other

---

[4]Examples of conceptual models are given in Figs. 5.1. and 5.5.

[5]Chambers, R. and Conway, G. *IDS Discussion Paper 296: Sustainable Rural Livelihoods. Practical Concepts for the 21st century.* Brighton: Institute for Development Studies, 1992.

[6]Modified from Bebbington, A. Capitals and capabilities: a framework for analysing peasant viability, rural livelihoods and poverty. *World Development*, **26** (1999), 2021–2044; Carney, D. *Sustainable Rural Livelihoods. What Contribution Can We Make?* London: Department for International Development, 1998.

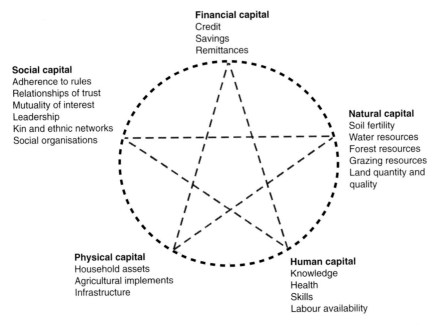

Financial capital
Credit
Savings
Remittances

Social capital
Adherence to rules
Relationships of trust
Mutuality of interest
Leadership
Kin and ethnic networks
Social organisations

Natural capital
Soil fertility
Water resources
Forest resources
Grazing resources
Land quantity and
quality

Physical capital
Household assets
Agricultural implements
Infrastructure

Human capital
Knowledge
Health
Skills
Labour availability

Fig. 10.1. The five capital assets. (Modified from Bebbington 1999. See footnote 6.)

capitals and has no value per se.[7] Principles for each of the five capital assets can be derived (Table 10.2.), and indicators could be selected to cover each of the principles. The tendency to bias indicator selection to one particular discipline is thus avoided. The advantage of using the sustainable livelihood concept is that it has been vigorously debated in the literature, and provides a framework for indicator selection.

Selecting and categorising indicators and organising them under principles should be done in ways that take account of the dynamic nature of the system. Over time, the desirable outcomes of management may change and this will require that indicators be modified. This brings back the importance of conceptual models, especially those stressing the dynamic nature of the system. Figure 10.2 illustrates that the capital assets are intimately linked to one another and focusses our attention on the dynamic nature of natural resource systems. Such a framework shows the interconnectedness of indicators in a dynamic system.

---

[7]See, for instance, Dasgupta, P. and Maler, K-M. *Beijer Institute Discussion Paper 139: Wealth as a criterion for Sustainable Development.* Stockholm: Beijer Institute, 2001; Pearce, D., Hamilton, K. and Atkinson, G. Measuring sustainable development: progress on indicators. *Environment and Development Economics* **1** (1996), 85–101; Hamilton, K. and Clemens, M. Genuine savings rates in developing countries. *World Bank Economic Review,* **13** (1999), 333–356.

Table 10.2. *Some suggested principles for each of the capital assets, with examples of criteria for each of the principles; The example is for illustrative purposes only*

Capital asset	Principle	An example of a criterion for each of the principles
Natural capital	Options for future use are maintained	Processes that maintain biodiversity are conserved
	Yield and quality of natural resource goods and services is maintained or improved	Ecosystem function is maintained
Financial capital	Financial capital is circulated within the system	Service and commodity outlets expand in the local and district centres
	Financial capital grows and is equitably distributed	Residents have a reasonable share in the economic benefits derived from resource use
Physical capital	Physical capital is maintained or improved over time	Housing condition is maintained or improved
Human capital	Ability to provide added value is improved over time	Greater array of added-value products are produced locally
	Improved and equitable distribution of human capital	Level of skills with respect to running committees and organisations is improved
Social capital	Maintenance of systems of social reciprocity	Economic and other shocks are buffered by systems of social reciprocity
	Maintenance of a set of dynamic rules and norms	Local rules are effective in controlling access to resources

In order to measure the performance of natural resource systems, the indicators selected must cover the full spectrum of capital assets. For example, financial capital may be very low because it has been invested in developing human and physical capital. The system then may be judged to be more acceptable than systems in which financial capital is higher but in which no financial resources have been transferred into other capital assets and natural, human, social and physical capital are depleted. There will be thresholds that the different capitals must not pass. For instance, spectacular growth in financial capital will not be sustainable if the other capitals are seriously depleted. Many of the problems of 'under-development' exist

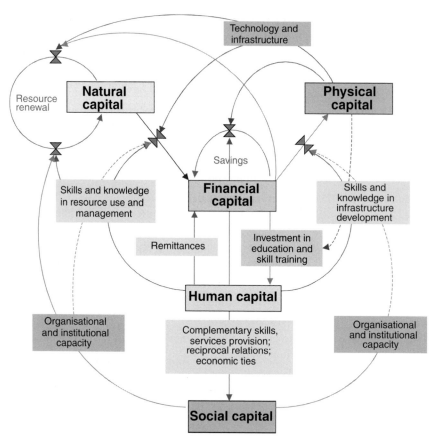

Fig. 10.2. The dynamic nature of capital assets. (From Campbell *et al.* See footnote 1.)

because natural capitals such as oil, minerals and forests have been converted into financial capital that has then been appropriated by the elite. Natural capital has been liquidated without any corresponding investment in education, health, infrastructure, etc. Financial capital is thereby maximised but human, social and physical capitals are depleted.

Simple indicator sets are desirable, but it would be foolish to expect simplicity when dealing with complex systems.[8] The process of examining potential indicators for each type of capital and each component of people's livelihoods will itself force the researcher and manager to ensure that their

[8]Pachico, D., Ashby, J., Farrow, A., Fujisaka, S., Johnson, N. and Winograd, M. Case study and empirical evidence for assessing natural resource management research: the experience of CIAT. In *Proceedings of a Workshop on Assessing Impacts in Natural Resource Management Research*, 27–29 April, 1999. Nairobi: World Agroforestry Centre.

activities are indeed addressing the natural resource problem in an integrated way.

Hierarchy theory indicates that work at a particular scale of organisation often requires insights from at least two other scales.[9] Thus work at the farm or household level may require component studies at lower levels, such as the plot level or the intrahousehold level, to understand the important processes that lead to outcomes at the household level. Similarly, work at the household level will also require work at higher levels, for example on the institutional framework established by local government. In the case of the ecological–economic simulation model of Mzola State Forest in Zimbabwe (see Fig. 10.3, below), much of the ecological work for establishing the model was derived from process-level work at the plot level.[10] The model outputs were more useful at the landscape and community level (e.g. the number of fires in the state forest, the value of goods and services derived under various scenarios). Natural resource assessment will invariably require that indicators be selected from at least two scales (Box 10.2).

Box 10.2. Criteria and indicators at the Chivi catchment area in Zimbabwe

Work at the Chivi catchment in Zimbabwe (Chapter 6) illustrates the fact that criteria and indicators attempting to capture similar phenomena vary according to the scale of analysis (Table 10.3.).[1] Much of the work in Chivi is being conducted at the scale of a 4.5 km² micro-catchment. This catchment contains a single well, but the social catchment for the well extends beyond the focus catchment into others, one of which supports a small dam. In spite of the focus on the micro-catchment, scale issues are being considered, both for larger biophysical units (e.g. what are the downstream impacts of the developments in the micro-catchments) and for larger institutional scales (e.g. how do the three traditional villages in the micro-catchment interact with the larger administrative units, up to the district level government, and with water governance units established at national, catchment and subcatchment levels). At lower scales, some key processes are being studied, for example tree–soil–water relations because trees are thought to be a major cause of groundwater recession in the catchment.

[1]Campbell, B., Sayer, J. A., Frost, P. *et al.* Assessing the performance of natural resource systems. *Conservation Ecology*, **5** (2001), 22. Online: http://www.consecol.org/vol5/iss2/art22.

---

[9]Allan, T. F. H. and Starr, T. B. *Hierarchy Perspectives for Ecological Complexity.* Chicago, IL: University of Chicago Press, 1982; Noss, R. F. Indicators for monitoring biodiversity: a hierarchical approach. *Conservation Biology*, **4** (1990), 355–364.

[10]Gambiza, J., Bond, W., Frost, P. and Higgins, S. A simulation model of miombo woodland dynamics under different management regimes. *Ecological Economics*, **33** (2000), 353–368.

Table 10.3. *Different scales at the Chivi site and some potential criteria for those scales, with one criterion shown for each of five capital assets*

| Principles for each capital asset | Potential criteria | | |
	Household/farm fields	Village/micro-catchments	District
Natural capital: yield and quality of natural resource goods and services is maintained or improved	Soil fertility in garden fields is maintained or improved	Groundwater resources for community well are maintained or improved	Siltation levels in main dams are reduced
Financial capital grows and is equitably distributed	Household savings grow and are equitably distributed	Micro-credit scheme is maintained and expanded	Council budgets increase
Physical capital is maintained or improved over time	Housing condition is maintained or improved	Water availability is improved	Road infrastructure is maintained or improved
Improved and equitable distribution of human capital	Educational status of households improves	Level of skills with respect to running committees and organisations is improved	Budgetary control is maintained and improved
Social capital: maintenance of a set of dynamic rules and norms		Local rules are effective in controlling access to resources	Leadership at the district level is respected

The impact assessment of resource management research will invariably include a qualitative component. Conventional monitoring systems often only help to inform us of outcomes that are expected or predictable. An outcome that was not predicted at the beginning of a research programme may not be revealed by a monitoring system.[11] In 1981, it would have been difficult to predict that gold panning would become one of the most important livelihood options in Chivi by the end of the decade. Similarly, nobody

[11] Pachico *et al.*, Case study and empirical evidence for assessing natural resource management research.

predicted that there would be a nearly fourfold increase of woodcraft markets after 1991 and that AIDS would wreak havoc in the community in the last five years of the millennium. End of project assessments may have to rely on qualitative indicators for unexpected phenomena that have occurred and for which quantitative data were not recorded during the project. Just as it is normal for the objectives of a resource management programme to change with time, so it is inevitable that indicator sets will need to be reviewed and adapted continuously. Indicators can be valuable as a basis for negotiation amongst interest groups about exactly which outcomes are desirable and for whom.

During the course of research, local people's feelings about the direction of change can be recorded (given that outcomes may only be measurable many years after the research has been completed). By capturing local people's perspectives, albeit often qualitative, we can integrate numerous variables. The political arena in any local venture is highly charged, and researchers are stakeholders with particular agendas that are being challenged and modified by local people. It, therefore, becomes particularly important for impact assessment to be informed by anthropological perspectives, which are often based upon qualitative data.

Incorporating simulation modelling

Research outcomes can be most simply defined as the difference between what happened as a consequence of the research activity and what would have happened anyway. In many cases, baseline data are collected at the start of a project in order to assess the impact. This is an inadequate approach, as the baseline data do not reflect the dynamics of 'what would have happened anyway'. Alternatively, impact assessment could be based on large-scale experimentation (i.e. implementing components of a programme in some localities but not in others), in conjunction with a statistical sampling programme. Such an approach is also unrealistic given the high expense.[12] The dynamism of natural resource management systems, and the fact that large-scale experimentation is usually not feasible, means that one of the few solutions for impact assessment is simulation modelling.

In terms of the learning cycle, simulation modelling should be implemented soon after the initiation of the research with data inputs being best estimates and the modelling results being used to set priorities and guide the action phase of the work. In the evaluation phase of the learning

[12] Walters, C. Challenges in adaptive management of riparian and coastal ecosystems. *Conservation Ecology*, **1** (1997), 1. Online: http://www.consecol.org/vol1/iss2/art1.

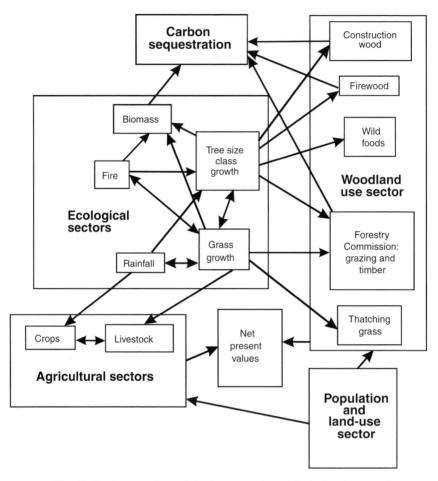

Fig. 10.3. An overview of the integrated model of a land use and forestry system built at a two-week workshop and subsequently refined, using STELLA (see footnote 13). The model was produced for the Mzola State Forest and surrounding communal areas, and was used to investigate the economic and ecological impacts of joint management.

cycle, the simulation model then becomes a tool for evaluation with more of the data needs satisfied and the modelling results then being used as a component for impact assessment. Models can help in the understanding of the counterfactual, what might have happened without the project (Fig. 10.3).[13]

[13]Campbell, B. M., Costanza, R. and van den Belt, M. Land use options in dry tropical woodland ecosystems in Zimbabwe: introduction, overview and synthesis. *Ecological Economics*, **33** (2000), 341–352.

Participatory approaches to assessment

Throughout this book, we have argued for a participatory approach within any natural resource management activity, and impact assessment is no exception. There is an extensive literature on participatory impact monitoring and the process by which indicators are identified and used.[14] Participatory impact assessment becomes a vital ingredient in a feedback or learning process that, in turn, increases the effectiveness of participatory natural resource management.[15] The Landcare programme in Australia (Chapter 9) is an example in which conservation extension groups involving a broad cross-section of rural people with a stake in catchment planning are using spatial modelling and remote sensing for monitoring and impact assessment. For researchers, pragmatism suggests using a participatory approach as it provides a cost-effective alternative to expensive statistical sampling programmes.

In participatory monitoring, local stakeholders must be involved both in the design of the monitoring system, including the selection of indicators,[16] and in the collection of information. Therefore, a fundamental aspect of the design and use of indicators requires negotiating a common framework that allows for maximal overlap between the information and the interests of the concerned stakeholders.

Local systems of monitoring can be rich in detail and incorporate indicators that satisfy several of the information demands of complex systems. There is, however, one fundamental problem with local information systems: they are developed in the context of a community of local users. By definition, the community has shared interests and paradigms and manages resources they consider their own. They will tend to exclude the needs and demands of other stakeholders. Consequently, feedback from off-site users may be inadequately captured. For example, downstream hydrological impacts or global biodiversity values may not be given sufficient consideration. It is important to ensure that planning takes account of external demands and needs. Assumptions about rights must be rigorously examined and the language and idiom of communication must not shut out external stakeholders.

For particular components of the system, detailed data may be required to assess the impact of natural resource management. The data may be more or less meaningless without further analysis (e.g. they may

---

[14] Abbot, J. and Guijt, I. *SARL Discussion Paper 2: Changing Views on Change: Participatory Approaches to Monitoring the Environment.* London: International Institute for Environmental Development, 1998.

[15] Pachico *et al.*, Case study and empirical evidence for assessing natural resource management research.

[16] Meadows, D. H. *Indicators and Information Systems for Sustainable Development. A report to the Balaton Group.* Hartland Four Corners: Sustainability Institute, 1998.

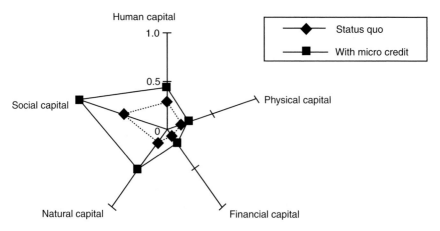

Fig. 10.4. Radar diagram showing the impact of micro-credit on the capital assets in a small catchment in southern Zimbabwe. The greatest changes were in relation to social capital (building community cooperative mechanisms). (From Campbell *et al.*, 2001. See footnote 1.)

act as points to calibrate a simulation model). To expect a community to participate in data collection that requires a considerable time outlay, without clear benefits to them, is unrealistic. In the Chivi site (Chapter 6) local people were hired to collect hydrological data that were considered key to assessing the impacts of land-use. The local monitors benefitted financially from this work and used some of the information to change their own activities or to convince others to change; however, they would not collect such information without financial reward. Thus, while we see a component of the assessment of natural resource management being undertaken within a participatory framework; other components would involve more formal data collection systems.

Integration of indicators

Given that a number of indicators are necessary for assessing impact, often at a variety of spatial and temporal scales, the question then becomes whether these can give an integrative summary of change in system performance across scales. By using simulation models, in which criteria are explicitly linked, some degree of integration will be achieved. We have examined further methods, not mutually exclusive, that can assist in ensuring integration.[17] These include simple additive indices in which indicators

[17] Campbell *et al.* Assessing the performance of natural resource systems.

are combined and derived indices in which principal components analysis is used to combine indicators. Indicator integration can also be visualised using two-dimensional plots derived from principal components analysis or radar diagrams (Fig. 10.4).

Keys to successful evaluation

Under most circumstances, it is not simple to measure impacts of research; however, in complex natural resource systems the difficulties are particularly great. If impact assessment frameworks are well conceived they should render the research more efficient and may reduce data requirements by suggesting redundancies in the overall research process. This approach is a radical departure from conventional impact assessment studies as they have been applied to agricultural research.

- Many of the components of impact assessment need to be initiated at the start of the learning cycle, e.g. bounding the system, developing a conceptual framework, selecting indicators and initiating the development of a simulation model.
- Given the numerous external influences on natural resource systems, just viewing the indicator data collected from the field may prove meaningless; it will be essential to integrate impact assessment with simulation modelling.
- Measuring system performance should be seen as central to the adaptive learning process rather than as an evaluation for external purposes. This has a number of implications, most notably the need for constant iteration between research, management practice and evaluation.
- To ensure a broad evaluation of a system, a sustainable livelihoods perspective is recommended.
- The approach to impact assessment should move from assessing technology adoption to assessing change in people's behaviour and their ability to learn and adapt.

11   Achieving research-based management

Science alone will not solve the problems of natural resource management. However, science has a role to play and there is an urgent need to strengthen the scientific basis for practical management programmes. Yet the potential for science-based management will not be realised simply by investing more resources in conventional research structures and approaches. On-station research that delivers fully fashioned products to be made available 'to whom it may concern' and that proceeds independently of day-to-day resource management has to be relegated to history. Richard Bell, a researcher-turned-manager who worked for many years in conservation programmes in southern Africa, pointed out that much natural resource management always has proceeded without the benefit of formal research. Research is expensive in time, money, equipment and trained personnel. Resources are limited – is research, therefore, really necessary? Bell's reply is that it is, but only under a new definition of the role of research. This role is to improve the understanding of the complex ecological, economic and social systems in which natural resource management operates. This, claims Bell, will allow management agencies to achieve their objectives more effectively. Research, in Bell's view, must become part of management. Yet focussing research efforts solely on those areas known to be of interest to management – biological inventories for example – may exclude scientific applications with potentially high pay-offs. Bell concludes:

> We can't tell in advance what research will turn up. So managing science is akin to gambling, a blend of caution and inspired rashness; it is best to study the form, hedge one's bets and play the occasional wild card. The idea is to formalise trial and error. Natural resource management requires a mastery of diverse disciplines – ecology, sociology, economics and so on. The relationship of resource management to those disciplines is exceedingly complex and poorly understood. Therefore managers operate in an environment where the outcomes of their actions are uncertain. Managers must adapt to these uncertainties, looking on everything that they do as a trial, with the appropriate recording of procedures and

monitoring of results. Management thereby becomes a type of research. This collision of opposites produces a vigorous hybrid of manager and researcher.[1]

However this vision requires a complete rethinking of the professions of resource managers and scientists.

Research cannot solve or bypass some of the intractable obstacles to improved resource management. In many countries, property and resource access rights are poorly defined or not easily defended through the law. In these situations, good resource management is difficult to achieve. Good resource management appears to be much more likely in countries with stronger economies and effective democratic processes. (This applies to impacts within the national jurisdiction; there are many examples of negative impacts from such countries on global commons such as the atmosphere or fisheries.) Many initiatives to improve natural resource management have come from 'civil society', citizen's groups rebelling at the injustice of bad resource management. These arguments have led many to claim that the key to better natural resource management is 'governance' and that science has a secondary and purely technological contribution to make.

We argue differently. We believe that science, the generation of better knowledge and the wide dissemination of knowledge and information are themselves key processes in the emergence of stronger civil societies and hence of democracy. These are essential foundations for the more equitable and sustainable management of natural resources. It is not by chance that political change in countries such as Thailand in the 1960s and Indonesia in the 1990s was partly stimulated by environmental groups protesting the inequities of bad and inequitable resource management. Science cannot provide all the answers but we believe that the right sort of science can be a major force for the emergence of the institutions and governance structures that are essential for good resource management.

There is a strong correlation between bad governance and bad resource management. Many major natural resource management crises are in badly governed countries. Amartya Sen has shown that famines never occur in democratic countries, for the same reasons chronic resource degradation does not occur in these countries.[2] The coming decades will see an intensification of the pressures on land in many poor countries. In many places, populations appear set to increase and resource endowments will be

[1] This quote is adapted from Adams, J. S. and McShane, T. O. *The Myth of Wild Africa*. New York: Norton, 1992.
[2] Sen, A. Democracy as a universal value. *Journal of Democracy* **10** (1999), 3–17. Online: http://muse.jhu.edu/demo/jod/10.3sen.html.

degraded. In other places, the elite is appropriating resources through corrupt practices. This results in resource degradation and few resource benefits to the poor. Such countries will either sink into a vortex of increased poverty and environmental destruction or they will have to establish good governance structures and use these to eliminate corruption. The latter is likely if science and society move forward in harmony. The revolutions in resource management are often not occurring as a result of actions from the top – from government research agencies or resource management organisations. They are coming from local action by groups of resource users, often energised by non-governmental organisations (NGOs); the best ones are those that have arisen spontaneously in response to local needs.

It is notable that many of the examples of science supporting improved resource management have occurred in spite of, not because of, the plans and policies of government agencies. Most of the new insights into better social organisation and better technologies for resource management have arisen through the work of individual scientists or resource users self-organising for change. Successful development projects are ones that have nurtured and accompanied local change processes rather than those that have sought to impose technological solutions. The work of Jürgen Hagmann and his colleagues in Zimbabwe (described in Chapter 3 and Box 10.1 (p. 213)) is an example of how development assistance can accompany a local initiative. Successful resource management practitioners are those who have been good at listening to and empathising with resource users; they have used their scientific skills to improve the available options for management and to empower households and communities. Most of the examples cited in this book come from poor countries in the south. However, in industrialised countries, the situation has evolved along similar lines. Initiatives for nature conservation and environmental protection legislation in Europe came from concerned citizens groups and only later did governments set up environment agencies and national parks. Even today, governments lag behind civil society in their willingness to accept the need for measures to protect natural resources. The examples of persistent organochlorinated pesticides in the 1950s and 1960s and later the problems of acid rain in the forests of North America and Europe are salutary.

So we see the processes of democratisation of societies as being inextricably linked to the processes of democratisation of science. In forestry and agriculture, the public sector research institutes have at times been an obstacle to the sort of changes that are needed. Almost none of the innovative science described in this book has come from the 'top down'; almost all has come from the 'bottom up', from concerned scientists working with and learning from the users of the resources. The erstwhile 'clients' of

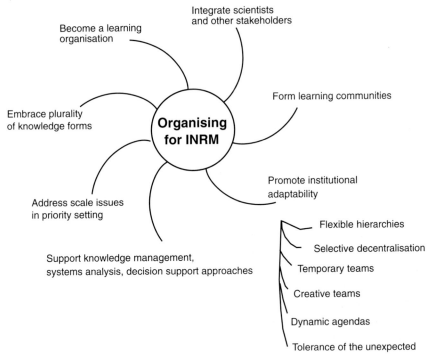

Fig. 11.1. Proposed characteristics of organisations undertaking integrated natural resource research and management (INRM). (Based on Ashby 2001. See footnote 3.)

the researchers have become their 'partners' and, in the words of Jürgen Hagmann, they have proceeded to 'learn and innovate together'.

The integrated approaches to natural resource management, as described in this volume, will require major changes in the culture and organisation of research (Fig. 11.1).[3] There are many parallels with developments in other branches of science where management has to deal with a future that is unknowable. This is the science that deals with non-equilibrium conditions, multiple aspirations and ambiguity. So, just as we see improved resource management being built on a process of social learning, so we see the need for organisations involved in natural resource management to be learning organisations. This means that top management promotes organisational flexibility and a culture favourable to learning, interaction of scientists with other stakeholders, experimentation and adaptability.

[3] Ashby, J. A. Integrating research on food and the environment: an exit strategy from the rational fool syndrome in agricultural science. *Conservation Ecology*, **5**(2000), 20. Online: http://www.consecol.org/vol5/iss2/art20.

Many of the arguments used in this book mirror the emerging paradigms for knowledge-based organisations that are at the cutting edge of the management science taught in business schools. Many of the problems of managing complex natural resource systems are similar to those of running a commercial company in a rapidly changing world. Yet, agricultural, forestry and other resource-based organisations have mostly evolved to deal with much simpler and more predictable conditions. They now have to change. Reconciling the need for increased supplies of food and fibres with the need to maintain the environment and to do this in a way that can bring a billion people out of absolute poverty is not a problem that can be solved by command and control science. We need a predictive science that can enable us to produce more goods and services, to do so sustainably and to do so on the basis of a limited and sometimes declining resource base: this is the modern science of natural resource management.

Integrated natural resource management research should lead to tangible impacts on the ground. If, however, we continue to evaluate the 'impact' of our research and development simply on the basis of the spread of specific technologies, we are likely to misdirect our efforts. Supporting farmers as managers may mean that informed non-adoption or adaptation-beyond-recognition may be better signs of success than reluctant adoption of a ready-made technology. If improving the ability of natural resource managers at all hierarchical levels is our target, we should measure our success and failure according to the adaptive learning capacity that our research fosters.

Ultimately, the value of science lies in its ability to improve decisions and negotiations by providing better (not necessarily more!) information to the various stakeholders so that more alternatives can be generated and evaluated. This runs counter to the conventional scientific value system where solutions are often selected that bear little relation to local stakeholders' perceptions of the problem. More equal access to information for the various stakeholders and a process where transparency becomes a requirement in public debate is essential if the information that we contribute is to be of actual value in the negotiation process.

In the process of researching this book, we have sought examples of successful organisational structures for science-based integrated natural resource management. We have found few that meet all of our criteria. None of these were in the developing world. One model that we do find attractive and that could be applied in developing country situations is that of the Wet Tropics Management Authority in North Queensland, Australia. Its essential features are outlined in Box 11.1.

Box 11.1. The Queensland Wet Tropics Management Authority

The rainforests of north Queensland in Australia are of outstanding global importance for their biodiversity. They have high levels of floral and faunal endemism and a unique assemblage of flowering plants of primitive families. The remaining forest areas are subdivided into a mosaic of management units under state and private ownership and subject to the control of numerous government departments. Many of the actual and potential uses of the area are incompatible: 80% of the area is subject to aboriginal land claims that could, in principle, be used to justify land-uses that are incompatible with biodiversity objectives. The original initiative to place the area on the World Heritage List and thus increase its level of protection came from urban-based conservation groups in the cities of the southern states of Australia and was resisted by the Queensland government and many local people. There are international public goods values that, at least until recently, were not considered important by people in the immediate vicinity of the World Heritage area. The protagonists of different uses of the area hold strong views and the situation has been highly charged politically. Minor violence and civil disobedience occurred at the time of the World Heritage listing.

The challenge of handling the negotiations and trade-offs amongst the different stakeholders was met through the establishment of the Wet Tropics Management Authority (WTMA).[1] WTMA has an independent board of six people appointed for their individual competence. The federal authorities and the state each appoint two members. The chief executive officer is jointly appointed by the federal and state authorities and serves as an ex-officio member and the chairman is also jointly appointed. WTMA is jointly funded by the central and state governments and allocates money to support conservation activities undertaken by the different agencies and private landholders operating in the World Heritage area. WTMA prepares management plans that are legally binding and undertakes strategic planning exercises that bring together stakeholders concerned by specific issues. All development plans for the area have to be agreed by WTMA. WTMA facilitates studies and negotiations between stakeholders on such issues as road and power line construction, tourism development, special measures for rare or endangered species, etc.

Special initiatives are being undertaken to facilitate the resolution of issues that may arise from aboriginal land claims. Aboriginals are being trained to facilitate discussions to explore economic activities based upon the natural values of the area for the benefit of the aboriginal people. Major disagreements exist as to the extent to which traditional hunting and gathering activities of aboriginals and commercial tourist development are compatible with conservation objectives.

The WTMA has been relatively successful in defusing the potential for conflict between all the objectives of the divergent stakeholders. Its perceived neutrality, ability to provide funding and broker deals and strong legal mandate have been key elements in its success. However, success has come during a period of dramatic growth in tourism revenues, which have boosted the local economy for the benefit of all. There were also generous compensation payments to loggers and farmers whose incomes were reduced by conservation measures. The WTMA model has potential for application in developing country situations, although it would certainly have less validity in situations where regulatory capacity is weaker, extensive areas are in common pool status, where land rights and claims are overlapping and little compensation can be paid.

---

[1]Based upon an interview with Russell Wilkinson, Executive Director of the Wet Tropics Management Authority and on our personal observations and discussions with stakeholders during a one month stay in the area in July 2001.

The democratisation of science

Some of the thinking on the need to overhaul science organisation comes from Jacqueline Ashby of the International Center for Tropical Agronomy (CIAT). She notes in her recent *Conservation Ecology* article that the 'democratization of science may be a prerequisite to improving both the quality of scientific understanding and to obtaining support and credibility for research'.[4] The involvement of extended peer communities in science, including the stakeholders impacted by an environmental problem, is essential when cause and effect relationships are unclear and research methods, and ethical considerations, have a high level of uncertainty.[5] Integrated approaches are changing the context of the debate: this heightens the need to include lay expertise in science and to cease restricting the conduct of research to technical specialists. The inclusion of citizen expertise in the reform of science bureaucracies is essential because integrated research requires a meeting point between different forms of knowledge and cross-fertilisation across diverse knowledge domains. New kinds of research organisation for carrying out research using integrated approaches must show a willingness to respect and use non-scientifically generated knowledge, to value a plurality of knowledge forms (not a unitary consensus) and to be open to engagement with stakeholders' concerns.

Organisational flexibility is required to enable diverse stakeholders to realise a paradigm shift towards integrated research approaches. Research organisations need to be learning organisations able to conduct research that is both strategic and capable of accompanying adaptive management. All interventions in agro-ecosystems must be monitored and the feedback used to adapt management. In this respect, there is a notable lack of fit between

---

[4]Ashby, Integrated research on food and the environment.

[5]Funtowicz, S. O. and Ravtz, J. R. Science for the post-normal age. *Futures,* **25**(1993), 739–55; Irwin, A. *Citizen Science. A Study of People, Expertise and Sustainable Development.* London: Routledge, 1995.

conventional management organisations and the ecosystems where adaptive management is required; some observers see this lack of fit as a 'crisis of organisational learning'.[6]

An important organisational feature needed for implementing integrated approaches is a flexible hierarchy that enables decision-makers to interact at different ecosystem levels. Researchers need to interact with non-scientists involved in extended learning communities. This organisational feature is missing in conventional natural resource science bureaucracies. Mintzberg and McHugh have described organisations with this potential for flexibility and learning as *adhocracies*.[7] An adhocracy is characterised by the production of complex outputs, demanding sophisticated innovation by combinations of experts deployed in temporary teams to work on projects. In an adhocracy, coordination is achieved less by direct supervision, performance controls and rules than by selective decentralisation. Power over different decisions is decentralised in uneven ways and devolved to the relevant source of expertise to deal with the issue at hand.

Various elements of organisational change can create the adhocracy needed for integrated approaches to natural resource science. In an adhocracy, management usually lets patterns of group work emerge in a self-organising way; innovative approaches can take root in improbable places in an organisation and management needs to judge when to 'step in' and support them when their value becomes apparent. Typically, periods with a proliferation of emergent ideas are interspersed with periods of continuity. Thus, management has to create a climate in which a wide variety of approaches can grow, to watch what comes up and to tolerate the unexpected. This organisational approach is consistent with the needs of research linked to the adaptive management of ecosystems.

Many of the organisational features of adhocracy coincide with those identified with learning organisations. For example, Senge defines the characteristics of learning organisations as being '*a willingness to take risks and to experiment, a decentralized decision making process, the use of effective systems for sharing learning and using it in the business and the frequent use of cross-functional work teams*'.[8] Such organisations value opportunities to learn

[6] Folke, C., Pritchard, Jr, L., Berkes, F., Coling, J. and Svedin, U. The problem of fit between ecosystems and institutions. *International Human Dimensions Program on Global Environmental Change Working Paper No 2*. Bonn, Germany: International Human Dimensions Program, 1998. Online: http://www.uni-bonn.de/ihdp/wp02m.htm.

[7] Mintzberg, H. and McHugh, A. Strategy formation in an adhocracy. *Administrative Science Quarterly*, **30**(1985), 160–197.

[8] Senge, P. M. *The Fifth Discipline: The Art and Practice of the Learning Organization*. New York: Doubleday-Currency, 1990.

from experience on a daily basis and foster a culture of feedback, disclosure and collective vision building. Finally, the learning organisation is closely connected to its environment: legislators, regulators, clients, competitors or communities.

The structural reform of science bureaucracies, which have been the home of agricultural, forestry and fishery research over the past 100–150 years, is occurring at breakneck speed in high- and low-income countries alike. This is occurring largely as a result of public disenchantment with, and loss of political support for, conventional agriculture and forestry. New organisational arrangements for integrated approaches to research are emerging spontaneously. Decentralised and networked research groups are organising themselves in order to respond to practical problems. Until recently, research planners and managers were ignoring this tendency. However the Consultative Group for International Agricultural Research and the European Union 6th Framework for Research are now allocating funds in ways that favour the formation of new alliances and consortia amongst researchers from different organisations and disciplines. Continuing research on the organisation of natural resource science is important to the future of ecosystems and human well-being.

The locus of control: local livelihoods versus public goods

Bottrall has discussed the dichotomy of ensuring 'local ownership' at the same time as ensuring equitable distribution and regulation of resources at the larger scale.[9] He has made the point that government departments address issues on a fragmented sector basis, and their attempts to promote the 'integration' of natural resource management tend to have high administrative costs (e.g. interdepartmental committees or new multi-sector units). By contrast, communities find it relatively easy to think and act holistically. The administrative costs of natural resource management will be kept within acceptable limits only by devolving significant management responsibility to community-based organisations and, where possible and appropriate, NGO intermediaries. The challenge is to link government departments effectively with each other and with local-level organisations. Interdepartmental committees are a poor compromise and fail where not properly supported by resources specifically allocated by each department. Instead, government allocations focussed on holistic programmes rather than

[9]Bottrall, A. Institutional aspects of watershed management. In *Proceedings of the Conference on Priorities for Water Resources Management*. Southampton: Overseas Development Administration, Natural Resources and Engineering, 1992, pp. 81–90.

conventional departmental top-ups may help to facilitate the cross-sector interfacing necessary.

The problems of intersector/interministerial collaboration are generally recognised to be easier to overcome through properly established decentralisation. However, this will require adequate capacity at lower and middle levels, and genuine social empowerment through devolution of authority as well as responsibility. Authority for management should be vested at the lowest appropriate level and only delegated upward where absolutely necessary. This resonates with the Catholic Church's dogma of subsidiarity, now much in vogue in European Union politics. The concept has a great deal of merit in defining the hierarchies of organisations needed for good integrated natural resource management. Each level must be functioning properly, and a missing level is essentially a block to information and authority flows. Parachuting to community level, as many external NGOs do, may inhibit the ability to scale-up.

Williams has discussed the emerging challenge of devising local governance arrangements that are supportive of the diverse needs of a variety of users, yet protective of the long-term productive capacity of the natural resource system.[10] In many countries, state property regimes in which central governments exercise exclusive decision-making powers are being de-emphasised in favour of decentralised and participatory management of natural resources. The specific approach used to encourage active local participation varies from one country to another. In some, it has taken the form of legislative reform of land tenure and natural resource management policy. In others, land-use planning based on 'village territories' has become very popular. In certain cases, new self-standing organisations may be created to facilitate the interactions of the various stakeholders (Box 11.1). In all cases, governments have sought to clarify tenure issues and reinforce the rights of local communities to manage their resources through granting of legal recognition and decision-making authority.

Van Zyl emphasised that integrated watershed management must be people centred. He also noted that: *'To succeed in managing . . . managers must be in a position to see the whole picture, understand the resources, the customers, their needs and aspirations and to make wise decisions in the interests of all'*.[11] This is natural resource management viewed from the top: the crucial missing element is the local ownership and incentive to implement those strategies

---

[10] Williams, T. O. Multiple uses of common pool resources in semi-arid West Africa: a survey of existing practices and options for sustainable resource management. *Natural Resource Perspectives 38.* London: ODI Overseas Development Institute, 1998.

[11] van Zyl, F. C. Integrated catchment management: is it wishful thinking or can it succeed? *Water Science and Technology*, **32**(1995), 27–35.

that have been developed through this top-down approach. An alternative view is from the bottom, whereby integrated resource management is seen as a means of scaling-up community-based schemes to the regional or catchment scale. While this approach has advantages in terms of achieving local ownership of the process, it has disadvantages with regard to structure, regulation and equity. For example, communities developing projects in headwater catchments are unlikely to put a high priority on ensuring that the resources of downstream users are not adversely affected.

As Chris Lovell and colleagues argue, the key issue that emerges is the need to link effectively community-based projects within larger, structured programmes.[12] Both are essential but they must be implemented in a package that meets in the middle (Fig. 11.2). Natural resource management needs to occur through a structured programme that provides overall planning, coordination and long-term financial support for activities at regional or local level. Equally it needs to occur at the scale of the common interest groups on contiguous areas of land the boundaries of which may be administrative, social or physical. At this level, the essential features are the *common interest group*, the *development process that facilitates participation in joint action*, and the *structured programme*. The lack of overlap between different physical areas and social groupings associated with the management of different resources can be overcome by this approach, since natural resource management in this participatory sense is at the scale of the common interest groups. The existence of a structured programme allows planning for downstream and off-site effects. While NGOs can often facilitate bottom-up processes, the government should be providing the enabling framework for local action (Table 11.1.).[13]

Elinor Ostrom has demonstrated that governance arrangements for natural resource management must be an appropriate mix of local and state organisations.[14] Assigning increased authority to local users without ascertaining the range of uses of a resource, the diversity of interests among users and the capability of local organisations to take on additional responsibilities will complicate rather than solve the problems.[15] The rights of individuals within legal entities are contractual arrangements that do little to secure

[12]Lovell, C., Mandondo, A. and Moriarty, P. The question of scale in integrated natural resource management. *Conservation Ecology*, **5**(2002), 25. Online: http://www.consecol.org/vol5/iss2/art25.

[13]Ostrom, E. Designing complexity to govern complexity. In *Property Rights and the Environment: Social and Ecological*, ed. S. Hanna and M. Munasinghe. Washington, DC: World Bank, 1995, pp. 33–46.

[14]Williams, T. O. Multiple use of common pool resources.

[15]Gonsalves, J. *Going to Scale: Can we Bring More Benefits to More People More Quickly? Highlights of a Workshop of the CGIAR–NGO Committee and The Global Forum for Agricultural Research with BMZ, MISEREOR, Rockefeller Foundation, IRRI and IIRR*, 10–14 April. Manila, Philippines: IIRR, 2000.

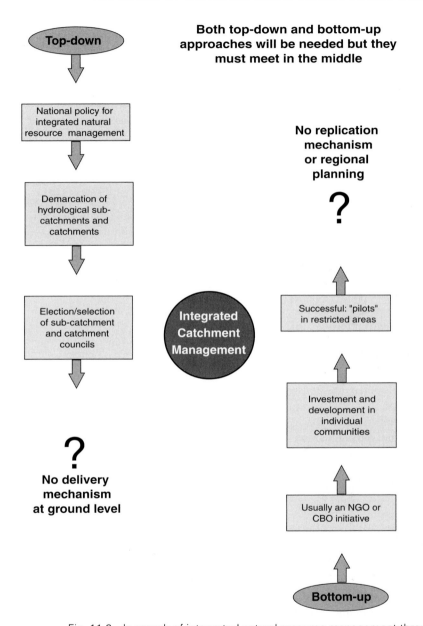

Fig. 11.2. In search of integrated natural resource management through reconciling top-down and bottom-up approaches (applied to catchment management). (NGO, non-government organisation; CBO, community-based organisation.) (From Lovell et al., 2002. See footnote 12.)

Table 11.1. *Undertakings by government and non-governmental organizations (NGOs) to help to bridge the gap between top-down and bottom-up approaches to integrated natural resource management*

On the part of government	On the part of NGOs
Provide a stable, supportive and enabling environment, and a political culture that allows democratic elections and rule of law	Forge strategic alliances to generate impact on a large scale
Provide long-term support to natural resource management agencies	Build up sufficient broad-based community pressure to influence policy
Implement meaningful devolution of control with organisational capacity building at middle and lower levels	Lobby politicians – invite them to see what is happening in the field and how this fits with their own mandates
Avoid top-down community manipulation and NGO tension by ensuring that programmes are led by and remain focussed on community priorities	Influence market forces and market development
	Encourage local champions
Provide clear mandates that allow NGOs to participate	Help to construct a shared vision for scaling-up through active participation by all
Provide clear mandates for state agencies	Strengthen community knowledge and skills in law, planning, decision making, marketing, team building, communication, conflict resolution and natural resource management
Develop infrastructure for disadvantaged communities	
Provide appropriate technical support	Strengthen community understanding of the government system in the scaling-up process
Ensure independent monitoring, evaluation and documentation of lessons learned and best practice	Build social capital, trust, cooperation and networks

Adapted from Gonsalves, 2000. See footnote 13.

property rights in the absence of demarcation, registration and records, all of which requires an institutional framework located in, and managed by, the state. Local organisations have a comparative advantage in dealing with resource use and preservation issues at community level, but they vary widely in their organisational and management capabilities. State organisations are needed to provide support for the formation or strengthening of these local organisations where they are non-existent or weak. In addition given the wide variety of users and the complex set of overlapping rights that are continuously contested, the need for conflict mediation will be fairly constant. State organisations will be important in resolving disputes and providing an appropriate legal framework to support and enforce resource use agreements worked out by different local groups.

Many of the problems of reconciling local livelihoods with the conservation of the global environment will only be solved if systems are put into place so that the global beneficiaries compensate local people for the direct and opportunity costs imposed by conservation programmes. Much has been written about this in recent years and practical examples are widespread in the developed world. Surprisingly, few sustainable systems of environmental payments have been put into place in the developing world. Costa Rica is taking the lead in establishing payments for the carbon sequestration values of trees. Payments for the provision of water do exist in a number of countries. Successful schemes that require users to pay for water are in place in Australia and India. User fees at water points in dry areas are one example. Unlike conventional water supplies, these are designed to provide water for domestic use and for income-generating projects such as small-scale irrigation. They are public water points implemented in a manner that promotes equity and empowers local groups to own the resource and assume responsibility for operation and maintenance. Income from production meets management costs and creates incentive for local management. In the longer term, re-investment of this income, and experience of collective action, creates wider benefits to the local economy and environment through diversification of livelihood strategies and intensification of farming.

Few developing countries have the domestic financial resources available to Australia and India for these sorts of scheme. International donors have been reluctant to make the very long-term commitments that such payments require. Some believe that alternatives to subsidies should be sought in most instances. However, many of the difficult problems of conserving endangered biodiversity in locations where it can have no conceivable local value would seem to us to require that such payments are made. There are major challenges in both valuing the resources and ensuring equitable sharing of payments that go beyond the scope of this book. We only note that the ongoing negotiations about payments for carbon sequestration under the Clean Development Mechanism will probably provide the arena in which this issue is explored (see Box 4.3, p. 88). Integrated natural resource management frameworks will be needed to address the problems of equity in sharing of costs and benefits. They will also help to address the difficult issue of leakage, where investments in one location create perverse incentives that lead to offsetting environmental damage in other locations.

Delivering science-based natural resource management: reinventing the development project

We have argued strenuously that forcing natural resource management interventions to conform to the rigid frameworks of conventional development assistance projects is unhelpful. However, we also recognise that donors have the right to expect accountability and to know what they are paying for. They will always need to know if and when the objectives of their interventions have been attained. Donor interventions will always have to be bounded in some way. So how can the present project approach be modified to increase the likelihood of achieving the dual goals of improving local livelihoods and conserving the natural resource base? The huge investments in natural resource management projects over the past decades have taught us many lessons. There are many examples of innovative approaches that contain the elements of success. The World Bank has experience in other sectors in using approaches such as 'Adaptive Program Loans' and 'Learning and Innovation Loans'. These have similarities with programmes of some bilateral donors who make long-term commitments to a general goal but manage the process continuously to ensure that their assistance adapts to changing circumstances.

One key to success is to commit for the long term to a general development goal that is genuinely shared by the donor and the host nation. It is neither necessary nor desirable to be too precise about the exact nature of the final outcome nor the pathway to getting there. This is the concept of the 'lighthouse' as formulated by Kai Lee in his book *Compass and Gyroscope*.[16] The lighthouse is the distant target towards which all efforts are directed. The compass and the gyroscope are metaphors for the management tools needed to get there. The lighthouse could be the goal of achieving an acceptable balance between local development benefits and global biodiversity values. The exact nature of the compromise that will eventually emerge cannot be known in advance – neither can the route that will be taken to arrive at the final outcome. Once an agreement has been reached on the ultimate goal, then the donors and their agents must slowly engage with the local stakeholders. Instead of project interventions being front-loaded, with major investments at the beginning, they should be back-loaded. A long time should be invested in getting to know the local situation, developing sensitivity to local

[16]Lee, K. *Compass and Gyroscope: Integrating Science and Politics for the Environment.* Washington DC: Island Press, 1993.

conditions and simply getting accepted as another stakeholder: being part of the system.

Donor views of desirable outcomes of a project may differ from those of many local stakeholders. This is especially true if the donor is committed to environmental values with benefits that do not accrue to the local interest groups. These differences in interests have to be made explicit from the beginning. In these situations, there will be a need for negotiations and trade-offs. In order to have legitimate grounds for attempting to influence local development pathways, the outside agencies have to bring something to the negotiating table. There has to be some plausible reason why the local interest groups should settle for outcomes that are less than ideal from their local perspective. There has to be something in it for them and it helps if some of these local benefits begin to flow reasonably early in the project process.

One of the biggest challenges is to persuade donors to cease seeing themselves as the owners of a project and to begin to see themselves as interest groups who are participants in a process. They must stop being dominant participants convinced of their superior knowledge and their right to exclusive control of resources. They must recognise that they are participants with different kinds of knowledge and interests and the ability, for a limited time period, to bring financial and technical resources. Local interest groups bring to the negotiating table their traditional rights and knowledge and a large degree of ownership over the natural resources whose conservation is at stake. Measures of success must not be defined in advance by the donor but negotiated continuously by the different interest groups.

It is difficult to escape from the model of the donor-controlled project. It has been part of the development landscape for too long. Yet, it is possible to see things differently. Government programmes to improve the livelihoods and conserve the local environments of aboriginal peoples in Australia have turned the project paradigm on its head. The government no longer contributes and manages projects; instead it makes funds available to the aboriginal peoples, who are then able to make their own choices about their conservation and development goals and to select and manage any experts that they might need to help them to achieve their desired outcomes. The donor, in this situation the government, sets the limits of the type of activities that may be supported but otherwise takes a back seat in the process.

We advocate the application of seven basic principles that could serve to modify classic projects in ways that would have significant impact on their likelihood of achieving improved natural resource management.

Set general goals but recognise that adaptability and learning will be required to reach them. It is counterproductive to attempt to define outcomes too precisely *ex-ante*. Goals should be expressed in general terms and negotiations and trade-offs should be accepted as part of the process leading to their attainment. All participants have to learn from the process and adaptation will be required at all stages.

There must be a fundamental commitment to an equitable relationship with local interest groups. Project staff must show humility and respect in their dealings with local interest groups. They must genuinely value local knowledge and have a commitment to local values and judgements. The arrogance of science and financial clout of donors must not be allowed to drive the process.

Outside interest groups must bring something to the table. The concept of a 'donor' is itself outmoded. Aid agencies and research institutes are interested parties. They have an agenda and they must negotiate like everyone else. Instead of adopting the stance of donors or ivory tower scientists, they should be contributors who will provide money and expertise in order to achieve specified outcomes.

All parties must commit to the process for as long as it takes. It is too easy for a donor to walk away after a fixed period of time and leave the local interest groups with 'their' problem. If it is a genuinely shared problem, then all parties must stick with it until it is solved.

All must move at the pace of the slowest. The sorts of changes in resource management practices that projects seek to bring about will inevitably take time. One is seeking to change the behaviour of cautious and conservative people. Some interest groups may be exposed to risks and will justifiably be cautious about accepting change. Externally determined deadlines should not be allowed to predominate.

Everyone's expectations must be realistic. The rate and extent of change that is possible in resource management systems is often much less than outside experts tend to imagine. Proponents of projects must avoid the exuberant hyperbole that often goes with effective fund raising. Too many projects have totally unrealistic expectations.

Funding must follow process. The amount and rate of disbursement of funds must be driven by the above principles. Generally, a gradual build-up and a long tail-off period will be consistent with the sorts of change that are required. The allocation of money between outside experts and local people must be fair and transparent.

Towards a revolution in natural resource science?

In practice, few, if any, scientists today would ever see farmers as completely passive adopters of a message. Nevertheless, most people would probably agree that positivist–realism, rather than constructivism (Chapter 3), is still the dominant paradigm in most development projects and research institutes. Boru Douthwaite, in his *Conservation Ecology* article,[17] gives us some examples of very different kinds of research effort (Box 11.2).[18] We need to look for different models of natural resource management research. It will require a paradigm shift for constructivist research to become a mainstream activity in natural resource management. Paradigm changes are not easy, as Thomas Kuhn points out in his highly influential book *The Structure of Scientific Revolutions*.[19] Kuhn says, 'scientists will go to great lengths to defend their belief structure to the extent that research is not about discovering the unknown, but rather "a strenuous and devoted attempt to force nature into the conceptual boxes supplied by professional education"'. To this end, a research and development community will often suppress novelties that undermine its foundations. Our contention is that resource management requires collaboration between scientists from both 'hard' and 'soft' science backgrounds. This will require that they negotiate a shared understanding of the two paradigms and develop a conceptual model that can be a basis for project design, implementation and evaluation.

Box 11.2. Alternative science

Democratic user-led innovation is able to harness the innovative potential of people who are directly affected by technology.[1] For example, a grassroots development process in Denmark was able to produce a wind turbine industry with a 55% share of a billion dollar a year world market, beating the USA who spent over US$300 million funding a top-down development programme led by the National Aeronautics and Space

---

[17] Douthwaite, B., de Haan, N. C., Manyong, V. and Keatinge, D. Blending 'hard' and 'soft' science: the 'follow-the-technology' approach to catalyzing and evaluating technology change. *Conservation Ecology*, **5**(2001), 13. Online: http://www.consecol.org/vol5/iss2/art13.

[18] See also Douthwaite, B. *Enabling Innovation: A Practical Guide to Understanding and Fostering Technological Change.* London: Zed Books, 2002.

[19] Kuhn, T. S. *The Structure of Scientific Revolutions*, revised edn. Chicago, IL: University of Chicago Press, 1970.

Administration (NASA). The origins of the Danish industry were a few agricultural machinery manufacturers and ideologically motivated 'hobbyists' who began building, owning and tinkering with wind turbines. There were many early teething problems, but the owners organised themselves into a group who lobbied successfully for design improvements, working closely with manufacturers to solve the problems. The owners' group developed a cooperative ownership model and pressured politicians to support the sale of their electricity to the national grid at a fair price. In contrast, NASA led a 'hard' science development approach that implicitly assumed that scientists could develop the 'perfect' wind turbine with little input from the owners and users. NASA's approach failed.

A further example of the power that a grassroots innovation model can harness is the development of the computer-operating system Linux, which is a 'a world-class operating system' that has coalesced 'as if by magic out of part-time hacking by several thousand developers all over the planet connected only by the tenuous strands of the Internet'. Linux started life when Torvalds, a Finnish computer science student, started to write a Unix-like operating system that he could run on his PC: he had become tired of having to queue for hours to gain access to Unix on the University's main frame. When he finally got the core of an operating system working, he posted it on the Internet so that others could try it out. Importantly he gave the source-code so other people could understand the program and modify it if they wanted. Just like the first Danish wind turbines, early versions of Linux were not technically sophisticated or elegant, but they were simple, understandable and they touched a chord with 'hackers': people like Torvalds himself who got a kick out of generating novelty for the sake of being creative, not for money.

Torvalds' main role in the development of Linux after the first release was not to write code for features people wanted but to select and propagate improvements to the system from the ideas that streamed in. Ten people downloaded version 0.02 and five of these sent him bug fixes, code improvements and new features. Torvalds added the best of these to the existing program along with others he had written himself and released the composite as version 0.12. The rate of learning selection accelerated as the number of Linux users increased and, to cope with the volume of hacks (novelties) coming in, Torvalds began choosing and relying on a type of peer review. Rather than evaluate every modification himself, he based his decisions on the recommendations of people he trusted and on whether people were already using the patch (modification) successfully. He, in fact, played a similar role to that of an editor of an academic journal, who makes sure articles are reviewed but retains final control over what is published and what is not. This approach has allowed Torvalds to keep the programme on track as it has grown from 10 000 lines of code to 1.5 million, all written by volunteers.

[1]Douthwaite, B., de Haan, N. C., Manyong, V. and Keatinge, D. Blending 'hard' and 'soft' science: the 'follow-the-technology' approach to catalyzing and evaluating technology change. *Conservation Ecology*, **5**(2001), 13. Online: http://www.consecol.org/vol5/iss2/art13.

[2]Douthwaite *et al.* Blending 'hard' and 'soft' science; Raymond, E. S. *The Cathedral and the Bazaar*, 1997. Online: http://www.openresouces.com/documents/cathedral-bazaar/index.htm.

We need radical new approaches to natural resource management research. Research has to support an evolving environmental agenda. It requires a changed relationship between the scientist and the practitioner. It has to move away from the 'total control' paradigm of conventional on-station agricultural and forestry research. The process of scoping and definition of the research agenda has to be much more inclusive: neither exclusively bottom-up nor excessively top-down but rather a process of negotiation between all the participants. It has to lead to the emergence of products to meet a range of possible future scenarios. The days when the research establishment could provide farmers with a single technological option are gone. It is astonishing that, as recently as the 1990s, reputable international research agencies were promoting the widespread adoption of alley cropping (growing arable crops between rows of nitrogen-fixing leguminous trees to enhance soil fertility) in the face of compelling evidence that there were relatively few real-life situations where this technology made sense for farmers.

The search for scaling-up and generalisability is itself a symptom of an outmoded view of natural resources research. It is a myth that many technologies or management methods will be uniformly applicable over very large areas. The objective is to develop suites of technologies and manage information and knowledge in such a way that locally adapted solutions can emerge. Every farm, forest and fishery is unique and, in the long term, success will depend upon the ability of the users of these resources to design management systems that exploit the comparative advantage of their location. These must be finely tuned to the opportunities and constraints imposed by the resource base. Precision farming is a modern concept that we find attractive. However, in reality, all traditional resource management systems are 'precise'. In many cases, people have developed management systems over long periods of time and have an enormous accumulated knowledge of what will and will not work. Precision resource management is already a reality for many traditional societies. The role of science is not to try and replace these systems but rather to build upon them so that they can yield more, adapt to market demand and do this sustainably.

High-technology 'bench science' still has a vitally important role to play. Emerging technologies have the potential to bring huge improvements to the lives of the poor and to do so in ways that sustain or enhance the natural capital of soils, water and biodiversity upon which all production ultimately depends. However, the flow of knowledge between the ivory towers of high science and the citizen in the field or forest needs to be strengthened. Natural resources research in developing countries still does not have the capacity to determine where the real opportunities and constraints for innovation lie. The locus of research decision making has to move down the continuum from the 'Science Council' towards the farmer's field or the forest-dependent community. The real world has to complement the research plot or laboratory bench as the site for experimentation.

The sentiments expressed in this conclusion may seem self-evident. Participation and action research are beyond doubt where the cutting edge of natural resource management lie. There are numerous examples, many quoted in this book, of where these approaches are bringing real benefits to poor people and the environment. However, our scientific establishment is still not organised to adapt, learn and communicate. Funding is still allocated according to simplistic ideas of short-term impact. Projects are constrained by logical frameworks that are based upon the premise of total control and total predictability. Scientists are rewarded for disciplinary prowess and individual accomplishment. Science and scientists are proving remarkably resistant to change. The bureaucracy still prevails over the adhocracy. The merits of adaptive management have been extolled in the literature for a couple of decades and adaptive management has been the norm for resource users since time immemorial; in spite of this, departments of agriculture and forestry are still locked into the command and control world of total predictability.

The final conclusion of this book is anything but to advocate a 'silver bullet' approach to the science of natural resource management. We simply urge the research community to be more open to counter-intuitive ways of organising itself. Science managers must respect the principles of adhocracy, admit civil society to their ranks, reject the arrogance of technological perfection and actively seek to change and adapt.

The keys to science-based conservation and development

- A good understanding of the underlying changes taking place in the natural resources system is essential. Historical trends analysis and scenario building are useful tools for achieving this. The objective of management interventions will usually be to influence the trajectory of change and not to impose a predefined management model.
- Indicators for assessing the performance of the natural resource system are essential. These have to be negotiated amongst all stakeholders and should be subject to constant review. These indicators should provide the feedback for adaptive management.
- Good management of information about natural resource systems and their performance is essential. This must encompass traditional

knowledge as well as state of the art geo-referenced data sets and predictive models.

- Action research at a range of scales and with the genuine participation of all significant stakeholders is essential. Special measures are needed to ensure that participation and negotiation is equitable and that power differentials do not favour elite groups.

- It is essential that governance arrangements for the natural resources system are fair and that underlying systems of land tenure, property rights and access rights are appropriate and defensible.

- Natural resource management organisations should combine the functions of research and management. Scientists should occupy key senior management positions. Ideally, management organisations should have mandates for coherent natural resource systems and it helps if these do not include an excessive diversity of administrative jurisdictions. The best arrangement – seldom possible in practice – is when a natural resource management system – a river basin, agro-ecological zone, etc. – is covered by a single administrative jurisdiction.

- Incentive payments, subsidies and so on for the provision of environmental services are widely applied in the developed world; it is naïve to assume that land managers in developing countries will forego local benefits in favour of public goods if they do not receive such environmental payments.

Bibliography

Abbot, J. and Guijt, I. *SARL Discussion Paper No. 2: Changing Views on Change: Participatory Approaches to Monitoring the Environment*. London: International Institute for Environment and Development, 1998.

Adams, J. S. and McShane, T. O. *The Myth of Wild Africa*. New York: Norton, 1992.

Adams, W. M. *Green Development*. Oxford: Oxford University Press, 1990.

Adamowicz, W., Luckert, M. and Veeman, M. Issues in using valuation techniques cross-culturally: three cases in Zimbabwe using contingent valuation, observed behaviour and derived demand techniques. *Commonwealth Forestry Review*, **76** (1997), 194–197.

Agudelo, L. A. and Kaimowitz, D. *Serie Documentos de Discusión Sobre Agricultura Sostenible y Recursos Naturales No. 3: Tecnología agrícola sostenible: retos institucionales y metodológicos, dos estudios de caso en Colombia*. [*Sustainable Agricultural Technology: Institutional and Methodological Challenges, Two Case Studies from Colombia*.] San Jose, Costa Rica: IICA/GTZ, 1997.

Allan T. F. H. and Starr, T. B. *Hierarchy Perspectives for Ecological Complexity*. Chicago, IL: University of Chicago Press, 1982.

Amezquita, E., Ashby, J., Knapp, E. K. et al. *CIAT's Strategic Research for Sustainable Land Management on the Steep Hillsides of Latin America*. Unpublished document. Cali: CIAT, undated.

Anderson, J. R. Selected policy issues in international agricultural research. On striving for public goods in an era of donor fatigue. *World Development*, **26** (1998), 1149–1162.

Anderson, R. J., Jr., Da Franca Ribeiro dos Santos, N. and Diaz, H. F. *LATEN Dissemination Note 5: An Analysis of Flooding in the Parana/Paraguay River Basin*. Washington DC: World Bank, 1993.

Anon. *Report on the Workshop on Integrated Natural Resource Management Research in the CGIAR: Approaches and Lessons*. 21–25 August 2000, Penang: ICLARM. Online: http://www.inrm.cgiar.org/documents/workshop_2000.htm.

Arce, A. and Long, N. Bridging two worlds: an ethnography of bureaucrat peasant relations in Western Mexico. In *An Anthropological Critique of Development: The Growth of Ignorance*, ed. M. Horbart. London: Routledge, 1993.

Ashby, J., Estrada, R. D. and Pachico, D. An evaluation of strategies for reducing natural resource degradation in the hillsides of tropical America. In *Proceedings of The Annual Meeting of the International Association of Impact*

Assessment, Quebec, 1994. http://www.ciat.cgiar.org/inrm/workshop 2001/docs/titles/8-1BPaperJABeltron.

Ashby, J. A. Integrating research on food and the environment: an exit strategy from the rational fool syndrome in agricultural science. *Conservation Ecology*, **5** (2001), 20. Online: http://www.consecol.org/vol5/iss2/art20.

Barr, C., Wollenberg, E., Limberg, G. *et al*. Case study 3: The impacts of decentralisation on forests and forest-dependent communities in Malinau District, East Kalimantan. In *Case Studies on Decentralisation and Forests in Indonesia*. Bogor: Center for International Forestry Research, 2001, p. 48.

Bationo, A., Lompo, F. and Koala, S. Research on nutrient flows and balances in West Africa: state of the art. *Agriculture, Ecosystems and the Environment*, **71** (1998), 19–35.

Bawden, R. On the systems dimension in FSR. *Journal of Farming Systems Research-Extension*, **5** (1995), 1–18.

Bebbington, A. Capitals and capabilities: a framework for analysing peasant viability, rural livelihoods and poverty. *World Development*, **26** (1999), 2021–2044.

Beinert, W. Agricultural planning and the late colonial technical imagination: the lower shire valley in Malawi, 1940–1960. In *Proceedings of a Seminar on Malawi: An Alternative Pattern of Development*, Edinburgh 12 and 25 May, 1984. Edinburgh: Centre of African Studies, University of Edinburgh, 1985, pp. 95–148.

Belcher, B., Colfer, C. and MacDicken, K. Towards INRM: Three paths through the forest. In *Proceedings of the Workshop on Integrated Natural Resource Management in the CGIAR: Approaches and Lessons*, 21–25 August 2000, 1–19. Penang: ICLARM. Online: http://www.inmr.cgiar.org/documents/workshop_2000.htm.

Berger, P. L. and Luckmann, T. *The Social Construction of Reality. A Treatise in Sociology of Knowledge*. Garden City: Anchor Books, 1967.

Berkes, F., Colding, J. and Folke, C. Rediscovery of traditional ecological knowledge as adaptive management. *Ecological Applications*, **10** (2000), 1251–1262.

Blackmore, D. J. Murray–Darling Basin Commission: a case study in integrated catchment management. *Water Science and Technology*, **32** (1995), 15–25.

Bottrall, A. Institutional aspects of watershed management. In *Proceedings of the Conference on Priorities for Water Resources Management*. Southampton: Overseas Development Administration, Natural Resources and Engineering, 1992, pp. 81–90.

Bousquet, F., Barreteau, O., Le Page, C., Mullon, C. and Weber, J. An environmental modelling approach: the use of multi-agent simulations. In *Advances in Environmental Modelling*, ed. F. Blasco and A. Weill. New York: Elsevier, 1999, pp. 113–122.

Bradley, N. L. A man for all seasons. *National Wildlife* (1998). Online: http://www.nwf.org/nationalwildlife/1998/tableam8.html.

Bromley, J. A., Butterworth, J. A., MacDonald, D. M. J., Lovell, C. J., Mharapara, I. and Batchelor, C. H. Hydrological processes and water resources management in a dryland environment I: an introduction to the Romwe catchment study in southern Zimbabwe. *Hydrology and Earth Sciences*, **3** (1999), 322–332.

Bronson Knapp, E., Ashby, J. A., Ravnborg, H. M. and Bell, W. C. A landscape that unites: community lead management of Andean watershed resources. In *Integrated Watershed Management in the Global Ecosystem. Soil and Water Conservation Society*, ed. L. Rattan. New York: CRC Press, 2000.

Bruijnzeel, S. *Hydrology of Moist Tropical Forests and conversion: A State of Knowledge Review*. Paris: UNESCO International Hydrological Programme, 1990.

Hydrology of montane cloud forests: a re-evaluation. Paper presented at second International Colloquium on Hydrology and Water Management in the Humid Tropics, Panama, 22–24 March, 1999.

Buck, L. E., Geisler, C. C., Schelhas, J. and Wollenberg, E. (eds.) *Biological Diversity: Balancing Interests through Adaptive Collaborative Management*. Boca Raton, FL: CRC Press, 2001.

Cain, J., Moriarty, P. and Lynam, T. *Designing Integrated Models for the Participatory Formulation of Water Management Strategies*. UK: Centre for Ecology and Hydrology, 2001.

Calder, I. R. *The Blue Revolution, Land Use and Integrated Water Resources Management*. London: Earthscan, 1999.

Campbell, A. Fomenting synergy: experiences with facilitating landcare in Australia. In *Sustainable Agriculture and Participatory Learning*, ed. N. G. Röling and M. A. E. Wagemakers. Cambridge: Cambridge University Press, 1998, pp. 232–249.

Campbell, B. and Shackleton, S. The organisational structures for community-based natural resources management in southern Africa. *Africa Studies Quarterly*, **5** (2001). Online: http://web.africa.ufl.edu/asq/v5/v5i3a6.htm.

Campbell, B., Sayer, J. A., Frost, P. et al. Assessing the performance of natural resource systems. *Conservation Ecology*, **5** (2001), 22. Online: http://www.consecol.org/vol5/iss2/art22.

Campbell, B. M., Luckert, M. and Scoones, I. Local-level valuation of savanna: a case study from Zimbabwe. *Economic Botany*, **51** (1997), 59–77.

Campbell, B. M., Chuma, E., Frost, P., Mandondo, A. and Sithole, B. Interdisciplinary challenges for environmental researchers in rural farming systems. *Transactions of the Zimbabwe Scientific Association*, **73** (1999), 39–57.

Campbell, B. M., Costanza, R. and van den Belt, M. Land use options in dry tropical woodland ecosystems in Zimbabwe: introduction, overview and synthesis. *Ecological Economics*, **33** (2000), 341–352.

Campbell, B. M., Jeffrey, S., Kozanayi, W., Luckert, M., Mutamba, M. and Zindi, C. *Household Livelihoods in Semi-arid Regions: Options and Constraints*. Bogor: Center for International Forestry Research, 2002.

Carney, D. *Sustainable Rural Livelihoods. What Contribution Can We Make?* London: Department for International Development, 1998.

Cassells, D. S., Bonell, M., Hamilton, L. S. and Gilmour, D. A. The protective role of tropical forests: a state of knowledge review. In *Agroforestry in the Humid Tropics: Its Protective and Ameliorative Roles to Enhance Productivity and Sustainability*, ed. N. T. Vergara and N. D. Briones. Honolulu: East-West Center, 1985, pp. 111–129.

Chambers, R. *Rural Development: Putting the Last First*. Harlow: Longman, 1983. *Whose Reality Counts? Putting the Last First*. London: Intermediate Technology, 1997.

Chambers, R. and Conway, G. *IDS Discussion Paper 296: Sustainable Rural Livelihoods. Practical Concepts for the 21st Century*. Brighton: Institute for Development Studies, 1992.

Chambers, R. and Jiggins, J. *Discussion Paper 220: Agricultural Research for Resource Poor Farmers: A Parsimonious Paradigm*. Brighton: Institute of Development Studies, 1986.

Checkland, P. and Scholes, J. *Soft Systems Methodology in Action*. New York: Wiley, 1990.

Checkland, P. B. From optimising to learning: a development of systems thinking for the 1990's. *Journal of Operational Research and Society*, **36** (1985), 757–767.

Chomitz, K. M. and Kumari, K. The domestic benefits of tropical forests, a critical review. *World Bank Research Observer*, **13** (1998), 13–35.

CIFOR. *Local People, Devolution and Adaptive Collaborative Management of Forests. Researching Conditions, Processes and Impacts*. Bogor: Center for International Forestry Research. Online: http://www.cifor.cgiar.org/acm/download/ACMFlyer.zip.

CIFOR C&I Team. *The CIFOR Criteria and Indicators Generic Template*. Bogor: Center for International Forestry Research, 1999.

Conway, G. R. The properties of agroecosystems. *Agricultural Systems*, **24** (1987), 95–117. *The Doubly Green Revolution: Food for All in the 21st Century*. London: Penguin, 1997.

Cook, B. and Kothari, U. *Participation: The New Tyranny*. London: ZED Books, 2001.

Corbett, J. D. and O'Brien, R. F. The spatial characterization tool – Africa v 1.0. *Blackland Research Center Report No. 97-03*. [CD-ROM Publication.] Houston, TX: Texas Agricultural Experiment Station, Texas A&M University, 1997.

Corbett, J. D., Collis, S., Bush, B. et al. USAID's African country almanac. Version 2.0.1. *Blackland Research Center Report No. 99-06*. Houston, TX: Agricultural Research Station, Texas A&M University, 1999.

Daniels, S. and Walker, G. Rethinking public participation in natural resources management: concepts from pluralism and five emerging approaches. In *Pluralism and Sustainable Forestry and Rural Development. Proceedings of an International Workshop*. Rome: Food and Agriculture Organization, 1999.

Daniels, S. E. and Walker G. B. *Working Through Environmental Conflict: The Collab-orative Learning Approach.* Westport, CT: Praeger, 2001.

Dasgupta, P. and Maler, K-M. *Beijer Institute Discussion Paper 139: Wealth as a Criterion for Sustainable Development.* Stockholm: Beijer Institute, 2001.

de Boef, W. S. Tales of the unpredictable. Learning about institutional frameworks that support farmer management of agro-biodiversity. Thesis, Wageningen University, 2000.

Department of Research and Specialists Services. *Annual Report of Division of Live-stock and Pastures 1992–93.* Harare, Department of Research and Specialist Services, Government of Zimbabwe, 1995.

Douthwaite, B. *Enabling Innovation: A Practical Guide to Understanding and Fostering Technological Change.* London: Zed Books, 2002.

Douthwaite, B., de Haan, N. C., Manyong, V. and Keatinge, D. Blending 'hard' and 'soft' science: the 'follow-the-technology' approach to catalyzing and eval-uating technology change. Conservation Ecology, **5** (2001), 13. Online: http://www.consecol.org/vol5/iss2/art13.

Edmunds, D. and Wollenberg, E. A strategic approach to multistakeholder negoti-ations. *Development and Change,* **32** (2001), 231–253.

Enters, T. *Methods for the Economic Assessment of the On- and Off-site Impacts of Soils Erosion,* 2nd edn. Bangkok: International Board for Soil Research and Management, 2000.

Farrington, J. and Boyd, C. Scaling-up the participatory management of common pool resources. *Development Policy Review,* **15** (1997), 371–391.

Farrington, J. and Lobo, C. *ODI Natural Resource Perspectives No. 17: Scaling-up Participatory Catchment Development in India: Lessons from the Indo-German Watershed Development Program.* London: Overseas Development Institute, 1997.

Folke, C., Pritchard, L., Jr., Berkes, F., Coling, J. and Svedin, U. *International Human Dimensions Program on Global Environmental Change Working Paper No 2: The Problem of Fit Between Ecosystems and Institutions.* Bonn, Germany, 1998. Online: http://www.uni-bonn.de/ihdp/wp02m.htm.

Fortmann, L. and Nabane (Nemarundwe), N. *NRM Occasional Paper 7: The Fruits of their Labours: Gender, Property and Trees in Mhondoro district.* Harare: Centre for Applied Social Sciences, University of Zimbabwe, 1992.

Franks, P. and Blomley, T. Fitting ICD into a project framework: the CARE expe-rience. In *Getting Biodiversity Projects to Work: Towards More Effective Con-servation and Development,* ed. T. O. McShane and M. P. Wells. New York: Columbia University Press, 2004, in press.

Freire, P. *Pedagogy of Hope. Reliving Pedagogy of the Oppressed.* New York: Continuum, 1997.

Fresco, L. O. *Cassava in Shifting Cultivation. A Systems Approach to Agricultural Technology Development in Africa.* Wageningen: Royal Tropical Institute, Amsterdam, 1986, p. 240.

Fujisaka, S., Harrington, L. and Hobbs, P. Rice–wheat in South Asia: systems and long-term priorities established through diagnostic research. *Agricultural Systems*, **46** (1994), 169–187.

Funtowicz, S. O., and Ravtz, J. R. Science for the post-normal age. *Futures*, **25** (1993), 739–955.

Gambiza, J., Bond, W., Frost, P. and Higgins, S. A simulation model of miombo woodland dynamics under different management regimes. *Ecological Economics*, **33** (2000), 353–368.

Garrity, D. P., Amoroso, V. B., Koffa, S. et al. Landcare on the poverty–protection interface in an Asian watershed. *Conservation Ecology*, **6** (2002), 12. Online: http://www.consecol.org/vol6/iss1/art12.

Giampetro, M. and Pastore, G. Multi-dimensional reading of the dynamics of rural intensification in China: the amoeba approach. *Critical Reviews in Plant Sciences*, **18** (1999), 299–329.

Gibbs, C. J. N. Institutional and organizational concerns in upper watershed management. In *Watershed Resources Management: An Integrated Framework with Studies from Asia and the Pacific*, ed. K. W. Easter, J. A. Dixon and M. M. Hufschmidt. Boulder, CO: Westview Press, 1986, pp. 145–156.

Gilmour, D. A., Bonell, M., Cassells, D. S. The effects of forestation on soil hydraulic properties in the middle hills of Nepal: a preliminary assessment. *Mountain Resources Development*, **7** (1987), 239–249.

Goleman, D. What makes a leader? *Harvard Business Review*, **Nov/Dec** (1998), 92–102.

Gonsalves, J. *Highlights of the Workshop Going to Scale: Can We Bring More Benefits to More People More Quickly?* Presented by the CGIAR-NGO Committee and The Global Forum for Agricultural Research with BMZ, MISEREOR, Rockefeller Foundation, IRRI and IIRR, 10–14 April, 2000. Silong, Philippines: International Institute of Rural Reconstruction.

Gottret, M. A. V. N. and White, D. Assessing the impact of integrated natural resource management: Challenges and experiences. *Conservation Ecology*, **5** (2001), 17. Online: http://www.consecol.org/vol5/iss2/art17.

Groot, A. and Marleveld, M. *Gatekeeper Series No. 89: Demystifying Facilitation in Participatory Development*. London: International Institute for Environment and Development, 2000.

Gunderson, L. and Holling, C. S. (eds.) *Panarchy: Understanding Transformations in Human and Natural Systems*. Washington, DC: Island Press, 2002.

Hagmann, J. *Learning Together for Change. Facilitating Innovation in Natural Resource Management Through Learning Process Approaches in Rural Livelihoods in Zimbabwe*. Weikersheim: Margraf Verlag, 1999.

Hagmann, J., Chuma, E. and Murwira, K. Kuturaya: participatory research, innovation and extension. In: *Farmers' Research in Practice: Lessons from the Field*, ed. L. van Veldhuizen, A. Waters-Bayer, R. Ramirez, D. Johnson and J. Thompson. London: Intermediate Technology, 1997, pp. 153–173.

Hagmann, J. R., Chuma, E., Murwira, K., Connolly, M. and Ficarelli, P. Success factors in integrated natural resource management R&D: lessons from practice. *Conservation Ecology*, **5** (2002), 29. Online: http://www.consecol.org/vol5/iss2/art29.

Hamilton, K. and Clemens, M. Genuine savings rates in developing countries. *World Bank Economic Review*, **13** (1999), 333–356.

Hamilton, L. S. and King, P. N. *Tropical Forested Watersheds, Hydrological and Soils Response to Major Uses or Conversions*. Boulder, CO: Westview Press, 1983.

Hamilton, N. A. Learning to learn with farmers. [A case study of an adult learning project conducted in Queensland, Australia 1990–1995.] Thesis, Wageningen University, 1995.

Harrington, L., Fujisaka, S., Hobbs, P., Adhikary, C., Giri, G. S. and Cassaday, K. *Rice–Wheat Cropping Systems in Rupandehi District of the Nepal Terai: Diagnostic Surveys of Farmers' Practices and Problems, and Needs for Further Research*. Nepal and Mexico City: International Maize and Wheat Improvement Center and Agricultural Research Council/International Rice Research Institute, 1993.

Harrington, L., White, J., Grace, P. et al. Delivering the goods: scaling out results of natural resource management research. *Conservation Ecology*, **5** (2001), 19. Online: http://www.consecol.org/vol5/iss2/art19.

Hartkamp, A. D., White, J. W. and Hoogenboom, G. Interfacing geographic information systems with agronomic modeling: a review. *Agronomy Journal*, **91** (1999), 761–772.

Henderson-Sellers, B. Decision support systems for stored water quality: 1. The environmental decision support system. *Environment International*, **17** (1991), 595–599.

Hinchcliffe, F., Thompson, J., Pretty, J., Guijt, I. and Shah, P. (eds.) *Fertile Ground: the Impacts of Participatory Watershed Management*. London: Intermediate Technology, 1999.

Hodson, D., Corbett, J. D., Wall, P. C. and White, J. W. *NRG–GIS Paper 98-01: An Agro-climatological Overview of Wheat Production Regions of Bolivia*. Mexico, DF: International Maize and Wheat Improvement Center, 1998.

Holland, J. H. *Hidden Order. How Adaptations Build Complexity*. New York: Addison-Wesley, 1995.

Holling, C. Investing in research for sustainability. *Ecological Applications*, **3** (1993), 552–555.

Holling, C. S. (ed.) *Adaptive Environmental Assessment and Management*. International Series on Applied Systems Analysis. New York: Wiley, 1978.

Holling, C. S., Berkes, F. and Folke, C. Science, sustainability and resource management. In *Linking Social and Ecological Systems. Management Practices and Social Mechanisms for Building Resilience*, ed. F. Berkes and C. Folke. Cambridge: Cambridge University Press, 1998.

Holling, C. S., Schindler, D. W., Walker, B. H. and Roughgarden, J. Biodiversity in the functioning of ecosystems: an ecological synthesis. In *Biodiversity Loss:*

Economic and Ecological Issues, ed. C. A. Perrings, K. G. Maler, C. Folke, C. S. Holling and B. O. Jansson. Cambridge: Cambridge University Press, 1995, 44–83.

Holling, C. S., Folke, C., Gunderson, L. and Maler, K-G. *Resilience of Ecosystems, Economic Systems and Institutions.* Final report submitted to John D. and Catherine T. MacArthur Foundation. Gainesville: Resilience Alliance, 2000.

Hope, A. and Timmel, S. *Training for Transformation, a Handbook for Community Workers.* Gweru: Mambo Press, 1984.

Hot Springs Working Group. *Research Series 3. Local-level Economic Valuation of Savanna Woodland Resources: Village Cases from Zimbabwe.* London: International Institute for Environment and Development, 1995.

Irwin, A. *Citizen Science. A Study of People, Expertise and Sustainable Development.* London: Routledge, 1995.

Jensen, F. V. *An Introduction to Bayesian Networks.* London: UCL Press, 1996.

Johannes, R. E. The case for data-less marine resource management: examples from tropical near shore fisheries. *Trends in Ecology and Evolution,* **13**(1998), 243–246.

Jones, P. G. and Thornton, P. K. Spatial modeling of risk in natural resource management. *Conservation Ecology,* **5** (2002), 27. Online: http://www.consecol.org/vol5/iss2/art27.

Kaimowitz, D. Useful myths and intractable truths: the politics of the link between forests and water in Central America. In *Forests–Water–People in the Humid Tropics.* Cambridge: Cambridge University Press, 2003.

Kaimowitz D., Snyder, M. and Engel, P. *Linkage Theme Paper No. 1: A Conceptual Framework for Studying the Links between Agricultural Research and Technology Transfer in Developing Countries.* The Hague: International Service for National Agricultural Research (ISNAR), 1989.

Kain, R. J. P. and Baigent, E. *The Cadastral Map in the Service of the State.* Chicago, IL: Chicago University Press, 1992.

Kates, R. W., Clark, W. C., Corell, R. et al. Sustainability science. *Science,* **292** (2001), 641–642.

Kinzig, A. P., Carpenter, S., Dove, M. et al. *Nature and Society: An Imperative for Integrated Environmental Research,* 2000. [Executive Summary of a report prepared for the National Science Foundation]. Online: http://lsweb.la.asu.edu/akinzig/report.htm.

Kolb, D. A. *Experiential Learning. Experience as a Source of Learning and Development.* Englewood Cliffs, NJ: Prentice Hall, 1984.

Korten, D. C. *When Corporations Rule the World.* London: Earthscan, 1995.

Kuby, T. *Innovation is a social process. What does this Mean for Impact Assessment in Agricultural Research?* Eschborn: German Development Corporation, 1999.

Kuhn, T. S. *The Structure of Scientific Revolutions.* Chicago, IL: University of Chicago Press, 1970.

Lal, P., Lim-Applegate, H. and Scoccimarro, M. The adaptive decision-making process as a tool for integrated natural resource management: focus, attitudes, and approach. *Conservation Ecology*, **5** (2001), 11. Online: http://www.consecol.org/vol5/iss2/art11.

Larson, C. Erosion and sediment yield as affected by land use and slope in the Panama Canal watershed. In *Proceedings of the Second World Congress on Water and Resources of the International Water Resources Association*. Mexico, 1979, pp. 1086–1095.

Lawton, J. Earth science systems. *Science*, **292** (2001), 1965.

Lee, K. L. *Compass and Gyroscope: Integrating Science and Politics for the Environment*. Washington DC: Island Press, 1993.

Leonard, H. J. *Natural Resources and Economic Development in Central America*. New Brunswick: Transactions Books, 1985.

Lewin, K. Action research and minority problems. *Journal of Social Issues*, **2** (1946), 34–46.

Lomborg, B. *The Sceptical Environmentalist*. Cambridge: Cambridge University Press, 2001.

Long, N. *Encounters at the Interface: A Perspective on Social Discontinuities in Rural Development*. Wageningen: Wageningen Agricultural University, 1989.

   From paradigm lost to paradigm regained. The case of actor-oriented sociology of development. In *Battlefields of Knowledge: The Interlocking of Theory and Practice in Social Research and Development*, ed. N. Long and A. Long. London: Routledge, 1992, pp. 16–43.

   Agency and constraint, perceptions and practice. In *Images and Realities of Rural Life*, ed. H. de Haan and N. Long. Assen, the Netherlands: van Gorcum, 1997, pp. 1–20.

Lopez Cordovez, L. Trends and recent changes in Latin American agriculture: a cross country analysis. *Cepal Review*, **16** (1982), 7–42.

Lovell, C., Mandondo, A. and Moriarty, P. The question of scale in integrated natural resource management. *Conservation Ecology*, **5** (2002), 25. Online: http://www.consecol.org/vol5/iss2/art25.

Lynam, T. J. P. Adaptive analysis of locally complex systems in a globally complex world. *Conservation Ecology*, **3** (1999), 1. Online: http://www.consecol.org/Journal/vol3/iss2/art13.

Lynam, T., Bousquet, F., Le Page, C. et al. Adapting science to adaptive managers: spidergrams, belief models, and multi-agent systems modelling. *Conservation Ecology*, **5** (2002), 24. Online: http://www.consecol.org/vol5/iss2/art24.

Maarleveld, M. and Dangbegnon, C. Managing natural resources: a social learning perspective. *Agriculture and Human Values*, **16** (1999), 267–280.

MacDicken, K. and Smith, J. *Capturing the Value of Forest Carbon for Local Livelihoods: Opportunities Under the Clean Development Mechanisms of the Kyoto Protocol*. Bogor: Center for International Forestry Research and University of Maryland, 2000.

Mandondo, A. *CIFOR Working Paper 32: Situating Zimbabwe's Natural Resource Governance Systems in History*. Bogor: Centre for International Forestry Research, 2000. Online: http://www.cifor.cgiar.org/publications/pdf_files/OccPapers/OP-32.pdf.

Martin, R. B. *Communal Areas Management Program for Indigenous Resources (CAMPFIRE)*. Harare: Department of National Parks and Wildlife Management, Branch of Terrestrial Ecology, Government of Zimbabwe, 1986.

Matose, F. and Wily, L. Institutional arrangements governing the use and management of miombo woodlands. In *The Miombo in Transition: Woodlands and Welfare in Africa*, ed. B. Campbell. Bogor: Center for International Forestry Research, 1996, pp. 195–219.

McShane, T. O. and Wells, M. P. *Getting Biodiversity Projects to Work: Towards More Effective Conservation and Development*. New York: Columbia University Press. 2004, in press.

Meadows, D. H. *Indicators and Information Systems for Sustainable Development*. [A report to the Balaton Group.] Hartland Four Corners: Sustainability Institute, 1998.

Meisner, C., Sufian, A., Smith, M., O'Donoghue, M., Razzaque, M. and Shaha, N. *Non-gender biased, innovative approaches for accelerated adoption of agricultural technologies, especially for wheat seed production and preservation. In Proceedings of The POWER-sponsored Workshop on Women in Seed*, May 2000.

Miller, W. L. and Morris, L. *Fourth Generation R&D: Managing Knowledge, Technology, and Innovation*. New York: Wiley, 1999.

Mintzberg, H. and McHugh, A. Strategy formation in an adhocracy. *Administrative Science Quarterly*, **30** (1985), 160–197.

Mokyr, J. *The Lever of Riches: Technological Creativity and Economic Progress*. Oxford: Oxford University Press, 1990.

Moriarty, P. B. *Integrated catchment management and sustainable water resource development in semi-arid Zimbabwe*. Dissertation. University of Reading, 2000.

Murombedzi, J. The need for appropriate local level common property resource management institutions in communal tenure regimes. In *CASS Occasional Paper Series – NRM 1990*. Harare: Center for Applied Social Sciences, University of Zimbabwe, 1990.

Murphree, M. W. Decentralising the proprietorship of wildlife resources in Zimbabwe's Communal Lands. In *CASS Occasional Paper Series – NRM 1990*. Harare: Centre for Applied Social Sciences, University of Zimbabwe, 1990.

Gatekeeper Series 36: Communities as Resource Management Institutions. London: International Institute for Environment and Development, 1993.

Boundaries and borders: the question of scale in the theory and practice of common property resource management. In *Proceedings of the Eighth Biennial Conference of the International Association for the Study of Common Property*. 31 May to 4 June 2000, Bloomington, Indiana pp. 1–35.

Nagle, G. N., Fahey, T. J. and Lassoie, J. P. Management of sedimentation in tropical watersheds. *Environmental Management,* **23** (1999), 441–452.

Nemarundwe, N. Negotiating resource access: Institutional arrangements for woodlands and water use in southern Zimbabwe. Dissertation. Swedish Agricultural University, 2003.

Nemarundwe, N. and Kozanayi, W. Institutional arrangements for water for household use: a case study from Southern Zimbabwe. *Journal of Southern African Studies,* **29** (2003), 193–206.

Nemarundwe, N. and Richards, M. Participatory methods for exploring livelihood values derived from forests: potential and limitation. In *Uncovering the Hidden Harvest. Valuation Methods for Woodland and Forest Resources,* ed. B. M. Campbell and M. Luckert. People and Plants Conservation Series. London: Earthscan, 2002.

North, D. C. *Institutions, Institutional Change and Economic Performance.* Cambridge: University of Cambridge Press, 1990, pp. 168–196.

Noss, R. F. Indicators for monitoring biodiversity: a hierarchical approach. *Conservation Biology,* **4** (1990), 355–364.

Ostrom, E. Designing complexity to govern complexity. In *Property Rights and the Environment: Social and Ecological,* ed. S. Hanna and M. Munasinghe Washington, DC: World Bank, 1995, pp. 33–46.

Pachico, D., Ashby, J., Farrow, A., Fujisaka, S., Johnson, N. and Winograd, M. Case study and empirical evidence for assessing natural resource management research: the experience of CIAT. In *Workshop on Assessing Impacts in Natural Resource Management Research* 27–29 April 1999. Nairobi: World Agroforestry Center, 1999.

Pearce, D., Barbier, A. and Markandya, A. *Sustainable Development: Economics and Environment in the Third World.* Aldershot: Edward Elgar, 1990.

Pearce, D., Hamilton, K. and Atkinson, G. Measuring sustainable development: progress on indicators. *Environment and Development Economics* **1** (1996), 85–101.

Pretty, J. N. *Regenerating Agriculture: Policies and Practice for Sustainability and Self-reliance.* London: Earthscan, 1995.

Raymond, E. S. *The Cathedral and the Bazaar,* 1997. Online: http://www. openresouces.com/documents/cathedral-bazaar/index.htm.

Ravnborg, H. M. and Ashby, J. A. *AGREN Network Paper 65: Organizing for Local-level Watershed Management: Lessons from Rio Cabuyal Watershed, Colombia.* London: Overseas Development Institute-Agricultural Research and Extension Network, 1996.

Reich, R. B. (ed.) *The Power of Public Ideas.* Cambridge, MA: Harvard University Press, 1988.

Rhoades, R. E. *Gatekeeper Series No. SA81: Participatory Watershed Research and Management: Where the Shadow Falls.* London: International Institute for Environment and Development, 1998.

Rhoades, R. E. and Booth, R. H. Farmer-back-to-farmer: a model for generating acceptable agricultural technology. *Agricultural Administration*, **11** (1982), 127–137.

Röling, N. G. Towards an interactive agricultural science. *European Journal of Agricultural Education and Extension*, **2** (1996), 35–48.

Röling, N. and de Jong, F. Learning: shifting paradigms in education and extension studies. *Journal of Agricultural Education and Extension*, **5** (1998), 143–161.

Röling, N. G. and Jiggins, J. The ecological knowledge system. In *Facilitating Sustainable Agriculture*, ed. N. G. Röling and M. A. E. Wagemakers. Cambridge: Cambridge University Press, 1998, pp. 283–311.

Roussel, P. A., Saad, K. N. and Erickson, T. J. *Third Generation R&D: Managing the Link to Corporate Strategy*. Boston, MA: Harvard Business School Press, 1991.

Rozemeijer, N. and van der Jagt, C. Botswana case study: community-based natural resources management (CBNRM) in Botswana: How community based is CBNRM in Botswana? In *Empowering Communities to Manage Natural Resources: Case Studies from Southern Africa*, ed. S. E. Shackleton and B. Campbell. Lilongwe: SADC Wildlife Sector Natural Resource Management Programme, Pretoria: CSIR, Harare: WWF (Southern Africa), Bogor: Center for International Forestry Research, 2000. Online: http://www.cifor.cgiar.org/publications/pdf_files/Books/Empowering.pdf.

Sanchez, P. Science in agroforestry. *Agroforestry Systems*, **30** (1995), 5–55.

Saxena, K. G., Rao, K. S., Sen, K. K., Maikhuri, R. K. and Semwal, R. L. Integrated natural resource management: approaches and lessons from the Himalayas. *Conservation Ecology*, **5** (2001), 14. Online: http://www.consecol.org/vol5/iss2/art14.

Schütz, A. and Luckmann, T. *The Structures of the Life-world*, Vol. 1. London: Heinemann, 1974.

Scoones, I. A visit to ICRISAT. *Haramata Bulletin*, **12** (1991), 19.

Scoones, I. *et al. Hazards and Opportunities. Farming Livelihoods in Dryland Africa: Lessons from Zimbabwe*. London: Zed Books, 1996.

Scott, J. C. *Seeing Like a State: How Certain Schemes to Improve the Human Condition have Failed*. New Haven, CT: Yale University Press, 1998.

Secretariat of the Convention on Biological Diversity. *Conference of the Parties Decisions. Decision V/6 Ecosystem Approach*. Paris: United Nations Environment Programme, 2001. Online: http://www.biodiv.org/decisions.

Sedjo, R. A. Towards an operational approach to public forest management. *Journal of Forestry*, **94** (1996), 24–27.

Sen, A. Democracy as a universal value. *Journal of Democracy*, **10** (1999), 3–17. Online: http://muse.jhu.edu/demo/jod/10.3sen.html.

Senge, P. M. *The Fifth Discipline: The Art and Practice of the Learning Organization*. New York: Doubleday-Currency, 1990.

Shackleton, S., Campbell, B., Edmunds, D. and Wollenberg, L. Devolution and community-based natural resource management: creating space for local people to participate and benefit? *ODI Natural Resource Perspectives*, **76** (2002), 1–7. Online: http://www.odi.org.uk/nrp/76.pdf.

Sheil, D., Puri, R. K., Basuki, I. et al. *Exploring Biological Diversity, Environment and Local People's Perspectives in Forest Landscapes*. Bogor: Center for International Forestry Research, 2002.

Simberloff, D., Farr, J. A., Cox, J. and Mehlman, D. W. Movement corridors: Conservation bargains or poor investments. *Conservation Biology*, **6** (1992), 493–504.

Simonovic, S. P. Decision support systems for sustainable management of water resources: 2. Case studies. *Water International* **21** (1996), 233–244.

Sinclair, F. L. and Walker, D. H. Acquiring qualitative knowledge about complex agroecosystems. Representation as natural language. *Agricultural Systems*, **56** (1998), 341–363.

Sithole, B. *Access to and use of dambos in communal areas of Zimbabwe: institutional considerations*. Ph.D. Thesis, Centre for Applied Social Sciences, University of Zimbabwe, 1999.

Sithole, B., Frost, P. and Veeman, T. Searching for synthesis: integrating economic perspectives with those from other disciplines. In *Uncovering the Hidden Harvest: Valuation Methods for Woodland and Forest Resources*, ed. B. M. Campbell and M. Luckert. [People and Plants' Conservation Series.] London: Earthscan, 2002.

Smyle, J. *Disaster Mitigation and Vulnerability Reduction: Perspectives on the Prospects for Vetiver Grass Technology (VGT)*. San Jose; Costa Rica: Regional Unit for Technical Assistance, World Bank, 1999.

Spilsbury, M. J. CIFOR – using a 'systems' approach to research evaluation. In *The Future of Impact Assessment in the CGIAR: Needs, Constraints and Options. Proceedings of a Workshop Organised by the Standing Panel on Impact Assessment (SPIA) of the Technical Advisory Committee, 3–5 May, 2001*. Rome: Food and Agriculture Organization, pp. 11–17. Online: http://www.cgiar.org/tac/spia0500/cifor.pdf.

Stür, W. W., Horne, P. M., Hacker, J. B. and Kerridge, P. C. (eds.) Working with farmers: the key to adoption of forage technologies. In *ACIAR Proceedings No. 95*. Canberra: ACIAR, 2000.

Swift, M. J., Bohren, L., Carter, S. E., Izac, A. M. and Woomer, P. L. Biological management of tropical soils: integrating process research and farm practice. In *The Biological Management of Tropical Soil Fertility*, ed. P. L. Woomer and M. J. Swift. Chichester, UK: Wiley, 1994, pp. 209–227.

Tomich T. P., Kilby P. and Johnston, B. F. *Transforming Agrarian Economies: Opportunities Seized, Opportunities Missed*. Ithaca, NY: Cornell University Press, 1995.

Tomich, T. P., van Noordwijk, M. and Thomas, D. E. (eds.) *ASB-Indonesia Report 10: Research Abstracts and Key Policy Questions on Environmental Services and Land Use Change, Bridging the Gap Between Policy and Research in Southeast Asia.* Bogor: World Agroforestry Centre, 1999.

UNESCO. *IHP Humid Tropics Programme Series No. 5: Integrated Water Resource Management: Meeting the Sustainability Challenge.* Paris: UNESCO Press, 1993.

van Noordwijk, M. Agroforestry as reclamation pathway for *Imperata* grassland use by smallholders. In *Proceedings of a Panel Discussion on Management of Imperata Control and Transfer of Technology for Smallholder Rubber Farming System,* Indonesia: Balai Penelitian Sembawa, Pusat Penelitian Karet Indonesia, 1994, pp. 2–10.

van Noordwijk, M., Tomich, T. P. and Verbist, B. Negotiation support models for integrated natural resource management in tropical forest margins. *Conservation Ecology,* **5** (2001): 21. Online: http://www.consecol.org/vol5/iss2/art21.

van Zyl, F. C. Integrated catchment management: is it wishful thinking or can it succeed? *Water Science and Technology,* **32** (1995), 27–35.

Wadsworth, F. Deforestation: death to the Panama Canal. *United States Strategic Conference on Tropical Deforestation.* Washington: US State Department and US Agency for International Development, 1976, pp. 22–24.

Walker, B., Carpenter, S., Andreis, A. et al. Resilience management in social–ecological systems: a working hypothesis for a participatory approach. *Conservation Ecology,* **6** (2002), 14. Online: http://www.consecol.org/vo16/iss1/art14.

Walters, C. *Adaptive Management of Renewable Resources.* New York: Macmillan, 1986.

Challenges in adaptive management of riparian and coastal ecosystems. *Conservation Ecology,* **1** (1997), 1. Online: http://www.consecol.org/vol1/iss2/art1.

Walters, C., Korman, J., Stevens, L. E. and Gold, B. Ecosystem modeling for evaluation of adaptive management policies in the Grand Canyon. *Conservation Ecology,* **4** (2000), 1. Online: http://www.consecol.org/vol4/iss2/art1.

Wheatley, M. *Leadership and the New Science. Discovering Order in a Chaotic World,* 2nd edn. San Francisco, CA: Berrett-Koehler, 1999.

Wollenberg, E., Edmunds, D. and Buck, L. Using scenarios to make decisions about the future: anticipatory learning for the adaptive co-management of community forests. *Landscape and Urban Planning,* **47** (2000), 65–77.

Williams, T. O. *Natural Resource Perspectives No. 38: Multiple Uses of Common Pool Resources in Semi-arid West Africa: A Survey of Existing Practices and Options for Sustainable Resource Management.* London: Overseas Development Institute, 1998.

Index